The Floure and the Leafe

AND

The Assembly of Ladies

Edited by
D. A. PEARSALL, M.A.
Lecturer in English Language and Literature
University of London,
King's College

THOMAS NELSON AND SONS LTD
London and Edinburgh

THOMAS NELSON AND SONS LTD

Parkside Works Edinburgh 9
36 Park Street London W1
117 Latrobe Street Melbourne C1

302–304 Barclays Bank Building
Commissioner and Kruis Streets
Johannesburg

THOMAS NELSON AND SONS (CANADA) LTD
91–93 Wellington Street West Toronto 1

THOMAS NELSON AND SONS
18 East 41st Street New York 17, N.Y.

SOCIÉTÉ FRANÇAISE D'ÉDITIONS NELSON
97 rue Monge Paris 5

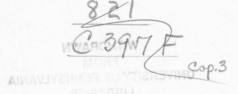

First published 1962

CONTENTS

v

ABBREVIATIONS

Pilg.—Lydgate's *Pilgrimage of the Life of Man*, translated from Deguile-ville. Edited by Furnivall and K. B. Locock, EETS (E.S.) 77, 83, 92 (1899–1904).

Pity—Chaucer's *Complaint unto Pity.*

P.Pl.—William Langland's *Vision of Piers the Plowman.* Edited by Skeat, 2 vols. (1886).

RR—*The Romaunt of the Rose.*

RS—Lydgate's *Reson and Sensuallyte.* Edited by E. Sieper, EETS (O.S.) 84, 89 (1901–3).

Secrees—Lydgate's *Secrees of the old Philisoffres* (completed by Benedict Burgh). Edited by R. Steele, EETS (E.S.) 66 (1894).

Suffolk—Poems attributed to the Duke of Suffolk and edited by H. N. MacCracken in *PMLA* 26 (1911), 142–80.

TC—Chaucer's *Troilus and Criseyde.*

TG—Lydgate's *Temple of Glass.* Edited by J. Schick, EETS (E.S.) 60 (1891).

Thebes—Lydgate's *Siege of Thebes.* Edited by A. Erdmann, EETS (E.S.) 108, 125 (1911–30).

Troy—Lydgate's *Troy-Book.* Edited by H. Bergen, EETS (E.S.) 97, 103, 106, 126 (1906–35).

(*b*) *Other abbreviations*

A—The text of AL in British Museum MS Addit. 34360

CFMA—Classiques Français du Moyen Age

CHEL—*Cambridge History of English Literature*

EETS (O.S., E.S.)—Publications of the Early English Text Society (Original Series, Extra Series)

EM—The East Midland dialect of ME

Hammond—*English Verse between Chaucer and Surrey*, ed. E. P. Hammond (Duke University Press, 1927)

JEGP—*Journal of English and Germanic Philology*

L—The text of AL in Longleat MS 258

ME—Middle English

MED—*Middle English Dictionary*, ed. Kurath and Kuhn

MLN—*Modern Language Notes*

MLR—*Modern Language Review*

MnE—Modern English

MP—*Modern Philology*

NQ—*Notes and Queries*

OE—Old English

OED—*Oxford English Dictionary*

OFr—Old French

PL—*Patrologia Latina*, ed. J. P. Migne

PMLA—*Publications of the Modern Language Association of America*

RDM—*Revue des Deux Mondes*

RES—*Review of English Studies*

Rom.—*Le Roman de la Rose*, ed. E. Langlois, SATF (5 vols., 1914–24)

SATF—Publications de la Société des Anciens Textes Français

SP—*Studies in Philology*

T—The texts of AL in the group Tr, L, Th

Th—The text of AL in Thynne's edition of Chaucer 1532

Tr—The text of AL in Trinity College (Cambridge) MS R.3.19

INTRODUCTION

The Flower and the Leaf was added by Thomas Speght to his collected edition of Chaucer's *Works* in 1598, and during the period of its inclusion in the canon the poem was much admired. It was paraphrased by Dryden and Wordsworth, singled out for special praise by Pope and Hazlitt, and, partly through Dryden's influence, by all the critics and historians of literature; it was the subject of a sonnet by Keats, and was generally regarded as the best of Chaucer's allegories, if not his best poem; and finally, in the last days of its glory (1868), subjects from the poem were chosen for inclusion in the Chaucer window in Westminster Abbey. About 1870 the poem was expelled from the canon, and, though some tried staunchly to retain it, by the end of the century its fall from grace was complete. Since then the poem has rarely been given the attention it deserves, and Skeat's slurs (' pretty ', ' tinsel ', ' flashy attractiveness ') have died hard. To any student of Chaucer, of course, the poem is full of echoes, which is one of its many delights; but it is a good deal more than an imitation of Chaucer: the grace and charm of its evocation of an ideal world, the serenely sensible view of life implicit in its allegory, the ease and delicacy of the handling, a pervading sweet reasonableness—all these will be immediately apparent to any reader, and give it the right to an independent existence outside an appendix to Chaucer. Further than this, *The Flower and the Leaf*, by working within the fixed tradition of the allegorical vision poem, shows how new life is breathed into a dying poetic convention, how the worn currency of generations of poets can be transmuted into the stuff of art, into pattern, beauty, and ' sentence '. *The Flower and the Leaf* imparts a bright lustre to a departing age, and is in no way eclipsed by Dryden's masterly paraphrase. It is hoped that the present edition, besides providing a text which has not been, in Saintsbury's phrase, ' vamped up to a possible or

impossible Chaucerian norm ' (*CHEL*, ii, 218), will do something to restore the poem to its rightful place in critical
estimation.

The Assembly of Ladies has been closely associated with
FL since the time of Skeat. It will be seen later that the
closeness of this association is here questioned, but AL is
still a most valuable pendant to FL in that it illuminates
many aspects of a common tradition, and also demonstrates
the break-up of that tradition.   Where FL accepts with
serenity an age, a civilisation, a scheme of values, a poetic,
AL is all bustle and movement, ever reaching after the new
though rooted in the old.   Its very shortcomings throw into
relief the remarkable qualities of FL.

TEXT

The sole extant authority for the text of FL is the print of
the poem added by Speght to his collected edition of the
works of Chaucer in 1598.   The text that he prints has been
much corrupted by transmission, as can be seen in the
spelling, which shows an improbable admixture of fifteenth-
and sixteenth-century forms, in the metre, often spoilt
through modernisation of spelling and loss of final -*e*, and
in rhymes like *should/gold* 427, *yes/this* 471, *pleasure* (ME
plesir)/*desire* 113; *wold* is modernised to *would* throughout,
but is preserved on two occasions for the sake of rhyme
(95, 445).   The possibility and extent of this kind of textual
corruption, both in MS and print, are well attested:
Chaucer's comments are famous, and Hawes echoes him in
the printing era, while further evidence is provided by the
careless copying habits of an otherwise reputable scribe like
John Shirley, and by the gradual degeneration of the suc-
cessive prints of Chaucer.[1]

The source of Speght's text of FL is not known, but it
is possible to speculate.   The library of Longleat House,
near Warminster, the ancestral home of the Marquesses of

---

[1] Chaucer, *TC*, v, 1795, *Adam Scriveyn*; Hawes, *Past. Pleas.*, 5804.
For Shirley see Brusendorff, *Chaucer Tradition* (Copenhagen, 1925), pp.
207–36.

Bath, contains a MS (Longleat 258) on the last leaf of which is a list of contents in the scribe's hand. The fourth entry in this list is ' De folio et flore ' (the titles of all the poems are Latinised), but unfortunately the pages of the MS which should contain FL, a complete quire (ff. 33–48), are missing. The lacuna was first indicated by Henry Bradshaw, who inserted this note in the MS: ' The missing quire consisted of 16 leaves each containing 3 stanzas on a page. *The Flower and the Leaf* would begin on the first page, and end on the last leaf but one with one stanza only on the page, the rest of the page and the back of the leaf being blank. The last leaf of the quire contained the first six stanzas of the *Complaint of Mars*.' The MS, which is dated about or a little after 1500, also contains AL, and is further described in the account of the text of that poem.

If the connection between the missing quire and Speght's print were a straightforward one, we might expect that the print would reproduce some at least of the spelling and other peculiarities of Longleat 258; but these peculiarities, which may be deduced from an examination of the Longleat texts of, for instance, AL and Chaucer's *Pity*, are not in evidence in the present text of FL. The quire was evidently removed by someone who liked the poem, or thought it might make a good addition to the collected Chaucer, and it was probably copied and circulated freely, the text becoming more and more corrupt in the process of transmission. The practice of circulating poems in separate quires, which were afterwards bound together in a single MS, was well known in the fifteenth century, while John Audelay's malediction upon those who cut pages from his MS indicates that the fate of FL is not unique.[1]

A tantalising inscription, much faded, at the beginning of Longleat 258 appears to mention Thomas Godfray, the printer responsible for William Thynne's first collected edition of Chaucer in 1532; the MS probably went through

[1] Examples of fascicular MSS are Trinity R.3.19, 21 and the famous Auchinleck MS. See Brusendorff, *op. cit.*, pp. 178–91; E. P. Hammond in *MP* 3 (1905–6), 159–78. The poem by Audelay is on p. 224 of the EETS edition by E. K. Whiting (O.S.), 184 (1931).

the hands of William himself, since he appears to have printed AL from it, and it would then have passed to Long-leat House, which was built by his nephew, Sir John Thynne. Sir John was the overseer of his uncle's will, and his name appears in Longleat 258 ('Constat John Thynne', f. 1r). The fate of the missing quire is perhaps suggested by some remarks of Francis Thynne, William's son. In 1599 Francis, zealous for his father's reputation as the original editor of Chaucer, and probably annoyed at being fore-stalled in his own plans for an edition, produced his *Animad-versions* upon Speght's edition (ed. Furnivall, Chaucer Society (1876)). He says here that he inherited from his father about twenty-five MSS, some of them very corrupt, and that these MSS were dispersed or stolen about twenty-six years previously ('yt maye happen soome of them to coome to somme of your frendes handes'), and he warns that the MSS are worse than useless (p. 12; cf. p. 7). Francis appeared to believe that Speght had based his alterations and additions on these 'false copyes', which we may conjecture to have included a corrupt copy of FL from the loose quire; and the mention of 'your frendes handes' is on this reckoning a veiled allusion to John Stow, the ubiquitous Elizabethan bibliophile, from whom it appears Speght took many of his notes and also his additions.[1] Stow was careless what poems he attributed to Chaucer, and Speght's own remarks in his second edition of 1602 (in the section on 'His Bookes') suggest that Stow presented him with a mass of material for inclusion from which he sifted the likeliest pieces.

A speculative connection between the missing quire, Francis Thynne's 'false copyes', and John Stow is all that can be deduced of the textual history of FL; such a con-nection would certainly explain the corrupt state of the text.

Some further description of Speght's edition is now

[1] See Stow, *Survey of London* (ed. C. L. Kingsford, 2 vols., 1908), ii, 111; Speght, f. 340r. It is worth noting that one of the two known MSS of the *Isle of Ladies*, Speght's other main 1598 addition, is Longleat 256.

necessary. It is a large folio volume, printed in black-letter in double column, and, like all the preceding collected editions of Chaucer, contains a large number of spurious works. It is the first edition with any sort of critical apparatus, but Speght's claim to have corrected the text ' by old written Copies ' is scarcely true, since it has been largely set up, as was the usual practice, from the previous edition, namely Stow's of 1561, and it is unlikely that Speght is responsible for much more than the apparatus and the additions.[1] The volume is in fact another bookseller's reprint: Speght himself tells us, in his address ' To the Readers ', that he did not take over as editor until the work was three-quarters through the press.

FL appears on ff. 365v–368v. The title given is 'The Floure and the Leafe', and the initial letter of the poem is decorated. No divisions are indicated in the text, which, except for the French (177f, 350), is in black-letter. The following spellings occur, and have been modernised in the present edition: v for initial u , u for medial v (but see 233n), i for j . Certain contractions have been silently expanded, viz. y^t for *that*; ye , y^e for *the*; $\tilde{e}$, $\tilde{a}$ for *en*, *an*; qd. for *quod*. The use of $_3$ for *gh* has been retained (47, 203, 500). The punctuation in Speght consists of eighteen commas, which are used to indicate rhetorical pauses, questions, exclamations, etc. (e.g. 52, 391, 553, 573), and not grammatical divisions. Capitals are sometimes used for important substantives (e.g. 29, 40, 86, 133); speech-prefixes are abbreviated and bracketed, e.g. (qd. she). The punctuation of the present edition is modernised throughout.

Speght published a revised edition in 1602, with an enlarged apparatus incorporating many of the changes suggested by Francis Thynne, who is referred to most respectfully. Again he claims to have consulted the MSS (Dedication), but again the claims are largely unfounded. AL, for instance, has been set up afresh from the 1561 edition, and many of the 1561 mistakes corrected in 1598 reappear. In FL certain errors, real (37, 238, 296, 300, *shold* 427, 563) or supposed (109, 142, *ware* 208 and 267, 246, 461), are

[1] See T. R. Lounsbury, *Studies in Chaucer* (3 vols., 1892), i, 270ff.

corrected, and there are the usual sporadic and inconsequential spelling changes. Such emendations and alterations are habitual with sixteenth-century printers and do not imply editorial revision. The punctuation is heavy and often inept, for instance the commas at the end of 201, 355, 502, 586, and the full stops at the end of 224, 329, 382, 495. The 1602 edition, for all its virtues, cannot be accepted as an authority.

Subsequent editions of Chaucer containing FL are listed in the Bibliography, and may be briefly dismissed. The black-letter edition of 1687 is another booksellers' reprint, and worthless. Urry embarked on his edition (1721) with a conviction that 'Chaucer's Verses originally consisted of an equal number of feet' (Preface), and proposed to 'restore him to his feet' by extensive emendation. In FL this resulted in some 1,400 changes, with a litter of corrections to final -e and of endings in -id, -ith, -is, Urry's peculiarly disfiguring trade mark. However, many of his emendations were adopted, without acknowledgment, in subsequent editions, and his principles, if not his methods, of textual reconstruction were generally observed. The endeavour was, by emending freely in accordance with a preconceived pattern of metre and grammar, to make FL look as much like Chaucer as possible, even after it had been proved that the poem was not Chaucer's. Skeat's edition, for instance, the most skilful and most important of these reconstructed texts, introduces some 750 emendations of Speght. Over 300 of these involve final -e, about one-fifth are for the sake of metre, and the tendency of all of them is to substitute a Chaucerian form for a more modern one. Such a text rests on two main assumptions: that the language, grammar, and spelling of the author's copy were more or less identical with those of Chaucer; and that the metre of the original was syllabically regular in the modern sense. Both assumptions are untenable, and must be rejected by the modern editor. The text we have is evidently not the author's, but we are not certain to get closer to the author's text by large-scale emendation, and so it is best to leave it alone. Speght's text is therefore here presented conservatively.

There are three MSS of AL : British Museum MS Addit. 34360 (A), Trinity College (Cambridge), MS R.3.19 (Tr), and MS Longleat 258 (L); [1] and one print of inferior authority, that of Thynne's collected Chaucer 1532 (Th). MS A has been taken as the basis of the present text, and is described more fully later ; the other three texts agree in a large number of inferior readings, and form a distinct group.

Trinity MS R.3.19 is a fascicular collection, written and compiled in the last quarter of the fifteenth century. It was the source of many of Stow's additions, and contains, amongst other works, the *Parlement of Foules*, the *Legend of Good Women*, *Pity*, *La Belle Dame sans Merci*, the *Assembly of Gods*, and the *Court of Love*. AL appears on ff. 55r–65v. The text, probably copied by an East Anglian scribe, is of little value, but it is older than L and, partly for that reason, occasionally agrees with A in minor details against L and Th (e.g. 7 *fyft*, L *fifthe*; 31 *besynes*, L *besinesses*; 181 *thys*, L *his*, Th *her* ; 335 *tell*, L *shewe*; 612 *euyll*, A *ill*, L *wele*), and is therefore used in the present edition where A fails. Otherwise Tr is related to L, though it has many eccentric readings of its own.

MS Longleat 258 is a homogeneous collection of poems (e.g. the *Temple of Glass*, *Pity*, *Anelida and Arcite*, the *Parlement of Foules*, the *Eye and the Heart*, *La Belle Dame sans Merci*) written, probably for private purposes, by a neat but inaccurate and unprofessional scribe about 1500. AL appears on ff. 58r–75v; the text of the poem, like that of *Pity*, is related to that of Tr, and of little or no value. The connection of L with Thynne's print is even closer, for reasons suggested above (pp. 3–4): in fact, Th was probably set up from L. However, Thynne treated his copy text with considerable freedom, and in correcting the numerous errors of L he sometimes hit on the authentic A reading (e.g. 339 *her*, L *him*; 512 *lady her*, L *lady thaire*; 674 *porte*, L *parte*). These readings are, of course, of no significance whatsoever, but they do demonstrate one important fact:

[1] For a full description of Tr see M. R. James, *The Western MSS. in the Library of Trinity College, Cambridge* (4 vols., 1900–4), ii, 69–74; for L see E. P. Hammond in *MLN* 20 (1905), 77–9.

that a late, inferior text may be superficially smoother than an earlier MS, solely through scribal or editorial emendation. Because of its fluency and freedom from error, Skeat chose Th as the basis for his eclectic text of AL in *Chaucerian and Other Pieces*.

MS Addit. 34360 is a codex of the late fifteenth century, but probably not later than about 1485; it is closely associated with MS Harley 2251, and the two MSS are said to be based on a lost Shirley codex. There are further associations with the group of MSS called by Brusendorff the ' Hammond Group ', including Trinity R.3.19; but Miss Hammond, in analysing the textual links of the MSS, expressly exempts the text of AL from all her remarks.[1] The contents of A are mostly Lydgate, though there is a little Chaucer, including *Pity*. AL is found on ff. 37r–49r. It has been carelessly copied: a line (33) and two whole stanzas (519–32) are omitted, two pairs of lines transposed (124f, 580f), several words left out (e.g. 29, 241, 260, 310, 377, 461, 617, 694), and other mistakes made (e.g. 50, 57, 167, 281, 311, 345, 720). However, there are many unique readings, two of them quite conclusive (61, 463), and others of considerable value (e.g. 64, 86, 225, 248, 298f, 628, 636), and for this reason, and the others stated above, A is presented here, with the minimum of emendation, as the authentic text of AL.[2]

The following spellings in A have been modernised: *v* for initial *u*, *u* for *v* (used in abbreviations only), *i* for *j*; and all the contractions involving *r* (a curl, or a small raised *r*) silently expanded, viz. -*ver*, *per*-, *ser*-, -*ner*, *mer*-, *pro*-, *your*, *our*, -*ar*-, *pray*, *part*. The flourishes after certain final consonants (e.g. *d*, *t*, *n*) mean nothing, and are ignored. The punctuation in the MS, except for the caesura virgule,

[1] E. P. Hammond, ' Two British Museum MSS.', *Anglia* **28** (1905), 1–28; ' A Scribe of Chaucer ', *MP* **27** (1929–30), 27–33; Brusendorff, pp. 178ff.

[2] Neither a critical text nor a genealogy of MSS is provided, since either misrepresents the nature of medieval MS production. See Hammond, *Bibliographical Manual*, pp. 106–13; Brusendorff, pp. 53–63; Saintsbury *History of English Prosody* (3 vols., 1906), i, 165–9.

which is used throughout, is restricted to where there is a change of speaker within the line (96, 98, 571, 753). The mottoes and the allegorical and other names are written in a bold hand and underlined (italics are used for the mottoes in this edition). There are no stanza headings in A such as are provided in the other three texts, e.g. *Discrecion purvyour* (Tr, L, Th, before 260), *Countenaunce porter* (L, Th, 274), *Belchere Marchall* (Tr, 316), *Largesse stewarde* (L, Th, 316).

The title of the poem is given in l. 752; there is no heading or explicit in A, though Stow has written ' Chauser ' (in one margin), ' la semble des dames ' (in the other), at the beginning of the poem. The heading and explicit in Tr refer to the *Assemble de Damys*. Thynne's title is *The assemble of ladies* (as also a late hand in L).

LANGUAGE

Both FL and AL are written in the literary dialect of fifteenth-century London English. This literary dialect tended to act as a preservative of sounds, spellings, and grammatical forms, especially when they were useful for rhythm or rhyme, and it differed considerably from colloquial English. No systematic account of it is given here, since the text of FL is for linguistic purposes of little value; the following remarks are intended primarily to help with questions of date and authorship. (In the Introduction and Glossary line-references without prefix are to FL, unless the context shows otherwise.)

Grammar

In both poems the verbal endings demonstrate a late stage in the break-up of the ME system. In the infinitive and present singular and plural, forms with and without *-e* are used indiscriminately. Survivals of infinitive *-en* (9, 68, 157n; AL 391) and present plural *-en* (478, 535; AL 288, 688, 719, also *b(i)en*, throughout) are rare. An apparent instance of the Southern plural *-eth* (363, cf. 8, 11) is probably a loose singular. The present 3 singular is *-(e)th* throughout. The final *-e* of the weak preterite is usually omitted in FL, and inorganic *-e* often added to the weak past participle. The

B

participial prefix *y-* appears in FL merely in imitation of
Chaucer (49, 375, 424; no instance in AL). Strong preterite
singular and plural generally fall together under one form,
whether modelled on the singular (e.g. *rode* 449) or the
plural (e.g. *found* 44). In FL there are two instances of the
preterite plural in *-en* (34, 71). The strong past participle
usually preserves *-e(n)*, though there are examples with no
ending (e.g. 31, 258), and some abbreviated forms (e.g. *be,
do, go*). *Shape(n)* is the obsolete strong past participle of a
verb now weak (64, 167). The present participle ends in
-ing, -yng; occasional forms in *-eng* (AL) are scribal.

Other points worth noting are the penetration of *ar(e)* as
the plural of the verb *to be* (536, AL 248), a characteristic
EM form not common in London until the late fifteenth
century; and the distinction of *shal*, singular, and *shul*, plural,
in AL (not FL), a distinction not often preserved after
c. 1475.

The pronouns are generally as in Chaucer, except in the
3 plural, where the EM *their, theyr*, etc. is firmly established
(in FL, 45 instances against 6 of *her, hir*; AL has *her* only
twice); *hem*, the accusative form, survived more strongly,
and *them* (AL *theym*) tends to be used only in stressed
positions (in FL, 11 instances against 24 of *hem*; AL, 3
against 17). The precise distinction of 2 singular and plural
in FL (591n) is worth noting, and the case-distinction of *ye*
and *you/yow* in both poems (a distinction not made by
Hawes, *c.* 1500).

In nouns and adjectives, as in verbs, final *-e* is no longer
a significant inflexion, and is added or omitted indiscriminately merely as a spelling, though of course Chaucerian
usage is frequently observed. AL is perhaps more liberal
in adding final *-e*, but no less arbitrary.

Pronunciation and spelling

The rhymes of FL, though often demonstrating the persist-
ence of Chaucerian habits, give clear evidence of the decay
of the stricter Chaucerian linguistic tradition in the fifteenth
century. Close and open $\bar{e}$, distinguished in rhyme by
Chaucer, fall together in *breade/weede* 45 (also 303), *grene/*

clene 292 (also AL 48); such rhymes are probably based on variant dialectal pronunciations (Dobson, *English Pronunciation 1500–1700* (1957), pp. 611–13). The rhyme *tre/pretile* 89 indicates development of close *ē* to [i], a change probably complete by the mid-fifteenth century. The rhymes of FL, like those of Chaucer, distinguish close from open *ō*, but AL rhymes *everichone/don* 435, and frequently takes advantage of Chaucer's licence of rhyming close and open *ō* finally (*do/so/go* 415, etc.). AL has several rhymes of short and long *o* (*upon/alon* 83, cf. 118, 237, 562) which have no parallel in FL, and others of long and short *a* (*yaate/therate* 274, cf. 484, 540). Rhymes in FL of *was, compas* with *pace, face* etc. (e.g. 51, 163, 342) indicate the retention of a short vowel in the French words (Dobson, *op. cit.*, p. 468). Chaucer uses such rhymes only in *Sir Thopas*, which suggests that he thought them suitable only for hacks.

Rhymes indicating that final *-e* was no longer pronounced (e.g. *passe/was* 28) are common in both poems. Earlier in the fifteenth century Lydgate had used sonant final *-e* under much the same conditions as Chaucer; but in the later poetry of the Chaucerian tradition the sounding of final *-e* was fitful and arbitrary; [1] it was a deliberate archaism, probably regarded as an ornament, rather like *-ed* in modern verse, and not certain to observe Chaucer's grammatical usage. However, Chaucer's influence was still powerful, and metrical evidence in FL shows 46 clear instances of sounded final *-e* (e.g. *brode* 33, *heare* 40), of which two-thirds conform with Chaucer's usage. Of these 46 examples (it is obviously bound to be an arbitrary count) 34 occur in the first half of the poem, which suggests that the author's language, or the scribe's, or the printer's, gradually got the better of Chaucer's. Final *-e*, to judge from the evidence of the scansion, has probably often been lost through scribal omission (e.g. *small* 8, *eat* 95, *green* 297). In AL there are only 23 instances of sonant final *-e*. Medial *-e-* is occasionally sounded in both poems, as in *chapelet* (154, 159, etc.), *commaundement* (422, AL 106, etc.).

[1] See C. F. Babcock, ' Inflectional *-e* in ME ', *PMLA* **29** (1914), 59–92.

Associated with the decline of sonant -*e* is the practice of rhyming words in -*ly* (also *by*, *I*, etc.) with foreign terminations originally in -*ie*, a licence from which Chaucer scrupulously refrained. FL has 15 instances of such rhymes, AL 6.

Final -*ed* and -*es* are, like final -*e*, treated far more conservatively in FL than in AL: the latter frequently has rhymes indicating complete lapse of *e* (e.g. *rubies/wise* 533; cf. 9, 193, 205, 380, 610), whereas FL has only one (75). Metrical evidence confirms this distinction between the two poems. However, the treatment of final -*es*, as of final -*e*, is not systematic enough to warrant emendation.

The spelling of FL, as one might expect in a text so corrupted by transmission, is on the whole very late, though each individual spelling has fifteenth-century support. Common examples are the distinction of open and close *ē*, *ō*, as *ea*, *ee* and *oa*, *oo* respectively; and the spellings *ar* for *er* (e.g. 41, 127), *an* for *aun* (e.g. 58, 188), -*ll* for -*l* (e.g. *all*, *full*), *who*- for *ho*- (e.g. 356n), -*ty* for -*te* in French words (e.g. 76, 138). These spellings occur rarely or not at all in AL; in FL they exist side by side with the more normal fifteenth-century spellings and with conservative forms like *avaunce* 578, *avise* 187 (*advise*, AL 331), *gadering* 411, *whider* 47 (*whethir*, AL 612), *hegge* 54, *brenning* 408, *thred* 257.

A feature of AL is the frequent use of *i* for *e* in unstressed syllables, especially -*is*, -*id* (also *aftir* 86, *bettir* 51, etc.). This is usually accounted a Northern or EM tendency, but is too common in the fifteenth century for any conclusions to be drawn from it (though see the notes to AL 332, 607, 674, 689). The spelling of the scribe of manuscript A is interesting as indicating the pronunciation of certain glide-vowels, viz. *terewe* 137, *chayer* 476, *suerte* 605 (cf. *flower* in FL 444). There is evidence that the development of this extra syllable, especially before *r* and *l*, was more common in the fifteenth century than the occasional spellings would suggest (see Bergen's Introduction to Lydgate's *Fall*, p. xxxv), and if we assume that this was the case, then such words as the following may well have been pronounced with an extra syllable: in FL, *birds* 119, 127, *earth* 199, *forth* 585, *hearb(s)* 407, 477, *h(e)arts* 20, 488, *hurt* 312, *lords* 254, 263, *word* 586, *world* 74, *worth* 255; *child* 259, *field* 75, 325, *old* 509, *shield* 256 (see Dobson, *op. cit.*, pp. 913, 925); and in AL, *ernest* 614, *nere* 484, *surely* 318, 329, 673 (cf. *suerte* 605).

The pronunciation of the following words should be noted: *acértained* 568, *answéred* 100, etc., *comfórted* 433, *créatúre* AL 50, etc., *départed* 193n, *notáble* 513, *persévering* 548, *rémembraunce* 579, *velüet* 233n. In both poems, as in Chaucer, *maner* can add -*e* and be used for rhyme, pronounced *manére*. In present participles, the last syllable may bear a stress (92n).

AUTHORSHIP AND DATE

The only reason for the attribution of FL and AL to Chaucer is their inclusion in the sixteenth-century collected editions of Chaucer. These editions are notoriously unreliable: about twenty authors in all are laid under contribution, some of them actually being named. It is clear that editors tended to regard a collected Chaucer as something in the nature of an anthology, and to put in it ' Chaucerian ' poems which might otherwise not get printed. Of course there was also a good deal of genuine confusion, as there had been in the fifteenth century, when scribes would blithely ascribe to Chaucer doggerel verse in broad Scots.[1] Furthermore, an editor, to be worth his salt, was expected to add some new finding to the Chaucerian corpus, much as a modern editor of a standard author will set some store by his addition of minor unpublished fragments; and Thynne's scrutiny of the MSS was so careful and his taste so good that later editors were left ' glenyng here and there '. There is no reason to doubt, however, the sincerity of Thynne and Speght in ascribing, respectively, AL and FL to Chaucer.

AL was summarily rejected from the canon in 1778 by Tyrwhitt in the ' Account of the Works of Chaucer ' (p. xxii)

---

[1] See F. W. Bonner, ' Genesis of the Chaucer Apocrypha ', *SP* **48** (1951), 461–81. Full accounts of the sixteenth-century editions are given in Skeat, Oxford *Chaucer*, i, 27–46; Lounsbury, i, 263ff; and of course in Hammond's *Bibliographical Manual*.

appended to his great edition of the *Canterbury Tales* (1775–1778), but it was kept in the collected editions of Chaucer until 1810 (Chalmers edition), when it was relegated to a section for spurious poems; in 1822 (Chiswick edition) it was finally dismissed. Tyrwhitt had his doubts about FL: ' I do not think its authenticity so clear as that of the preceding poem ', viz. *The Isle of Ladies* (*op. cit.*, p. xi); but his doubts earned him nothing but scorn until 1868, when, on the basis of the *y/ie* rhyme-test, Bradshaw pronounced it spurious.[1] Soon after, Ten Brink confirmed his opinion, with a mass of further evidence, linguistic, metrical, and aesthetic, and thereafter the poem was fair game for Skeat, who attributed it to the same poetess as AL, and for Furnivall.[2] It was separated from Chaucer's authentic works in Skeat's revised edition of Bell (1878).

It will not be necessary to recapitulate here the arguments against the Chaucerian authorship of FL and AL. There is no worth-while external testimony to support the ascriptions, and the internal evidence of language, rhyme, and metre, as has been seen, is all against it.

Both poems purport to be by women (see 462, 467, 500, 547, AL 7, 18, 259, etc.), though whether they are or not is a matter for little more than speculation. There is nothing ' absurd ' in supposing ' that a fifteenth-century male poet would give himself out to be a woman ', as Skeat suggests (*Chaucer Canon*, p. 110); in fact there are many examples of this particular *prosopopeia* in English and French verse, as for instance in the work of Lydgate (*Minor Poems*, ii, 418)

---

[1] Bradshaw's views were communicated by Furnivall, *Temp. Pref. to the 6-text ed. of CT* (1868), pp. 107–11. Having discovered the test, Bradshaw was reluctant to make it too dogmatic (see G. W. Prothero, *Memoir of Henry Bradshaw* (1888), p. 354), but others were very ready to do so.

[2] Ten Brink, *Chaucer: Studien zur Geschichte seiner Entwicklung und zur Chronologie seiner Schriften* (Münster, 1870), pp. 156–64; Skeat, Oxford *Chaucer*, i, 44, vii, lxii–lxx (also AL); *Chaucer Canon* (1900), pp. 139–41 (AL, pp. 110–11); Furnivall, *Athenaeum* (1872) ii, 49–50. Skeat develops his theory of common female authorship in *Academy* **35** (1889), 448–9; **41** (1892), 592; *Modern Language Quarterly* **3** (1900), 111–12; *Athenaeum* (1903), i, 340.

and Deschamps (Poems 426, 432, 434, etc.). The pre-dominance of women in the Court of Love tradition and in the orders of the flower and the leaf would provide a motive for the dramatic fiction. On the other hand, if we do accept that both poems are by women, there is certainly no need to assume, with Skeat, that poetesses were so rare in the fifteenth century that they must be by the same woman. Girls were not usually given an academic education, but a woman of birth in a noble household would acquire a know-ledge of reading and writing, and be able to write letters and short verses. Several poems in the manuscript which R. H. Robbins calls ' the Findern anthology ', and which he edits in *PMLA* **69** (1954), 610–42, are by women, while in France there was the celebrated Christine de Pisan, and also a group of women poets of the mid-fifteenth century, some of them ladies-in-waiting at the court of Margaret of Scot-land, wife of the Dauphin Louis, herself an enthusiastic patroness of literature and a poetess in her own right.[1]

Furthermore, if both FL and AL are by the same woman, then she has shown a rare, not to say unlikely, talent in projecting two such totally different dramatic *personae*. The narrator in FL is charmingly modest and self-effacing, as in her epilogue (also 461, 566–7, 574–5, 585), while her questions to the lady are full of humility, and elaborately polite (491–9, 544). The lady in AL, on the other hand, is very pleased with her work (AL 743–7, 753), almost rude to Lady Loyalty (680–93), obstinate about not wearing a motto (311–15, 411–413), always stealing surreptitious glances at other women's clothes (204–5, 302–3), and saying how well she herself looks (255, 259). The differences, for what they are worth, are striking.

Apart from the supposition of female authorship, Skeat offered further comparisons between FL and AL to support the theory of common authorship : he noted the use of *very* as an adverb, the descriptions of gardens and arbours, and the use of scraps of French (the first feature is common in the later fifteenth century, the others are dealt with in the

[1] *Rondeaux du XVᵉ siècle*, ed. G. Raynaud (SATF, 1889), pp. vii, xv, xxviii.

notes to 43, 49, 177, AL 85). He also compared 148–53
and AL 526–32; 295 and AL 350; 567 and AL 729; 26
and AL 241, 253; 391 and AL 447; and pointed out many
phrases common to the two poems (see, e.g., notes to 20, 25,
59, 60, 98, 144, 458, 459, 589). These resemblances are
mostly trivial, and all have a common source in Chaucer or
Lydgate. Skeat replied to critics who said that the verbal
resemblances he quoted were only common tags by referring
to the phrase *twain and twain*, appearing both in 295 and
AL 350, which he said did not occur in Chaucer or Shakespeare and which he could find nowhere else (*Athenaeum*
(1903), i, 340); but in Lydgate he would have found it at
least 8 times (see 295n). Internal evidence of this kind is
valueless in determining authorship. Skeat's later speculations, attributing the two poems to Margaret Neville,
Countess of Oxford, on the basis of certain stylistic resemblances to a poem of eight rhyme-royal stanzas, which was
mistakenly supposed to be by the Countess, in the Paston
letters, are best forgotten.

The main objections to the theory of common authorship
are linguistic and stylistic. Some marked differences between
the language and rhymes of the two poems have already
been noted. Further distinctions follow, for which reference
may be made to the Glossary; these barely conscious features
of style are the best kind of internal evidence. So, in FL,
after that, *at the last*, are frequently used for narrative
transition, but not in AL; phrases like *a little throw*, *by
manifold*, contracted negative verbs like *nad*, *nas*, *nis*, the use
of *even* as an intensive adverb, are all peculiar to FL; *swete*,
in its various forms, is used 13 times in FL, never in AL.
On the other hand, certain expressions particularly favoured
in AL are hardly used in FL: vague phrases with *case*;
certayne, *in* (*for*) *certayne*, *forsoth*, *forthwithal*, as tags;
phrases with *wise*; and the word *creature*. In most of these
differences the usage of FL is more archaic: *do* is used as
an auxiliary only twice, against 9 times in AL, and *that* is
far more frequently used to form or support conjunctions in
FL; a significant point is that in FL the preterite of *see* is
sie, *see* throughout, while in AL it is *sawe* throughout. The

use of certain archaic words is interesting: *eke* occurs 17 times in FL, never in AL; *yede(n)* 12 times in FL, never in AL; *wight* 10 times in FL, once in AL. Textual corruption is out of the question with these differences, nor are they due to differences of genre, or to changes of technique or habit on the part of a single poet. Less significant are differences which might be due to textual corruption in FL: the distinction of *shal*, sg. and *shul*, pl., and of *to* and *til* as used before consonants and vowels respectively, distinctions observed in AL but not in FL; the more conservative use of the Northern 3 plural pronoun *theym* in AL; and the preservation of *must* as an impersonal verb in AL. The evidence as a whole, it will be seen, is emphatically against common authorship, and, although we cannot discount the possibility of skilful archaism on the part of the poet of FL, suggests that FL is somewhat earlier than AL.

Some wider distinctions of style, to be treated later (see pp. 59ff, may be anticipated. The main one, briefly, is that in AL the line and the stanza are treated as sense units, while in FL the freest of run-on lines and stanzas abound. The poet of AL, with his rhyming tags and meaningless line-fillers, makes versifying look easy; this could hardly be said of FL. A persistent and distinctive feature of the style of the latter poem is its use of comparative constructions with an idealising tendency, as we shall see; these are far less frequent in AL. There are, furthermore, differences of quality which are readily apparent, such differences as are not to be accounted for in terms of individual poetic development.

G. L. Marsh, in his article on ' The Authorship of FL ' (*JEGP* **6** (1906–7), 373–94), states his view that FL is by Lydgate, but the resemblances of metre, style, themes, and imagery that he points out are commonplaces of the Chaucerian tradition (some of them are commonplaces of the Middle Ages), and in any case MacCracken shows that the evidence of rhymes is decisively against Lydgate's authorship (*Lydgate's Minor Poems*, vol. i, pp. vii, l), since he very rarely rhymes *y/ie* (15 instances in FL), and never rhymes *-y* with *-ory* (FL 518, 523), or the penultimate syllable of words in *-oun* (FL 564). There is of course much imitation of Lydgate, as of Chaucer, in FL.

FL has also been linked with *The Isle of Ladies* by C. F. McClumpha in his note in *MLN* 4 (1889), 203, but the resemblances to which he draws attention are trivial. There is much more to be said for the grouping of FL, AL, *The Court of Love*, and *The Kingis Quair* made by W. M. Mackenzie in the introduction to his edition (1939) of the last-named poem. That the poet of FL knew *The Kingis Quair* seems likely, while it is more or less certain that the clever and sophisticated author of *The Court of Love* was acquainted with AL; reference to the notes of the present edition will bear out these statements. Beyond this, however, the parallels between the poems are no more than one might expect in works written at about the same time within a strictly conventionalised poetic tradition.

In AL there are many similarities in theme, style, and diction to the English poems of Charles of Orleans, and to the poems attributed by MacCracken to the Duke of Suffolk, while the colloquial idiom and rapid exchange of dialogue seem to owe something to the *Assembly of Gods*.[1] Far more striking than any of these, however, are the extraordinarily close parallels between AL and *Generydes*, a conventional and professionally competent romance in rhyme royal (6,995 lines) of the mid-fifteenth century or later, based on a French original now lost. Not only are there precise and unmistakable parallels of phraseology, but also the treatment of stanza and line, the language and grammar, and minor tricks of style like the use of *case*, *certayne*, *furthwithall*, *wise* are in all respects alike.[2] This kind of internal evidence, where the resemblances are exact and detailed, and where

[1] Orleans, ed. R. Steele, EETS(O.S.) 215, 220 (1941–6): see notes to AL, 62, 63, 85, 170, 171, 225, 243, 515, 526, 533, 649; Suffolk, ed. MacCracken, *PMLA* 26 (1911), 142–80 (see notes to AL 593, 649, 668, 720); *Assembly of Gods*, ed. O. L. Triggs, EETS(E.S.) 69 (1896) (see especially 15–35, 1975–95).

[2] *Generydes*, ed. W. Aldis Wright, EETS(O.S.) 55, 70 (1873–8); for some parallels see notes to 14, 95, 137, 220, 225, 294, 311, 394, 406, 443, 478, 510, 511, 538, 539, 665, 674. The evidence is more fully set forth in my article in *RES* 12 (1961), 229–37.

imitation or the influence of a common tradition is not involved, should be distinguished from the kind dismissed above. AL and *Generydes* may well be by the same hand, in which case it is unlikely to be a woman's.

Perhaps mention should be made here of the ingenious theory of Miss Ethel Seaton, propounded in her book *Sir Richard Roos: Lancastrian Poet* (1961), that FL and AL, as well as most other fifteenth-century poetry, are by Sir Richard Roos, known to us in the past only as the translator of Alain Chartier's *La Belle Dame sans Merci*. Her case is based on the supposed existence of obscure and hitherto unrecognised double acrostic anagrams in the poems she ascribes to him. There is no real analogue for this device; but in any case Miss Seaton's methods of going to work on the poems are so preposterous that it would be tedious to embark on a criticism of them. However, putting aside the question of authorship, it would be churlish not to recognise the liveliness with which Miss Seaton writes; she has little to add to our knowledge of FL, but her account of the neglected AL (pp. 294–308) has some shrewd insights and is particularly interesting in its analysis of the social background.

It remains now to assemble the evidence as to the date of FL and AL. Of the two, making due allowance for scribal corruption and modernisation, and for the possibility of deliberate archaism, FL appears to be the earlier: the more conservative treatment of final -*e*, -*es*, -*ed*, and the more archaic vocabulary, grammar, and syntax all support this conclusion, though AL occasionally preserves an older linguistic usage, and makes less use of *y*/*ie* rhymes. The more formal garden of AL, the maze and arbour, the architecture of Plesaunt Regard, and the dress of Lady Loyalty also seem to suggest that the poem is later, since they reflect the fashions of the later reign of Edward IV, when, during a period of comparative calm (1472–83), England was much influenced by the closer association with Burgundy and the Continent.[1] The garden and arbour in FL, the dresses of the ladies, the accoutrements of the knights, could all come

[1] See notes to AL 10, 32, 53, 55, 70, 161, 162, 165 (see Berdan, *Early Tudor Poetry*, p. 66), 523, 526 (cf. FL 141, 152).

from Chaucer, or even earlier, though again we have to reckon with archaism in FL: AL tends to reflect everyday, contemporary life and habits, whereas FL seeks its expression in the conventions of the past.

However, grammar, rhymes, vocabulary,[1] versification, literary borrowings, social setting, the allusion to the Garter (FL 519) and (in AL) MSS all combine to indicate a date for both poems in the third quarter of the fifteenth century, AL possibly even a little later. AL, with its smooth versifying and effortless padding, must be the work of a practising poet, another salvo in the interminable feminist controversy of the fifteenth century (see below, pp. 53–4); it may, like *Generydes*, be based on a French original (see 61, 62, 86, 225, 471, 707, 752, and notes). FL looks more like the work of a non-professional poet, perhaps a woman.

THEMES AND CONVENTIONS

In FL the narrator, unable to sleep, goes out for a walk: from an oak-grove a little path leads to an arbour, where she sees a nightingale singing in a laurel, a goldfinch in a medlar tree (126). She hears singing and sees a company of ladies, dressed in white and wearing chaplets of laurel, woodbine, and agnus castus; their singing and dancing are led by a beautiful lady carrying a branch of agnus castus (189). Then a great company of knights appear, all dressed in white, some with crowns of laurel, others with chaplets and branches of laurel, oak, hawthorn, and woodbine; first come trumpeters, then kings of arms, heralds, and pursuivants, nine knights, each with three henchmen, and finally a great rout of knights (273). They joust, and then go to meet the ladies, and singing and dancing begin afresh under a huge laurel tree (322). Then she sees another company, of knights and ladies together, dressed in green, with chaplets of flowers; they sing in praise of the daisy (353). But as the sun grows hot the second company faint in the heat, while a sudden storm drenches them; they are comforted in their distress by the

[1] See notes to FL 10, 65, 160, 245, 252, 348, 395, 406, 459; AL 6, 47, 82, 165, 192, 225, 471, 550.

company of the leaf, who have been sheltered by the laurel, and the lady of the leaf invites them all to be her guests (433). As they all ride away the nightingale flies to the lady of the leaf and settles on her hand, while the goldfinch flies to the lady of the flower (448). The narrator, emerging from her arbour, meets a lady in white, who explains that the followers of the leaf are the chaste, the faithful, and the valorous; their queen is Diana, and those crowned in laurel are the Nine Worthies. The followers of the flower are the idle and pleasure-loving, led by Flora (543). She explains why the leaf and flower have this significance, and questions the narrator as to her allegiance; then she hurries off to catch up her company, leaving the narrator to her epilogue.

The lady in AL is telling her story to a knight (28). She tells how one afternoon she lost her friends in a maze and found her way to an arbour, where she fell asleep (77). In a dream a lady, Perseveraunce, comes to tell her that an assembly is to be held by Lady Loyalty to hear women's grievances, and that she must come, dressed in blue, with her friends, to the palace of Pleasaunt Regard. Diligence will act as her guide, but no men are to come (190). After Perseveraunce has left Diligence arrives, and they journey to the palace (231). She puts on a blue dress which a friend has brought for her, and they are admitted to the palace by the porter, Countenaunce, who tells her the names of other officers of Lady Loyalty's court, and how she is to present her complaint (364). Her friends arrive, followed by many other ladies, and Perseveraunce busies herself with the formalities of admission to the court (427). The chamberlain, Remembraunce, leads them to the throne-room, where Lady Loyalty presently makes her entrance (539). She commands that the petitions be read to her by her secretary Avisenesse (581), and this is done (707). Having heard the petitions, Lady Loyalty says that a further parliament will soon be held to remedy their grievances. They thank her, but just as they set out to depart (735) the lady woke up. The knight to whom she has been relating her dream compliments her on her story, and she leaves to rejoin her friends.

The remarks that follow are devoted mainly to FL, and they are intended to illuminate the complex of social and literary conventions from which the poem is drawn. Particularisation of individual sources has been made only incidentally, since the poem springs from such a long and complex tradition: to say that FL is an imitation of Deschamps's *Lay de Franchise*, or of Machaut's *Dit dou Vergier*, can be grossly misleading.[1]

The cult of the flower and the leaf

In the earlier version (F) of the Prologue to *LGW*, Chaucer, after offering his homage to the daisy, begs for help from lovers in praising the flower, saying it is part of their duty to do so,

> Whethir ye ben with the leef or with the flour.
>
> (72)

There is the suggestion here of another cult which that of the daisy transcends. He continues with his praise of the daisy, admitting his indebtedness to earlier poets, and then describes how he went out on May morning to worship the daisy. He lies on the ground gazing at it.

> I pray to God that faire mote she falle,
> And alle that loven floures, for hire sake.
>
> (187)

This suggests to him a possible misinterpretation of his lines, which he hastens to correct.

> But natheles, ne wene nat that I make
> In preysing of the flour agayn the leef,
> No more than of the corn agayn the sheef;
> For, as to me, nys lever noon ne lother.
> I nam withholden yit with never nother;
> Ne I not who serveth leef, ne who the flour.
> Wel browken they her service or labour;

---

[1] Such statements are made by McClumpha, ' Origin of FL ', *MLN* 4 (1889), 201–3; E. G. Sandras, *Étude sur Chaucer* (Paris, 1859), pp. 95–106. G. L. Marsh's valuable article on ' The Sources and Analogues of FL ', *MP* 4 (1906–7), 121–68, 281–328, to which the following pages are much indebted, avoids this error.

For this thing is al of another tonne,
Of olde storye, er swich stryf was begonne.

(188–96)

Chaucer is evidently referring to another cult which had
been introduced at the court of Richard II, a cult by which
lovers offered their service either to the flower or to the leaf;
his tone towards the new fad is sarcastic (190, 194). However, in the later version (G) of the Prologue the first easy
dismissal of the cult (F 72) is removed, and in its place we
find an assurance that no one need be offended by his praise
of the daisy,

> Sith it is seyd in fortheryng and honour
> Of hem that eyther serven lef or flour,
>
> (70)

and he has moved his earlier defence against possible accusa-
tions of partiality (F 188–96) so that it follows immediately
afterwards (G 71–80), with the sarcasm noticeably toned
down. This is tidier, of course, but there is another infer-
ence to be drawn: that the cult of the flower and the leaf
had grown in influence since the Prologue was first written,
and that Chaucer was more than ever concerned to remove
any suggestion that by praising the daisy he was participating
in the flower–leaf strife, or that he thought the latter of
ephemeral significance.

Chaucer may well have been acquainted with the poems
written by Deschamps about the cult, in which the existence
of two orders is clearly indicated.[1] The first poem declares
that the flower, for its beauty and scent, and for the fruit it
produces, far surpasses the leaf which, though green and
pleasant, is less beautiful, and exists only to serve and protect
the flower. The second opens:

> Pour ce que j'ay oy parler en France
> De deux ordres en l'amoureuse loy,
> Que dames ont chascune en defferance

---

[1] Poems 764–7 (SATF edition, iv, 257–64). See G. L. Kittredge,
' Chaucer and some of his Friends ', *MP* 1 (1903–4), 1–18; Marsh, *op.
cit.*, pp. 126–31.

L'une fueille et l'autre fleur, j'octroy
Mon corps, mon cuer a la fleur;

the reasons he gives for offering his allegiance to the flower
are similar to those in the first poem. The particular
association of the orders with women—though men were
not excluded—is to be noted, since it is what we find in FL.
Later in the poem Philippa of Lancaster, daughter of John
of Gaunt, is named as patroness of the order of the flower.
In the third poem a woman addresses ' Tresdouce flour,
Elyon de Nillac ', and to the flower, symbolising the person,
allegiance is given. The fourth poem, however, takes the
side of the leaf: the flower fades but the leaf remains ' forte,
ferme et loyaulx ', offering shelter from the sun, healing the
sick, and freshening the air; everyone wears green leaves in
May time, and even in winter ivy has leaves still; in any
case, fruit is not very good for you. The envoy names several
French noblemen who were adherents of the order of the
leaf.

It may be assumed, then, that one of the diversions of
court society in England and France at the end of the
fourteenth century was to divide into two amorous orders,
and to argue, no doubt with great subtlety, the comparative
merits of the flower and the leaf. It is clear, however, that
no symbolic association was made between the properties
of the flower or leaf and the moral qualities of their adherents,
though it can readily be seen, from Deschamps's arguments
for the leaf, how natural the moral interpretation was to be.

Evidence for the survival of the cult into the fifteenth
century is provided by two poems of Charles of Orleans,
probably written about 1435, during his long imprisonment
in England.[1] The first describes a May-day game in which
each member of the company chose either the flower or the
leaf as emblem for the coming year; there appears to have
been an element of chance in the choice, and to his lot fell
the leaf, which he concludes is appropriate enough, since
the only flower he was interested in, his lady, is dead. A

[1] For the French version see *Poésies*, ed. P. Champion (CFMA,
1923–7), *Ballades* 61–2 (i, 85–8); for the English version, probably also
by Charles, see *English Poems*, ed. Steele, *Ballades* 65–6 (pp. 75–7).

rather sad envoy rejects both leaf and flower as transitory
(see FL, 562n). In the second poem he tells how, on the
second of May, in a dream, a flower comes to him, reproach-
ing him for changing his allegiance; he replies that it was
his fortune to choose the leaf, and in any case it is only a
playful custom. His true allegiance, he declares, is still, for
the sake of the flower that was taken from him, to the flower,

> Though that I levys were a thousand skore.

These poems may refer to English custom, or may be based
on reminiscences of the practice of the cult in France before
he was taken prisoner.

Another poem which may have reference to the flower–
leaf strife is one (B.XIX) of a group of poems attributed to
the Duke of Suffolk and edited by MacCracken in *PMLA*
26 (1911). It is re-edited separately in Hammond's *English
Verse between Chaucer and Surrey* (p. 200), where it is
entitled ' A Reproof to Lydgate '. It is a poem in praise of
the daisy, and contains these lines:

> And for the fayth I owe unto thys flour,
> I must of reson do my observaunce
> To flours all, both now and every our.

The poem ends with a reproof to Lydgate for doubting the
truth of women. MacCracken suggests that it is a love
poem addressed to Margaret of Anjou, whose device was a
daisy, and whom Suffolk brought over to marry Henry VI.
If there is a reference to the cult of the flower and the leaf,
the suggestion is that worship of the daisy was often associated, despite Chaucer, with adherence to the flower.

Gower has often been quoted as evidence that the followers
of the flower and the leaf sometimes appeared in force, as in
FL, at May-day festivities. At the end of the *Confessio
Amantis* the poet sees Youth leading a company of lovers,
who are wearing on their heads

> Garlandes noght of o colour,
> Some of the lef, some of the flour,
> And some of grete Perles were.
>
> (viii, 2467–9)

c

However, such references to the traditional May-day ceremony of wearing garlands of leaves and flowers are commonplace, and indicate the source rather than the practice of the cult. Similarly, in the *Knight's Tale* Manly sees a reference to the strife of the flower and the leaf in Arcite's song (*CT*, I, 1512); but Arcite is thinking of nothing more than the common practice of going out to gather branches of woodbine and hawthorn on May morning.[1]

There must have been many of these cults or ' games ' of love in the courts of fifteenth-century England and France. They were a kind of ritual as well as an amusement, part of a code of social behaviour in which the relationships between the sexes, in this rich, leisured society, were formalised as in a dance. St Valentine's Day, for instance, when birds and lovers choose their mates, was a courtly institution, a day of festival and diversion,[2] and the custom of choosing one's lover for the coming year on 14 February, and presenting him with a green chaplet, is mentioned by Christine de Pisan (*Virelay* X, *Dit de la Rose*, 638). May day was celebrated with many customs, and the cult of the daisy has been mentioned. A further analogue is provided by the symbolism of the holly and the ivy at Christmas festivities. The custom of creating ' orders ' as a form of literary and social amusement, quite apart from the genuine orders of chivalry like the Garter and the Golden Fleece, was also common. There was Christine de Pisan's order of the Rose, to be bestowed on those knights who defend the honour of women,[3] and Boucicaut's ' L'Escu vert a la dame blanche ', for the same purpose. Deschamps even suggests the names

---

[1] See H. Savage, ' Arcite's maying ', *MLN* 55 (1940), 207–9; Manly's note is in his edition of selected *CT* (1929).

[2] See *The Parlement of Foulys*, ed. D. S. Brewer (Nelson's Medieval and Renaissance Library, 1960), especially pp. 4–7. For the ' game of love ' in general in the fifteenth century, see the excellent chapter in J. Stevens, *Music and Poetry in the Early Tudor Court* (1961), pp. 154–202.

[3] *Dit de la Rose*. Tarbé (*Poètes de Champagne* (Reims, 1847–61), v, 80) gives further examples. He suggests that the emblem of the order of the flower was the rose, already a royal device in England, and consequently associated with John of Gaunt and Philippa his daughter.

of people who might become members of ' l'ordre de la
baboe [grimace] ' (Poem 927), an *élite* of hard drinkers.

The origins of the cult of the flower and the leaf, and
the practices associated with it described in FL, are closely
bound up with May-day observances and festivities.
Generally speaking, the custom on May morning was for
people to go out into the woods and fields before dawn, and
there to gather flowers and branches of greenery, especially
hawthorn, which were brought back to bedeck houses.
Chaplets and garlands of leaves and flowers were worn by
both sexes, and the gift of one was a token of love. Hawthorn
was so closely associated with these customs that in England
it came to be called simply ' may ', though in France ' le mai '
could be woodbine or honeysuckle or any spring greenery.
The gathering of branches and flowers and the journey home
were accompanied by singing and dancing. Young girls
going out would often wear white, though the more customary
colour was green (e.g. Deschamps, Poems 415, 419f):
Guenevere insisted that at her ' maying ' all her knights
should be clad in green and be accompanied by a squire and
two yeomen (cf. the three ' henshmen ' in FL).[1]

Courtly practice should be distinguished at this point from
the popular customs of which it was a delicate imitation.
The popular practice was for young people to go out at mid-
night to the woods, and to spend the night in ' plesant
pastimes ', with the result, as the Elizabethan moralist
Stubbes credibly reports, ' that of fortie, 3 score, or a 100
maides going to the wood over night, there have scaresly
the third parte of them returned home againe undefiled '.[2]
Some relaxation of morals certainly characterised May night,
though it may not have been the riot of licence the Puritan

[1] Malory, ed. Vinaver (3 vols., 1947), iii, 1121f. For descriptions of
May-day customs see *CT*, I, 1033–55; Douglas, *Aeneid*, xii, Prologue
(ed. Small (1874), iv, 80); *CL* 1431–42; Christine de Pisan (ed. SATF),
i, 235, 239; Orleans 1692; J. Bédier, ' Les Fêtes de Mai ', *RDM* (1896),
iii, 146–72; J. Brand, *Popular Antiquities* (ed. H. Ellis, 2 vols., 1813), i,
179–203; R. Tuve, *Seasons and Months* (Paris, 1933), pp. 115, 162–5;
A. R. Wright, *British Calendar Customs*, ii (1938), 195ff.

[2] *Anatomy of Abuses*, ed. Furnivall, New Shakespeare Society (1877),
p. 149.

imagination envisaged. Courtly imitation of the popular
festival was in some sense an escape from the artificial
complexities of court life to a more carefree, ' natural ' life,
and reflected the pastoral ideal, the idyllic vision of rustic
life which was as much part of French court society in the
fourteenth and fifteenth centuries as in the eighteenth.[1]

The May-day festivities were often very elaborate, with
performances of pageants and mumming plays, courtly ' dis-
gysings ', contests of archery, feasting, and jousting.[2] The
rich ceremonial so vividly and brilliantly described in FL,
the stately splendour of the procession, the sumptuous array,
all have their match in contemporary reality. Nor is it
difficult to imagine such an exodus of the court into the fields
of a May morning, where singing and dancing in companies
were followed by jousting and a courtly ' disgysing ' of the
Nine Worthies. In Deschamps's *Lay Amoureux*, after the
customary gathering of may and presentation of flower
chaplets, there follow singing, dancing, jousting, and feasting,
in groups and companies. This division into companies is
mentioned also by Stubbes. In Deschamps's *Lay de
Franchise*, a source of the Prologue to *LGW*, the poet goes
out to do his observance to the daisy, and comes to a garden
where he sees a company of ladies in green; he hides and
watches them singing and making chaplets. Then a great
company of knights come, in their midst a king in green;
they receive chaplets and branches from the ladies and then
engage in vigorous jousting, afterwards declaring their
allegiance to Love. The poem was inspired by the May
fêtes of Charles VI at the *château* of Beauté in 1385, when
the king went out in the midst of the company dressed all in
green. It was at some such festival, presumably, that the
orders of the flower and the leaf were inaugurated, taking over
and giving a further significance to the customs of May day.

---

[1] See Deschamps, *Lay de Franchise*, 268–312, and Poem 315; Pisan,
Dit de la Pastoure; Huizinga, *Waning of the Middle Ages* (1924), chap. x;
I. Siciliano, *Villon et les thèmes poétiques du moyen âge* (Paris, 1934),
pp. 407–20.
[2] Chambers, *Medieval Stage*, i, 160–81; G. Wickham, *Early English
Stages 1300–1660*, i (1959), 13–50, 191–228.

Many of the practices described in FL, quite apart from the origins of the cult, are thus bound up with May festivities: the wearing of chaplets of leaves and flowers, the carrying of branches of foliage, especially hawthorn, the homage to the daisy, the singing, dancing, and jousting, the distinctions of dress, as well as the original division into companies.

Significance of the allegory

In FL the cult of the flower and the leaf is taken as the symbolic basis of a moral antithesis, with the idle love of pleasure of the servants of the flower (536–9) contrasted with the chastity and constancy, the honour and valour, of the servants of the leaf. The leaves of different trees signify different virtues, and the only one specifically contrasted with the flower is the laurel (544–65), but it is clear that the poet of FL is infusing into a light-hearted courtly game (cf. Charles of Orleans's comments) a new significance, based on an age-old correspondence of the flower and the leaf with certain aspects of human life. This correspondence must now be examined.

The fundamental contrast is of the transitory beauty of the flower with the less beautiful but more enduring leaf. There is also a difference in operation: ' The main function of the flower is accomplished only in its death; that of the leaf depends on prolonged work during its life'. The leaf is eternal not in itself but in its contribution to the life of the individual tree, which the flower does not assist at all. Thus the leaf is a symbol of human life as it should be—' just, laborious, united in aim, beneficent in fulfilment '—while the flower is expressive of the fading away of mere pleasure and self-indulgence.[1]

The symbolism of the flower and the leaf was particularly powerful in the Middle Ages through Biblical associations.

[1] These quotations and comments are from Ruskin, viz. *A Lecture on Tree Twigs* (*Works*, ed. Cook and Wedderburn, vii, 474), where he refers to FL; *Modern Painters*, vol. v (vii, 99f); *Proserpina*, chap. iii (xxv, 247). Comparison may be made here with *The Owl and the Nightingale* (ed. E. G. Stanley, Nelson's Medieval and Renaissance Library, 1960), where the Owl, a sober bird, sits on a tree-stump covered with ivy, while the frivolous Nightingale is surrounded by blossoms (see Introduction, p. 23).

' All flesh is grass, and all the goodliness thereof is as the flower of the field. . . . The grass withereth, the flower fadeth: but the word of our God shall stand for ever ' (Isaiah 40:6–8; 1 Peter 1:24f). ' For the sun is no sooner risen with a burning heat, but it withereth the grass, and the flower thereof falleth, and the grace of the fashion of it perisheth : so also shall the rich man fade away in his ways ' (James 1:11). ' As for man, his days are as grass: as a flower of the field, so he flourisheth. For the wind passeth over it, and it is gone; and the place thereof shall know it no more' (Psalm 103:15f). Grass and flowers are the conventional images for the transitoriness of human life (e.g. Job 14:2; Isaiah 28:1, 4; Psalms 90:5, 102:4, 11). The unfading leaf, however, is the symbol of the godly man: ' And he shall be like a tree planted by the rivers of water, that bringeth forth his fruit in his season ; his leaf also shall not wither; and whatsoever he doeth shall prosper ' (Psalm 1:3). ' For he shall be as a tree planted by the waters, and that spreadeth out her roots by the river, and shall not see when heat cometh, but her leaf shall be green ' (Jeremiah 17:8). The righteous man is compared to a green olive tree (Psalm 52:8); he will flourish as the palm and the cedar (92:12). Evergreen trees are the special gift of God (Isaiah 41:19, 55:13, 60:13; Ezekiel 47:12). No doubt the symbolism of the leaf is to be associated with the unfading tree of life (Genesis 2:9; Revelation 22:2); the figure of the unfading leaf of the tree by the waters would also have greater potency for the Eastern mind.

These images were developed in the patristic commentaries, and occasionally an explicit contrast was drawn between the enduring leaf of the godly and the fading flower of the worldly, usually by bringing together two Biblical texts. Such a contrast appears ' in a position of prominence at the beginning of the most authoritative of all commentaries on the most widely read book of the Bible, Augustine's commentary on the Psalms ',[1] where Psalm 1 and Isaiah 40 are

---

[1] D. W. Robertson, ' The Doctrine of Charity in Medieval Literary Gardens ', *Speculum* 26 (1951), 30: a valuable article (24–49). For Augustine see Migne, *Patrologia Latina*, 36, col. 68.

associated. Elsewhere Isaiah's *flos foeni* is contrasted with the palm or cedar of the righteous, as by Augustine, Cassiodorus, and Peter Lombard on Psalm 92 (Migne, *PL*, 37, col. 1179; 70, col. 659; 191, col. 860), by Jerome on Job 8:12 (*PL*, 26, col. 637), by Bede and Martin of Leon on James 1 (*PL*, 93, col. 13; 209, col. 187), and by Bede on Psalm 1 (*PL*, 93, col. 187). The image of flowers and grass as representing the transitory desires and glory of the flesh was elaborately developed by many commentators,[1] and in a famous passage in Jerome's commentary on Isaiah 40 the flower symbolises the beauty of a young girl: at first she attracts hordes of admiring young men, but soon the freshness of her beauty fades, and she is disdained. So fade all worldly pleasures: ' foenumque est et flos praeteriens ' (*PL*, 24, col. 402). The unfading leaf of the tree of life, on the other hand, symbolises the word of God, the healing power of spiritual grace, as in the commentaries of Jerome (*PL*, 24, cols. 417, 536, 788; 25, col. 475), Ambrose (*PL*, 17, col. 963), Rufinus of Aquila (*PL*, 21, col. 647), Remigius of Auxerre (*PL*, 131, col. 153), Bruno the Carthusian (*PL*, 152, col. 641), Honorius of Autun (*PL*, 172, col. 277), Peter Lombard (*PL*, 191, col. 64), and Martin of Leon (*PL*, 209, col. 413).

It would be only right to point out that the explicit contrast of flower and leaf made by Augustine is rare, and that they could carry other meanings. Thus the leaf is also used as an image of human frailty (Isaiah 64:6), while the flower which in Adam was fading is eternal in Christ (e.g. Prosper of Aquitaine, in *PL*, 51, col. 286). The Virgin was *flos campi* or *flos florum*, and martyrs wore crowns of roses and lilies (e.g. *CT*, VIII, 220). Nevertheless, it is clear that the moral interpretation of the flower and the leaf in FL is in part simply a secularisation of a traditional symbolism associated with them in the Bible and in scriptural exegesis.

The imagery of the flower, which had classical warrant

---

[1] For example, Augustine (*PL*, 36, col. 607; 37, cols. 1242, 1333, 1909); Jerome (*PL*, 26, col. 1093); Ambrose (*PL*, 14, col. 167); Gregory (*PL*, 75, col. 983; 79, col. 606); Origen (Migne, *Patrologia Graeco-Latina*, 12, col. 1323).

too (e.g. *Iliad*, vi, 146; *Aeneid*, vi, 309; Horace, *Odes*, II, xi, 9; Ovid, *Ars Amatoria*, II, 115), is deeply rooted in medieval literature, particularly in moralising poets like Deschamps and Lydgate.   Lydgate often associates the flower of worldly beauty and pleasure with the *shoures* of adversity (cf. FL) which it cannot endure.

> He knew afforn & sauh bexperience
> That al beute shal waste a-wey & fade
> Lik somer flours in ther most excellence,
> That growe on hillis & lowe doun in the shade:
> The rose, the lilie, when thei be most glade,
> Upon ther stalkis—ther preef is alday seyn—
> Been beten doun with a stormy reyn.

The image is specifically applied to the daisy.

> Alcestis flowr, with whit, with red and greene,
> Displaieth hir crown geyn Phebus bemys briht,
> In stormys dreepith.[1]

Deschamps develops at length Jerome's comparison of a beautiful woman with a flower in the anti-feminist *Miroir de Mariage* (5805–65).   Chaplets of flowers, quite apart from their association with May day, were usually regarded as the signs of carnal or light love, as worn for instance by Venus (*HF*, 135; *RS*, 1572; *Troy*, ii, 5724), Priapus (*PF*, 259), Ydelnesse (*RR*, 566), or those who love *paramours* (*Pilg.*, 11603–9).

The imagery of the leaf was less firmly established, except in particular cases like the laurel and hawthorn, which will be dealt with later.   Hence we sometimes find the leaf used as a symbol of transience (e.g. *Conf. Am.*, viii, 2854; *Fall*, i, 4563), and also the Biblical contrast of fading with unfading leaves *and* flowers, as in Lydgate's description of Paradise (*Fall*, i, 540ff).   In *RS* the forest of Diana is full of trees whose leaves never fade, not for sun, frost, wind, hail, or rain (2727–49; cf. FL, 556), and of unfading flowers (2764–

---

[1] *Fall*, v, 57–63; *Minor Poems*, ii, 770.   See also *Minor Poems*, i, 5, 17, ii, 781; *Troy*, ii, 2008, v, 3568; *Fall*, i, 942, 6086, iii, 2201, vi, 20; Gower, *Conf. Am.*, Prologue, 937; Deschamps, Poem 280; and for the *shoures* of adversity, *Fall*, i, 6069, iii, 4856, iv, 1644, v, 1339, etc.

2772), while in the Garden of Deduyt, where people think of nothing but mirth and play (5554), the appearance of eternal freshness, Diana tells us, is illusory (3900–4).

In addition to the Biblical associations of the flower and the leaf, FL is perhaps also connected with popular customs in which the leaf symbolised virginity, the flower defloration. In the Italian Tyrol, reports Gubernatis (*Mythologie des Plantes* (Paris, 1878), i, 143), young girls wore a green leaf in their hair until their marriage, when it was replaced by artificial flowers; in the May-day rites of Brittany, the branch of may given to a girl as a token of love must bear no flower or bud, for flowers in bloom would mean that she was no longer a virgin.[1] In a Picard poem quoted by Marsh (*op. cit.*, p. 135), the flower and the leaf seem to symbolise love and honour respectively.

Apart from the fundamental contrast of the flower and the leaf expressed in the character of the two companies, the allegory of FL also acts out certain other aspects of the contrast. The shelter which the leaf affords to flowers is mentioned (365–7) and symbolised in the comfort Diana's company offers to Flora and her followers. The healing power of the leaf, another topic in Deschamps's praise, is symbolised by the ointments and salads (407–13) which are collected for the distressed company of the flower. The ordeal which the latter are made to undergo, of scorching sun followed by wind, hail, and rain (354–71), is in some sort an objectification of the carnal, worldly love which the flower typifies, the waves of passion, the alternate hot and cold.

> And thus with colde and with sodein hete
> Was Medea in hir silfe assailled.
> (*Troy*, i, 1964f; cf. *TC*, i, 420—a favourite oxymoron)

There is an interesting parallel with the *De Amore* of Andreas the Chaplain (trans. J. J. Parry, Columbia, 1941). In the fifth Dialogue Andreas describes three gardens, inhabited by different women. One, pleasant, shady, and well watered,

---

[1] Gubernatis, ii, 87. Cf. Hoffmann-Krayer, *Handwörterbuch des deutschen Aberglaubens* (10 vols., Berlin und Leipzig, 1927–42), iv, 495, v, 1512.

is for those who are faithful and discreet in the service of love; another, arid and scorching, is for those who deny love; and a third, soggy and marshy underfoot with the ice-cold waters of the overflowing fountain, but with the sun beating down mercilessly overhead, is for those who are lustful and who indulge the flesh without discrimination.

Accessories to the allegory

The symbolism of the leaf could be, as we have seen, somewhat ambiguous, and it is therefore strengthened in FL by association with two trees whose symbolism could not be mistaken, the laurel and the hawthorn. The laurel, in fact, is fundamental to the allegory of the leaf, and the agnus castus, oak, ' cereal oak ', and woodbine (for discussion of which see notes to 160, 269, 209, and 485), as well as the hawthorn, are subordinate to it. Chaplets of laurel are worn by both ladies (158) and knights (268), the Nine Worthies wear crowns of laurel (249), and some knights carry branches of it (271); the nightingale sings in a laurel tree (109), and the company of the leaf shelter under a huge bay-laurel (304; see note).

The laurel is an evergreen, its leaf unfading (*Anel.*, 19; *CT*, IV, 1466), and therefore symbolises endurance. It is an apt reward for military valour since it confers its own immortality on the glorious deeds of the recipient; this is the main association in FL (see 507n). It betokens also wisdom, long perseverance in virtue (548), and foresight (*Fall*, v, 533–46), and martyrs win the crown of laurel by their patient endurance of suffering and adversity (*Pilg.*, 7484–98). But the laurel is further appropriate to FL because it is an emblem of purity; the Greek name, Daphne, was that of a nymph who was turned into a laurel in order to preserve her virginity when she was being pursued by Apollo. The story is told by Gower (*Conf. Am.*, iii, 1716ff) after Ovid, and in *L'Espinette Amoureuse* (1571–1763) by Froissart, who associates the myth not only with the symbolism of military honour but also with loyal and pure love (2855–67).

Hawthorn, branches of which are carried by ladies of the leaf (272), is explicitly associated with constancy in love in

Lydgate's *Temple of Glass*. Venus, who is herself wearing a chaplet of hawthorn leaves instead of the usual roses, grants the lady's prayer for help in love, and gives her branches of hawthorn

> Which shul not fade ne nevir wexin old,

enjoining her to be faithful in love and unchanging,

> As ar these leves, the which mai not die
> Thuruȝ no dures of stormes, that be kene,
> No more in winter then in somer grene.
>
> (514–16)

Schick gives parallels in his note to this passage.

The other main accessory to the allegory of the leaf is the nightingale (109n). According to the legend of Philomena as told by Gower (*Conf. Am.*, v, 5943–6002; cf. *LGW*), the nightingale sings only in summer because she wants to be hidden by the foliage, for shame at her lost maidenhead, which her song bewails. A common motif of the Middle Ages was to make the song of the nightingale an allegory of the Passion. The idea was given currency in a Latin poem by John Peckham and is represented in the fifteenth century by two pseudo-Lydgatian nightingale poems (ed. EETS (E.S.) 80 (1900)). In the first, the nightingale sings ' upon a laurer grene ' (l. 63), and the poet hopes that his account of the song will discredit ' love unlawfle ' and ' fleschly lust ' (ll. 20f). The antithesis, of course, as in the second poem, is divine love, but there is certainly some idea of chaste and serious human love behind it. It is this association of the nightingale with the more serious aspects of love which we find in FL, and, although nightingales are always connected with love and its festivities (see 39n), it is clear that this particular association was widely accepted (see Marsh, *op. cit.*, p. 162).

The choice of the medlar and the goldfinch to symbolise indolence and frivolous pleasure in the allegory of the flower hardly needs explaining. ' As the fruit of the medlar is rotten before it is ripe, it may be the emblem of sensual pleasure, which palls before it confers real enjoyment. The goldfinch is remarkable for the beauty of its plumage, the sprightliness of its movements, and its gay tinkling song, and may be supposed to represent the showy and unsubstantial character of frivolous pleasures' (Bell's *Chaucer* (1856), iv, 236). The popular name of the medlar (see 86n) may indicate a vulgar association with loose women; the old editions of Chaucer have a poem beginning 'O mossie Quince', addressed to an ageing prostitute (Speght, f. 325v). The goldfinch is not often mentioned elsewhere, but it is associated with gaiety in Chaucer (*CT*, I, 4367) and in the *Tale of Beryn* (476). (In Christian iconography it is the bird of day, the bringer of light.)

The daisy, which is the only flower actually associated with the allegory of the flower in FL, was, as we have seen, the subject of a cult somewhat older than that of the flower and the leaf, probably originated by Machaut in his *Dit de la Marguerite*. Machaut's praise of the daisy was echoed by Deschamps in his *Lay de Franchise* and his *Eloge d'une Dame du Nom de Marguerite* (Poem 539), by Froissart in a *balade* in *Le Paradys d'Amour* (1627–53) and other poems, and by Chaucer in *LGW*.[1] With these poems, as will be seen further in the notes, FL is closely related, though the line quoted from the *bargaret* (350) is not from any of them. In Chaucer, as in the French poets, the daisy is praised as the symbol of true womanhood, in its humility, its purity, in its following of the light of the sun, whose image it bears at its heart. In FL this symbolism is forgotten or suppressed; the fall from grace was inevitable after the worship of the daisy had been identified (e.g. by Suffolk) with adherence to the flower. The leaf, it will be seen, has taken over some of the attributes of the daisy, just as the daisy in its turn ' had fallen in large measure heir to the possessions of the Rose ' (Lowes, p. 629).

The symbolism of FL is extended also to the dress of the two companies: the followers of the leaf wear white, as an emblem of purity, while those of the flower wear green, which signifies inconstancy and frivolity in love. The association of white with purity needs no illustration; as in

[1] See J. L. Lowes in *PMLA* **19** (1904), 593–683; also Marsh, pp. 157–60.

FL, so on her appearances in the *Dit de la Rose* (279–81) by Christine de Pisan and in Lydgate's *Reason and Sensuality* (2816) Diana is clad in dazzling white. Further associations of white with joy and with soldierly qualities are quoted by Marsh (pp. 144f), and it has already been mentioned in connection with May festivities. The symbolism of green, however, was not without its contradictions: Diana, for instance, as a huntress is usually clad in green (e.g. *CT*, I, 2079); Emely, when she goes out hunting (*CT*, I, 1686), and Alceste (*LGW*, 214) both wear green, though with the latter it is part of the allegory of the daisy. But in general it is clear that green came to be associated more and more closely with frivolity and pleasure, and further, with inconstancy, especially in contrast with blue (see *AL*, 83n). So Chaucer, *Against Women Unconstant*:

> In stede of blew, thus may ye were al grene;

and Lydgate:

> Wachet bleuh of feyned stedfastnesse . . .
> Meynt with liht greene for chaung & doubilnesse;

while for Machaut, ' Blanc est joie, vert est nouvellete '.[1] In the fifteenth century ' the symbolic meaning attached to blue and green was so marked and peculiar as to make them almost unfit for usual dress ' (blue, because of the suspicion of hypocrisy). This comment by Huizinga (*Waning of the Middle Ages*, p. 249) emphasises the need to appreciate that distinctions of dress in the Middle Ages were of deep and immediate significance. Rank and allegiance were proclaimed in colours and liveries and devices; dress was only one part of a tendency to embody every meaning in expressive forms (Huizinga, *op. cit.*, chap. I). For the poet of FL, the distinction in the dress of the two companies was not a sterile literary fancy but an effective means of enriching the allegory. Some sense of this change in habits of thought is

---

[1] *Fall*, vi, 44–6; Machaut, *La Loange des Dames*, Balade 272 (ed. Chichmaref, i, 235). Cf. also *CT*, V, 646; *Fall*, i, 6447, vii, 1240; *Thebes*, 73; Pisan, *Autres Balades*, IX (i, 217); Machaut, *Remede de Fortune*, 1909; Watriquet de Couvin, *Li Dis des VIII Couleurs*, 227; Marsh, pp. 150–1.

fundamental to the appreciation of FL: whatever symbolism
attaches now to colours, or flowers and plants, is residual or
trivial or ' poetic ', but for the late-medieval poet, surrounded
by the images of heraldry, by emblems and devices (see AL,
85n), familiar with the symbolic properties of plants to
which the natural historians devoted most of their attention
(see FL, 407n), and with their significance in religion and art,
it was very different.   The symbolism of colours and precious
stones was elaborately exploited in the ceremonial of tournaments, which doubtless influenced FL, while for plants a
' Blason des Herbes, Arbres et Fleurs ' was published as a
kind of dictionary of symbolic usage.   Like colours, flowers
were a language: Ophelia's skilfully gathered bouquet could
express sentiments of affection or of gentle reproach.

The distinguishing of the companies in FL reflects the
practice of tournaments, where it was the custom for knights
and squires to appear in groups and companies, clad in one
colour ' d'uns paremens ', and their ladies likewise (e.g.
Deschamps, Poems 357, 444, 501).   In the *fête de tournoi*
described in *Le Livre du Duc des Vrais Amans*, for instance,
by Christine de Pisan, the duke and his retinue, and twenty
ladies, are all in white, while the squires and their ladies are
all in green (1013, 1254).

Courtly tradition

The allegory of the flower and the leaf is intended to enforce
a moral contrast between, on the one hand, idle and frivolous
pleasure, and on the other, chastity, constancy in love, and
prowess in chivalry.   The striking features of this contrast
are the association of chastity with constancy in love, and the
fact that Diana leads a company which includes faithful
lovers as well as maidens; furthermore, even those who wear
chaplets of agnus castus are chaste lovers rather than dedicated
virgins (see 302f, 320, 322).   FL, in fact, confronts us with a
reversal of the familiar antitheses of courtly love, for we often
think of the true courtly lover holding constant war, as the
poet of the *Court of Love* puts it (682–3), with chastity and
with Diana.   This emphasis in FL on purity and fidelity in
love, however, is not new in the literature of courtly love: the

concept of courtly love, as one might expect, varies from
place to place and from time to time, and, indeed, from poet
to poet, and in England at least it is not usually adulterous
but is characteristically thought of as leading to marriage.
This is Chaucer's view, finding its richest and most complex
expression in the *Parlement of Foules*,[1] and, on a simpler
level, it is the view of his successors. In Lydgate's *Temple
of Glass*, Venus, after bringing the two lovers together,
exhorts them to be true to one another, having made it clear
to the knight that

> She shal not have, ne take of the non hede
> Ferther then longith unto hir womanhede.

> (875)

In the *Kingis Quair*, Venus, using imagery that contrasts
markedly with that of FL, says that showers are her tears for
untrue love, and the rain makes the flowers grow,

> That preyen men in thaire flouris wise
> Be trewe of lufe, and worship my servise.

> (818–19)

The main theme of her advice to the lover (890–966) is to be
true in love, and the poem ends with the marriage of the
lovers. In the *Pastime of Pleasure*, Hawes leaves us in no
doubt that the intentions of Graunde Amour towards his
lady are entirely honourable. On the whole, it is clear that
the esoteric courtly ideal of a yearning, quasi-divine, in-
satiable, adulterous passion was an extreme manifestation of
the complex code of behaviour known as courtly love, and
that its doctrines had long been modified, especially in
England, towards the ideal of a chaste, loyal love leading to
marriage—though with much of the former imagery retained.
It is this latter ideal which is expressed in FL.

In France much more of the subtle sophistry of the *De
Amore* survived, as in the long sequence of poems prompted
by Alain Chartier's *La Belle Dame sans Merci*, but there is a

---

[1] See *PF*, ed. Brewer, p. 8; also J. A. W. Bennett's discussion in *The
Parlement of Foules* (1957). As early as *The Owl and the Nightingale* a
similar modification of the more esoteric doctrine of Andreas can be
seen (1340–2, and the note in Stanley's edition).

similar tendency to ' raise the moral tone ' of courtly love.
A good example of this tendency is *Les Cent Ballades* (ed.
SATF (1905)), written by a group of noblemen about 1390.
This series of poems sets out to debate whether loyal, self-
denying service to a single lady brings greater happiness in
love than the infidelities of fashionable flirtation, and concludes in favour of loyalty. Boucicaut, one of the authors of
the *Cent Ballades*, gave further expression to these ideals of
love and womanhood by creating, on his return from the
East in 1399, the order of ' L'Escu vert a la dame blanche ',
whose thirteen members vowed to defend the honour and
reputation of women (*Les Cent Ballades*, p. xxxv). Then, on
St Valentine's Day 1401, the Duke of Burgundy eclipsed
him by founding an elaborate *Cour Amoureuse*, with many
officers drawn from royalty and nobility; the court was
founded on the virtues of humility and fidelity, and ' to the
honour, praise, commendation and service of all ladies '.[1]
Though it appears that the court did in fact meet to hear
poems and songs and questions of love, it was of course no
more than a social amusement, partly designed to draw attention from the terrible plagues at that time raging in Paris;
many of its members were notorious debauchees. However,
the ideals to which an age gives expression are just as important, in their way, as the realities.

The ideal of a loyal and honourable love can be found
earlier, as in Machaut's *Dit dou Lyon*, where the central
allegory concerns a beautiful garden of eternal spring and
unfading foliage, representing ' L'Esprueve de fines amours '
(1778), and demands chastity (1466) from lovers; but the
dissemination of the ideal seems to have owed most to
Christine de Pisan. In *Le Livre du Duc des Vrais Amans*,
for instance, she tells of a duke who falls in love with the
wife of a nearby noble; although she returns his affection,
neither wishes to compromise her honour, ' de faire chose
villaine ' (2744), and so, in the intervals of their writing long
epistles to each other, he goes off to find expression for his
love by jousting and fighting and engaging in crusades

[1] Huizinga, pp. 102–3. See especially A. Piaget in *Romania* 20 (1891),
417–54; also *PF*, ed. Brewer, pp. 4, 132.

abroad. Christine's *Cent Balades d'Amant et de Dame* again glorify the honourable love strengthened and purified by the lover's absence in wars. The emphasis on martial virtue is important, for it is taken over in FL as one of the main elements in the moral contrast. Military prowess is also emphasised in the earlier *Cent Ballades* (VII–XVI), and seems to have been an integral part of the new ideal of love. It will be discussed later.

It has been suggested[1] that the kind of courtly love praised in FL, as well as the emphasis on morals, had something to do with the changing tastes of the age, with the growth of a new bourgeois reading class who were less interested in the artificial conventions of love than in common-sense morality. No doubt the new class of readers did help to bring about the fifteenth-century fusion of moral and erotic allegory, but it would be well to guard against any implication that FL represents a break with tradition, for, as we have seen, the attitudes it reflects had, in England at least, long been current. Furthermore, whatever ' common sense ' there may be in the morality of FL, the life which it mirrors is still very much a courtly and conventional ideal.

Homiletic tradition

The allegory of FL, apart from its debt to the courtly tradition, owes something also to homiletic contrasts which were commonplaces of the age. Didactic poetry gives full expression to these contrasts. In Lydgate's translation of the *Pilgrimage of the Life of Man*, for instance, we find Idleness set against Industry (11230), Sensuality against Mortification of the Flesh (12291), and Venus against Virginity (13089), while the *Assembly of Gods* is largely concerned with the conflict of Reason and Sensuality, perhaps the most familiar of all these themes, and the closest parallel with FL. In Gower, Reason and Will (Sensuality) are frequently contrasted (e.g. *Conf. Am.*, iii, 1199, 1859, 1867, 2335, 2428,

---

[1] H. S. Bennett, *Chaucer and the Fifteenth Century*, p. 134; the changing tastes of the age are dealt with by Bennett in *Essays and Studies* **23** (1937), 7–24; *RES* **19** (1943), 113–19; *MLR* **39** (1944), 1–8.

etc.): usually Reason counsels the complete rejection of courtly love, though chaste and faithful connubial love is not scorned. Lydgate, however, quite apart from many scattered references in the *Fall of Princes* (i, 6200, 6257; ii, 2535, etc.), develops this moral contrast most fully in *Reason and Sensuality*, a translation from the French *Les Échecs Amoureux*, and a poem closely connected in theme and imagery with FL. Like FL, Lydgate's poem is a fusion of moral and courtly allegory. At the beginning Nature describes the two ways of life: of Reason, man's godlike gift, by which he transcends his humanity and is exalted to the divine, and of Sensuality, concerned only with bodily delights (637–896). This is the fundamental homiletic position; but some concession to courtly ideals is made in the subsequent contrast of Minerva and Venus. It is Minerva who gives honour and glory to knights who, eschewing idleness, lead the virtuous life (1024–94), while Venus leads ' the amerouse constablerye ' (1470), ruled by fleshly appetite, fickle and changeful (1549–54). Further penetration of courtly ideals is seen in the rivalry of Diana and Venus, which occupies most of the poem. Diana represents chastity, of course, but in one illuminating speech, lamenting the increasing power of Venus and carnal love, she looks back to the days of King Arthur, when love was chaste and honourable, and knights did virtuous deeds to win their ladies' favour (3118–240). The parallel with FL is striking.

The successful reconciliation of moral and erotic allegory is rare before the *Faerie Queene*, but in FL a most delicate balance is maintained. The rivalry of the two orders is seen as a friendly and courteous one, and, though the later part of the poem, where the symbolism of the orders is explained, comes down firmly and unequivocally on the side of the leaf, the harshness of the moral opposition is softened by the concentration of emphasis on the virtues of the leaf, while the follies of the flower are dismissed with good-natured brevity in four lines of mild euphemism. The tone of the whole, in fact, is so far from being solemn that it has been suggested (by Stevens, *Music and Poetry in the Early Tudor*

Court, p. 182) that the allegory is all part of a game on the poet's part, playfully slandering the adherents of the opposing order and so adding a new twist to an old pastime. Yet there is about the poem an undertone of sobriety which makes this view seem inadequate; it is, after all, possible to be serious without making a long face, and it is one of the poet's gifts to eschew the heavy moralising and stark contrasts of much medieval didactic poetry. The allegory is drawn out from the situation rather than imposed upon it, with an urbane and practical kindliness which is yet strong enough to pervade every line of the poem. It is strange that some writers (e.g. Taine, *Histoire de la littérature anglaise* (1866), i, 191), though praising FL, have considered the allegory an obstacle to appreciation, or at best an irrelevant addition—strange, because without the allegory the poem is nothing. This attitude towards allegory seems to be based on two misconceptions of the nature of medieval poetry, which are still prevalent.

The first is that poetry has its own sphere, and should not attempt, or at most only in a very indirect way, to deal in ethics, or to offer principles or examples of conduct. Allegory is regarded as a means of ' sugaring the pill ', a poetic form of decoration for fundamentally unpoetic material. In the Middle Ages art and life were not so separated. Art had no transcendental significance of its own, but existed as a part of life, offering pattern, beauty, and ' sentence '. Allegory was an attractive way of presenting truths about life without crude didacticism; it was the manifestation of a habit of mind which saw underlying meanings in every word of Scripture, and which could give an orthodox Christian interpretation not only to Homer and Virgil but also to Ovid's *Metamorphoses* and the *Roman de la Rose*. For Dante, Petrarch, Boccaccio, for Lydgate and Hawes, allegory was coterminous with poetry.[1]

The second misconception is that allegory is mechanical, and works from a system of correspondences which have no

[1] See C. G. Osgood, *Boccaccio on Poetry* (Princeton, 1930), p. xxxviii; *Fall*, iii, 3830f; *Past. Pleas.*, 40–2; Hammond, *Chaucer to Surrey*, pp. 29, 409, 488, 492.

more than a fanciful interest. To some extent this is true, for allegory does involve a tendency to crystallise symbolic relations, and in this crystallisation life is sometimes lost. It is especially true of the late fifteenth century, when allegory was a habit, rather than the manifestation of a habit of mind, and when its predominance as a literary form was such that it was used almost automatically (see C. S. Lewis, *Allegory of Love*, p. 232). Even Lydgate sometimes uses allegory as a mere framework, apparent only in the introduction of personified abstractions. But allegory is never mechanical when it is the expression of some deeply observed symbolic relation. In *Piers Plowman*, in the best books of the *Faerie Queene*, in Bunyan, the allegory enriches the ' meaning ', and, to compare great things with small, the same is true of FL.

The elaborate descriptions of the companies involved in the allegory of FL have also been criticised as tedious and unnecessary (see for example *The English Poets*, ed. T. H. Ward (1883), i, 85). However, it should be clear by now that the detail is meaningful; and furthermore, description of this kind, as well as being one of the main ornaments of poetry, was peculiarly adapted to an age which was used to the pictorial presentation of meaning not only in art (AL, 456n) but also in the pageants, tournaments, and rich ceremonial of real life, and which could trace accurately and with ease the significance of elaborate, static descriptions.

In a sense, the disdain for allegory is only one aspect of the modern objection to abstraction in poetry. So Skeat dismisses FL as ' devoid of any human interest, as regards revelation of character ' (*Academy*, 35 (1889), 448), ' wholly lacking in interesting touches of personal character ' (*Chaucer Canon*, p. 139), while Chaucer is remembered for little realistic touches, the hole for the cat in the door of Nicholas's garret, the friar pushing the cat off the bench so that he can sit down; the squawking of the ducks in *PF* raises a readier sympathy than the rich allegory of the garden. Some common ground of appreciation will always be found, but it will not always be of much value.

Chivalry

The early fifteenth-century ideals of love were accompanied, as we have seen in Christine de Pisan and the *Cent Ballades*, by a fresh emphasis on knightly prowess. This was part of a longing for the days of true chivalry which permeates the late Middle Ages. Whether such a chivalry had ever in fact existed is doubtful; it certainly makes little appearance in the life of the fifteenth century, though sporadic acts of quixotic courtesy are recorded, as in the past by Froissart. But the cruelty and wanton destruction of the Hundred Years' War and the Wars of the Roses made men pine even more strongly for the ideals of the past, and the kind of love and chivalry idealised in FL reflects this longing. Malory associates chivalry very closely with pure love.

> But nowadayes men can nat love sevennyght but they muste have all their desyres. That love may nat endure by reson, for where they bethe sone accorded and hasty, heete sone keelyth. And ryght so faryth the love nowadayes, sone hote sone colde. Thys ys no stabylyte. But the olde love was nat so. For men and women coude love togydirs seven yerys, and no lycoures lustis was betwyxte them, and than was love, trouthe and faythefulnes. And so in lyke wyse was used such love in Kynge Arthurs dayes.   (ed. Vinaver, iii, 1119)

Caxton, who, like Malory, tried to enshrine in literature the departing spirit of chivalry, reproaches, in his Prologue to the *Book of the Order of Chivalry*, the idle pleasure-loving knights of his day: ' O ye knyghtes of Englond where is the custome and usage of noble chyvalry that was used in the dayes, what do ye now, but go to the baynes & playe atte dyse' (*Prologues and Epilogues*, ed. Crotch, EETS (O.S.) 176 (1928), 82).

This contrast of the pure love and chivalric honour of the past with the idle luxury of the present had been familiar in French literature for much longer; nowhere does it appear more strongly than in Deschamps. For him, of course, it was part of the conventional moralist's contempt for the present age (Poems 12, 31, 95, 96, 329, 343, etc.), the ' former age' motif treated also by Chaucer and Lydgate (*Fall*, vii, 1153ff). In his *Lay de Franchise*, a poem closely associated with FL, the knights joust and afterwards declare their allegiance to love, which alone can inspire prowess in arms; the present day, however, is dedicated to 'Lascheté, Convoitise, Paresce' (228–34). The *Lay de Vaillance* pictures an ideal age of chivalry, with the noble, pure, and valiant knight free from worldly desires and fleshly appetites, and contrasts the present age, when knights seem to care only for preening themselves, idling away the days, and indulging the flesh (90, 194). Sometimes Deschamps would look back to Roman times as the golden age of chivalry (*Lay de Plour*, 39; Poem 380; cf. FL, 531), sometimes only a few years, to the time of the great John of Bohemia, killed at Crecy (*Plour*, 177–206), or of Bertrand du Guesclin (*Lay de Bertrand du Guesclin*, 253). Elsewhere he uses the Nine Worthies to show the superiority of olden times in moral virtues and valour (e.g. Poems 12, 239, 403).

In FL, which has evidently been influenced by this longing for the past, we find the same contrast of two kinds of love, the same contrast of knightly prowess with idle luxury, and the same illustration of the chivalric ideal by reference to the Romans, the knights of King Arthur, and the Nine Worthies. Even the pastimes of the two companies have been influenced. By the strict moralist, the jousting of the one as well as the hunting and hawking of the other would all have been rejected as worldly vanities (e.g. Deschamps, Poem 108); another might tolerate hunting as a way of eschewing idleness (*Fall*, i, 4684); but in FL hunting and hawking are despised, since they are idle pleasures, and jousting is praised, since it demands valour and fortitude.

Briefly, then, FL starts from a courtly game, originally associated with May festivities; the game is invested with new significance drawn from the Bible and from other familiar symbolic associations, and used as the vehicle for a particular view of life, courtly and chivalric in its essence, but markedly influenced by homiletic morality. These are the themes of the poem. The conventions of structure, the machinery of the poem, will now be examined.

Conventions of structure

The narrative of FL is conducted according to a familiar pattern, which may be called the ' processional ' motif. In this pattern the poet, hidden, sees companies of people riding past in a procession, which is elaborately described; while he wonders at its significance, one of the knights or ladies stops to explain the meaning of what the poet has seen, and to draw out the allegory. The closest parallel to FL is provided by a group of narratives describing the ' purgatory of cruel beauties '—the title given by W. A. Neilson to his article on them in *Romania* **29** (1900), 85–93. There is an example in Gower. Rosiphelee, who has scorned all love in the past, rises before dawn on May morning and goes walking in the park, and as she stands musing she sees a company of ladies richly clad in white and blue, and mounted on white steeds. Rosiphelee hides herself, and sees a woman riding behind them laden with halters. This woman stops to explain that the company before her was of ladies who served love truly, while she herself in her lifetime rejected love and was thus punished (*Conf. Am.*, iv, 1245–1446). FL differs from this genre, of which Neilson gives several other examples, in that its allegory is not bound by the procession, but permits of subsequent action, and in that the allegory of reward and punishment which it displays is moral rather than courtly (*Allegory of Love*, pp. 247–8), though the poet, with a characteristic gentleness of spirit, modifies the rigour of the ' purgatory ' (354–71) by reconciling the companies through human pity and charity (372–433).

The processional motif is illustrated also in poems like Petrarch's *Triumph of Love* and Douglas's *Palace of Honour*, and with FL we may compare further the many poems in which the poet, from his hidden vantage-point, sees the companies of lovers or the retinue of the God of Love himself. The Prologue to *LGW* is one example which has certainly influenced FL; another is *La Panthere d'Amors* (ed. SATF (1883)), in which the poet, after hearing singing and music, sees a fine company, some jousting, some singing and dancing (217–19), among them one who stands out surpassing all the others (cf. FL, 164); it is the God of Love, who gives to the poet the interpretation of the allegory of the panther (463 ff).[1]

The introduction to the narrative of FL (1–126) adheres to the conventional pattern of spring setting followed by description of the garden. Both elements are almost obligatory in courtly love-vision literature. The fashion was set by *RR*, and observed in the poems of Machaut, Jean and Baudouin de Condé, Watriquet de Couvin, Deschamps, Froissart, Chaucer, Lydgate, Alain Chartier, and others.[2] Many parallels to these poems are quoted in the notes; it would not be wise to single out an individual ' source ', though the debt to *RR*, Chaucer, and Lydgate, and to other poems of the Chaucerian tradition like the *Kingis Quair* and the *Cuckoo and the Nightingale* is clear.

The rich and varied tradition of the spring opening has been carefully analysed by Rosemond Tuve.[3] She distinguishes two main elements in the tradition: the French, where the description was a mere back-cloth to the love motive; and the English, where there was a delight in beauty, a picture of the year's labours, an interest in scientific detail, a symbol of resurrection, and a recognition of great Nature's system. In FL, as she says, ' the bones of the old formulae show under a covering of borrowed phraseology ' (*op. cit.*, p. 70). Conventional elements which may be easily identified are the astronomical periphrasis (1–3), the ' clothing ' of the earth (7), the rain renewing what was dead in winter (10–12) and causing germination (12f), and the gladness which all feel at the approach of spring (13f).

The astronomical periphrasis has perhaps the noblest ancestry. It was the epic way of indicating time, and Quintilian commented that no poet could afford not to know astronomy (*Institutio Oratoria*, I, iv, 4). The mannerism

---

[1] Cf. also *Conf. Am.*, viii, 2454ff; *KQ*, 540–651; Deschamps, *Lay Amoureux*; Machaut, *Dit dou Vergier*, 157; Froissart, *Paradys d'Amour*, 957.

[2] See Marsh, chap. iii; W. O. Sypherd, *Studies in Chaucer's House of Fame* (Chaucer Society, 1907), pp. 1–6.

[3] *Seasons and Months* (Paris, 1933); ' Spring in Chaucer and before him ', *MLN* **52** (1937), 9–16.

was ridiculed by Seneca, as it was later by Shakespeare in *Hamlet*; apparent burlesques in Chaucer (e.g. *CT*, V, 1018; *TC*, ii, 904) and other ME poets are echoes of rhetorical analysis of classical examples, as Miss Hammond has clearly shown (*English Verse between Chaucer and Surrey*, p. 447).

Two elements in the provenance of the spring opening need further emphasis. The first is the stimulus given to the practice by the precepts of medieval rhetoricians, the most influential of whom, Matthew of Vendôme and Geoffrey of Vinsauf, both suggest the description of seasons, especially *descriptio veris*, as an effective form of amplification.[1] One fourteenth-century reader of the *Roman de la Rose* was well aware of their influence, for he wrote in a MS, beside line 78: ' Totum istud punctum Matheus Vindocinensis de loci placidi descriptione '.

The development of the spring opening was further encouraged by the need, in poetry intended for oral delivery, for a standardised technique of entry, as of withdrawal. The seasons headpiece provided such a technique, and was consequently little disturbed, since in its conventional form it offered an effective means of *rapprochement* with the audience. For similar reasons the narrative would be punctuated in the same way, as in *Kyng Alisaunder*, where the twenty-four sections are introduced by means of descriptions of seasons which have little or no relevance to what follows. These devices of entry and transition would naturally tend to survive into the fifteenth century, even though private reading became much more common.

The development of the autumn opening should be noted as a refinement of the older tradition (see AL, 1n).

The description of the garden in FL, as can be seen from the notes, is full of conventional elements, such as the grove of trees, the birds singing, the little path, the arbour with its turf-benches and carpet of grass, and the fragrant scents. Again the tradition extends back to classical times, the tradition of the *locus amoenus* (Curtius, *European Literature and*

[1] Matthew, *Ars Versificatoria* (ed. Faral in *Les Arts poétiques du XIIe et du XIIIe siècle*, p. 146); Geoffrey, *Documentum* (ed. Faral, pp. 272, 274).

the Latin Middle Ages, pp. 183–202); again it was reinforced
by the precept and example of medieval rhetoricians (e.g.
Matthew, pp. 119, 143, 147f); and again the tradition was
focused for the later Middle Ages by *RR*. In this poem
was also introduced, not for the first time, the idea of the
' Earthly Paradise ' (648; cf. FL, 115), which, however it is
interpreted, is an indication of the symbolic significance of
the garden for the Middle Ages. The symbolism could be
devotional, as in the *hortus conclusus* sacred to the Virgin,
or perverted, as in the *Merchant's Tale* (see D. W. Robertson,
op. cit., pp. 40–6), but more commonly the garden represented, simply, civilisation. ' The walled garden became
the centre of all that was fair and peaceful in love, in life,
and in religion '.[1] *Paradisus* itself is the Persian *pairidaeza*,
a walled enclosure, and paradise is often pictured enclosed
or walled. The garden of FL is full of delights, but the
dominant impression is one of order and proportion (29, 31f,
53, 65), of harmony and ' mesure ' (58), aptly befitting the
sane and serene view of life to which the poem gives expression. There was not much taste in the Middle Ages for
the wild grandeur and melancholy beauty of nature; the
realities were a little too close for the exercise of such
refined appreciation. Admiration was reserved for the
' tender, bright, balanced, enclosed, symmetrical ',[2] the
images of human sway and human beauty; as in art, the
demand was for formality, brilliance of colour, and definition
of outline, and nature's forms were habitually modified in
the interests of ' order, light, intelligibility and symmetry '.
Nature, to be appreciated, had to be courteous. Tastes had
changed by the nineteenth century, and praise of FL was
thus qualified: ' But the love of nature, as exhibited in this
poem, is rather a matter of feeling than of intelligent appreciation or of refined taste; for the description of the
grove applies to the clipped and trimmed artificial plantation,
and not to the wild and free luxuriance of forest growth.

[1] Joan Evans, *Pattern: a Study in Ornament in W. Europe* (2 vols.,
1931), i, 58.
[2] Ruskin, ' Mediaeval Landscape ' in *Modern Painters*, vol. iii
(*Works*, v, 248–316), p. 257.

Chaucer here unfortunately followed his literary reminiscences, instead of trusting to his own instincts and his taste ' (G. P. Marsh, *Origin and History of the English Language* (1862), pp. 415f). The assumption that the poet's instincts were for the wild and ' Romantic ', but were trammelled by literary convention, is an interesting sign of the change of taste, and quite unwarranted.

Medieval landscape description was more a matter of literary technique than of personal observation or feeling for nature. Curtius has shown this clearly in his discussion of medieval Latin literature (*op. cit.*, e.g. pp. 159, 183f), and his observations are particularly valuable in that they correct a tendency to regard medieval *topographia* as simple and sweet and fresh, ' native woodnotes wild ', and emphasise the provenance of landscape description as a conventional technique of amplification. But however appropriate Curtius's views are to the Latin Middle Ages, it would not be wise to apply them too strictly to the vernacular literature of fifteenth-century England, where, although traditional patterns are still observed, there is a tendency to embellish the description with original details of observation, and the description of gardens moves gradually towards a realistic representation of the type of garden the poet would himself know. There is in Chaucer little sign of this movement, as Schaar points out; [1] in FL we may note the detail of the red oak-leaves (35n), set against much that is evidently purely literary in inspiration (see 56n, 209n, 304n); in AL the process is far advanced (see notes to 10, 32, 53, 55, etc.). There is also in FL, within the conventional framework, an evident delight in the natural scenes described which marks a further movement from rhetorical tradition, though the impression of ebullience is partly due to a particular technique of idealisation and should not be too closely associated with eighteenth- and nineteenth-century feeling for nature. [2]

FL is characterised by G. L. Marsh as ' a tissue of

[1] *The Golden Mirror* (Lund, 1955), pp. 421–3, 485.

[2] Interpretation from this point of view in Hazlitt, *Lectures on the English Poets* (*Works*, ed. Waller and Glover, v, 26–8); *Essay on Manners* (xi, 269–72); F. T. Palgrave, *Landscape in Poetry* (1897), p. 123.

conventionalities ', owing most to Chaucer (especially *LGW*, *PF*, the *Knight's Tale*) and his imitators (especially Lydgate), and much, no doubt partly through them, to *RR* and the French poems influenced by it.[1] The description is apt, for FL is entirely conventional in themes, imagery, and machinery, but it is unfortunate if Marsh's phrase should be permitted to bear a taint of disapproval. In the Middle Ages, when reproduction of MSS was so laborious and communications were so limited, originality was of little account, and imitation, or plagiarism, as by Chaucer of French and Italian poets, would be regarded as a tribute, and a form of publicising the original. Borrowing was often proclaimed, not guiltily concealed. Under such conditions literary traditions were far more powerful and persistent, ' periods ' of literature were longer, and convention was all-important, while personal and individual expression was less valued. The ' conventionalities ' of a poem like FL, with its roots deep in tradition, cannot be merely tolerated, for without them the poem is meaningless. No medieval poem is going to yield its richest rewards until we have explored and made some effort to understand the traditions which give it life.

On the other hand, of course, the pressure of literary convention can become stifling in an age of mediocrity such as the fifteenth century, when no great poet emerges to re-mould and reinvigorate tradition, and the result is a poem like AL. Berdan concludes that AL is inferior to FL ' largely because it is more conventional ' (*Early Tudor Poetry*, p. 65), but this is not so: AL is in fact less ' conventional ' than FL, and shows many signs of a most un-conventional realism. The distinction is that in AL the use of convention is automatic and superficial, the author's real interests lying elsewhere, while in FL convention is accepted and integrated in a rich, coherent, and meaningful pattern.

The Assembly of Ladies

Some references to AL have already been made. Its theme is simpler, its machinery cruder, and it may be somewhat

[1] ' The Sources and Analogues of FL ', *MP* 4 (1906–7), p. 321.

briefly dismissed. It seems to be in general an echo of the feminist controversy which preoccupied the later Middle Ages.[1] Its aim is to vindicate the truth and loyalty of women by describing an assembly at which they present their complaints against the neglect and unfaithfulness of men. Though there is little specific mention of love in the poem, the paintings in the palace (456–66) are of women unfortunate in love, and the genre of the complaints could hardly be mistaken.

The debate about women was, of course, not new—the *Wife of Bath's Prologue* is a good index to the previous course of the argument; but about 1400 the controversy was stimulated by the *Cent Ballades*, by the establishment of the *Cour Amoureuse*, and by the writings of Christine de Pisan. Her *Epistre au Dieu d'Amours*, for instance, translated by Hoccleve as the *Letter of Cupid*, is a vehement defence of the honour and fidelity of women, in which *RR* as well as Ovid is attacked for its slanders against women (e.g. 8455ff, 13265ff, 16323ff). This seems to have sparked off a lively controversy, with women as its theme and *RR* as its focus, in which bishops, scholars, and high state officials engaged as well as poets. This debate dragged on through the century, in poems like *Le Champion des Dames* by Martin le Franc, and overlapped the sequence of poems prompted by Chartier's portrait of *La Belle Dame sans Merci*. It was very much a debating game for the most part.

In England writers were polite but ironic. In his *Regement of Princes* (ed. EETS (E.S.) 72 (1897)) Hoccleve has a long passage on the superiority of women, pointing out that the rib she was made from was cleaner than the slime man came from, that like the rib, all the supreme things—heaven, sun, moon—are rounded, that woman was made inside Paradise, man outside it, and concludes that husbands ought always to be ruled by their wives (5104–94), a typical *reductio ad absurdum* of the feminist case. Lydgate, in his

---

[1] See Siciliano, *op. cit.*, pp. 349ff; Huizinga, *op. cit.*, chap. viii; F. L. Utley, *The Crooked Rib* (Ohio University, 1944)—an Index to poems in English on the woman question to 1568; J. Peter, *Complaint and Satire in Early English Literature* (1956), pp. 31–6, 86–91, 99–103.

translations, often apologises for the attacks on women in his original, and says that they do not apply to all women, and quotes examples of good women—but usually translates the offending passages with evident relish (e.g. *Troy*, i, 1840–1943, 2072–135; ii, 3536–68, 5814–19; iii, 4270–416, etc.). His irony is rare and rather charming. Caxton tempers the harshness towards women of the *Dictes of the Philosophres* in this way in his Prologue: ' For I wote wel, of what somever condicion women ben in Grece, the women of this contre ben right good, wyse, playsant, trewe, secrete, stedfast, ever besy and never ydle, Attemperat in speking, and vertuous in alle their werkis: or atte leste sholde be soo ' (ed. Crotch, p. 22).

The position allotted to women in AL is not very flattering to them, and hardly tolerable socially, and the poem is evidently the product of a purely literary convention. This convention, of the faithful but wronged woman, as in Ovid's *Heroides*, is almost as common as that of the adoring but despised lover; Chaucer's *Anelida* and *LGW* are examples which have evidently influenced AL (see 456–66). In French there are bitter laments by ladies who feel they have been betrayed in Christine de Pisan's *Cent Ballades* and *Duc des Vrais Amans*. Deschamps frequently adopts the guise of a woman complaining of unfaithfulness or unrequited love, and further examples of this convention are found in Lydgate and other English poets (see above, p. 14). These poems hardly fit in with the generally accepted idea of ' courtly love ', the essence of which is the humility of the lover before the idolised mistress, but there are enough of them to show that another convention of love coexisted with courtly love, in which the woman complains of the indifference of the man. The early lyric poetry of France, as Jeanroy points out (*Origines de la poésie lyrique* (1925), pp. 96, 225), was largely inspired by this conception, which survived strongly in popular tradition.

The framework of AL is the familiar Court of Love,[1]

[1] For full discussion see W. A. Neilson, ' The Origins and Sources of *The Court of Love* ' in *Harvard Studies in Philology and Literature*, vi (1899); Stevens, *op. cit.*, pp. 164–7.

presided over this time by Lady Loyalty, and combining two traditions, the court of love in the legal sense and the royal court of Venus or Cupid. The former tradition is most familiar to us through Andreas the Chaplain, who describes how courts of ladies were set up to debate and make judgments on subtle questions of love (see Bk. II, chap. vii, Questions 16, 18, 21 in the *De Amore*). Such courts may actually have been held, as an elegant diversion, by Eleanor of Aquitaine and her two daughters.[1] Reference may be made also to the *Cour Amoureuse* of 1400, and the *Arrets d'Amour* (*c.* 1463; ed. SATF (1951)) of Martial d'Auvergne, a minor legal official who makes his cases conform as closely as possible to the procedure and jargon of the *Parlement* of Paris. The result is an uproarious bourgeois travesty of the delicate debates of Andreas, without however, it appears, any specifically satirical intent. Literary references to deliberative courts of love include the early *Council of Remiremont*, where an assembly of nuns (of all people) debate whether *clercs* or *chevaliers* are better as lovers, Gower's *Confessio Amantis* (e.g. iii, 704, 829, 1673), and the *Wife of Bath's Tale* (*CT*, III, 1028). The legalistic conception of a debate survived also in the *jeux-partis*, in the popular *jugements d'amour* of Machaut and Christine de Pisan, and in the *questions d'amour* which occur so frequently in love-poems (e.g. *CT*, I, 1347, V, 1621; *PF*, ed. Brewer, pp. 10–12).

Even more closely associated with AL are those poems where the court of the God of Love or of Venus is described, and where we see lovers offering their complaints and petitions, or *bills*. In the *Kingis Quair* the poet sees in the Palace of Venus a great company,

> With billis in thaire handis, of one assent
> Unto the juge thaire playntis to present.
>
> (574)

Further examples are the *Court of Love* itself and the *Pastime of Pleasure*, where Venus and Cupid call a parliament on

[1] See Neilson, pp. 248f; A. Kelly in *Speculum* **12** (1937), 3–19; G. Paris, *Mélanges de littérature française du moyen âge* (1910), pp. 473–497.

22 September (cf. AL) to redress lovers' grievances (3748ff).
In some of these poems the complaints themselves are given
in detail, as in the *Temple of Glass* (143–246), and the *Parlement of Love* attributed to Suffolk (ed. MacCracken, B.XX),
which closely resembles AL.

> And upon this, thay present up thair byllys
> Upon her knes, wyth facys pale of hewe,
> Compleynyng sore for many dyverse skyllys:
> Sum sayed playnly, that fortune was untrew,
> And sum bygan a long proces to sewe
> Of seven yere enduryng in servyse
> Wythout coumfort in any maner wyse.
>
> (50–6)

The *complaintes d'amour* for which these assemblies provided
the occasion were in themselves a favourite literary genre
(see FL, 320n), and the examples in AL (582–707) are
full of echoes of Charles of Orleans, Suffolk, and other
poets.

The introduction of allegorical figures associated with
Love is another conventional feature of AL. The commonest usage was for these personifications to be grouped
in the retinue of Love, the medieval way of analysing its
attributes, as in *RR* (793ff) and *PF* (218–28). A refinement
of this usage was for the Court of Love to be envisaged as a
household, with these personifications as its officers, so that
we get not only a porter (as in *RR*) but also a chamberlain,
an usher, a butler, and so on. There is usually some attempt
to fit the allegorical attribute to the office held, as in AL 318,
322, 343, but it is not always easy. Many poems parallel
the usage of AL[1] and inevitably certain names are common
to several of them, but none of the coincidences with AL
is significant. It is interesting to note the contrasts between the allegorical figures in *RR*, such as Idleness,
Mirth, Beauty, Riches, and Courtesy, and those in AL, such
as Diligence, Discretion, Perseverance, and Temperance.

---

[1] E.g. *BK*, 498–511; *Past. Pleas.*, 302, 477–83, 4537 (*Perceveraunce*);
KQ, 673–7; Froissart, *Le Trésor Amoureux*, 404–48. A very elaborate
example is edited by P. Meyer in *Romania* **15** (1886), 241–6.

Evidently two very different conceptions of behaviour are involved, the latter having more to do with morality than courtly love. The choice of Loyalty as the chief figure in AL is in accordance with the general theme of the poem, but seems to owe something also to the appearance of the goddess Loyalty in Christine de Pisan's *Dit de la Rose* (91) to establish the order of the Rose for those who defend the honour of womanhood. Watriquet de Couvin has a *Dis de Loiauté* in which Lady Loyalty is praised, and referred to once as 'Dame azurée' (88).

The dream-framework of AL needs no explanation: the device was universal. Also medieval writers, and Chaucer among them, were full of speculation about dreams, and discussed their motivation, nature, and significance frequently and at length (e.g. *RR*, 1–20; *HF*, 1–58; *PF*, 95–108; *CT*, VII, 2921–3171; *TC*, v, 358–85). In the dream vision poem, the most careful writers would make the dream spring naturally from the circumstances of the narrator, as in AL: the narrator, unhappy in love, dreams of the court of Lady Loyalty, where the wrongs of all despised lovers will be set right. Both wish-fulfilment (*PF*, 99–105) and the increase in dream activity caused by anxiety (*HF*, 36–40) are involved. It might be added that as a point of literary technique the dream was useful, for it was not only a means of surmounting reality, but also gave unlimited flexibility to a narrative, doing away with the need for trivialities like sequence and coherence. The narrative of FL, it should be noted, is not a dream.

The allegory of AL has little vitality. The personifications drop dead from the pen, and the attempt to enliven the convention and show 'originality' by introducing them in the course of conversation (316–43), instead of merely describing them in a group, is not successful. In some parts of the poem, especially towards the end, in the complaints, the motions of versifying are automatic and empty. The author's real interest, as Professor C. S. Lewis points out, seems to have been in 'the stir and bustle of an actual court, the whispered consultations, the putting on of clothes, and the important comings and goings' (*Allegory of Love*,

p. 250). Here the narrative is sprightly, the dialogue has a
vivid colloquial vigour, and the narrator's pert self-confidence
comes over quite sharply. The poem is altogether thinner
in texture than FL, but it has its own charm.

FORM AND STYLE

Both FL and AL are written in the seven-line stanza,
rhyming *ababbcc*, known as Rhyme Royal. The origin of
this term was for long fancifully associated with the use of
the stanza by King James I of Scotland in the *Kingis Quair*
(see l. 1379), but it is clear that it derives originally from
the OF *chant royal, ballade royal*. The latter term was
naturalised in English in the fifteenth century to describe
the seven-line stanza, while the name *rhythm royal* is used
first by Gascoigne (1575).[1]

Rhyme royal was a mark of the ' high style ', and was
usually reserved for grave and serious poems. Thus Chaucer
uses it for the Tales of the Man of Law, the Clerk, the
Prioress and the second Nun, for *PF, TC*, and part of
Anelida. Gower introduces it at the end of the octosyllabic
Confessio Amantis for his supplication to Venus; Lydgate
uses it for his *Fall of Princes*, and for the complaints in the
Temple of Glass, though the narrative is in couplets. In
Hawes, rhyme royal is deliberately dropped for the Godfrey
Gobelive episodes, and in Skelton's *Magnyfycence* it is used
for formal and stately passages, with couplets for the ordinary
exchange of drama. In the sixteenth century it was mainly
reserved for poems like the *Mirror for Magistrates* and
Spenser's *Ruins of Time*. When sixteenth-century writers
associated Chaucer's decasyllabic couplet with the old loose
semi-alliterative four-stress couplet of drama and popular
verse, they expressly exempted rhyme royal: ' His meetre
Heroicall of Troilus and Cresseid is very grave and Stately,
keeping the Staffe of seven, and the verse of ten, his
other verses of the Canterbury tales be but riding ryme '
(Puttenham, quoted in Spurgeon, *Chaucer Criticism and
Allusion*, i, 125).

[1] See H. N. MacCracken, ' Rhyme Royal ', *MLN* 24 (1909), 31–2.

In his use of rhyme royal Chaucer observes scrupulously the innate tripartite structure of the stanza. Syntax and metre correspond more closely than in the couplet, and the stanza is treated as a unit, with little of the prolonged paragraph development that we find in his poems in couplets. Only rarely is one stanza linked to the next. Lydgate's use of rhyme royal is less strict, and he permits linking in about one stanza in eight. In FL the stanza is treated in most cavalier fashion: about thirty of the eighty-five stanzas are run on, and there is little attempt within the stanza to make sense and form obey a single logic, though examples of the balanced and economical use of the stanza as a unit are not wanting (85–91, 127–33, 288–94, 442–8, 533–539). Though Hawes and *CL* imitate Lydgate's usage in linking stanzas, the only poem which matches the licence of FL is the *Romans of Partenay* (see AL, 463n). In AL stanzas are rarely linked (see 49, 56, 133, 455, 637, 686, 721).

The analysis of the versification of FL is complicated by the corruption of the text and the problem of final -*e* (see p. 11 above): it was these two factors that were largely responsible for the misunderstanding of Chaucer's versification which began in the fifteenth century and continued until the eighteenth. Speght (To the Readers (1602)), perhaps prompted by Francis Thynne, and Urry (Preface), who had both seen MSS of Chaucer, suggested that the roughness of Chaucer's verse was due to faults of transcription; but imitations of Chaucer's verse by Wyatt and Spenser make it clear that by the early sixteenth century Chaucer's artificial decasyllables were not distinguished from the 'riding ryme' of native popular verse. The kindest view taken was that his verse, though rough, was manly and vigorous, that he was more interested in 'solid sense than jingle' (Dart, in Urry's edition), and that his verse did have the 'rude sweetness of a Scotch tune' (Dryden). It was not until Morell, Tyrwhitt, and Gray came again to the MSS and rediscovered the secrets of his versification that Chaucer was 'restored to his feet', though some critics, like Southey and Nott, went on advocating until nearly 1850 a rhythmical rather than a syllabic scansion, a view recently revived.

Textual corruption is in some measure responsible also for the low opinion held of fifteenth-century versification. Saintsbury refers to the ' prosaic, hobbling, broken-backed doggerel of Lydgate ' (*History of English Prosody*, i, 234), but the texts on which he based his opinion were of inferior quality, like that of the *Secrees*, and included genuinely rugged works like the *Assembly of Gods* which are not by Lydgate at all.   But no conceivable scribal corruption could account for some of the verse of the fifteenth century, and furthermore we possess two texts in autograph MSS, John Hardyng's *Chronicle* and George Cavendish's *Metrical Visions*, and they are as bad as any.

The usual explanation of fifteenth-century versification is that Chaucer's practice, especially with regard to final -*e*, was artificial and archaic even in his own day, and that after 1400 linguistic changes and the loss of final -*e* upset the balance he had achieved, and left poets in confusion, trying to use their own language and imitate Chaucer at the same time.   But there is no confusion in Lydgate.   His verse may not be musical to our ears, but it is certainly systematic, and so is his use, for most of his life, of final -*e*.   Even in the middle of the century we find two translations, possibly by the same author, one of Palladius's *De Re Rustica* (ed. EETS(O.S.) 52, 72) and one of Vegetius's *De Re Militari* (ed. EETS(O.S.) 201), in which the use of final -*e*, though rare, is perfectly correct, and the verse completely assured. AL is another example of regular versification. Confusion over final -*e* may have contributed to the decay of Chaucer's pentameter, but it hardly explains it.

Another similar view is that Chaucer's verse maintains a precarious balance of alien syllabic techniques with native rhythmical verse, and when the language changed and the weak inflexional syllables he had used to preserve that balance were lost, English poets reverted to the old alliterative-based measure, ' a long line divided by a sharp medial break into two half-lines, each half-line containing not less than two or more than three stresses, and most half-lines hovering

between two and three stresses '.[1] Certainly the old tunes
are never far away in Lydgate, and he is very much aware
of the half-line; and clearly the native four-stress line is
dominant in poets like Henry Bradshaw and George Ashby,
in popular drama, and in Skelton's *Magnyfycence*. But
equally clearly Lydgate, and the poet of FL, and Hawes were
trying to write pentameters: unfortunately for theory, con-
verting pentameters into ' Up the airy mountain ' jingle is
dangerously easy.

Clòse by those mèads, for èver crowned with flòwers,

Whère Thames with prìde survèys his rising tòwers,

Thère stands a strùcture òf majestic fràme,

Whìch from the nèighbouring Hàmpton takes its nàme.[2]

A useful corrective to this too-free ' rhythmical ' reading is
Licklider's work on *ictus* or ' pitch-accent ' (*Chapters on the
Metric of the Chaucerian Tradition*, Baltimore, 1910). He
points out that the decasyllable is an artificial, not a natural
form, and a mark in itself of the high style: artificial
accentuation of unstressed syllables by raising of pitch
and increase of length is a way of heightening style, and
is clearly used by Chaucer and his followers for this purpose.

Lydgate's systematic irregularity can be explained only in
one way. In the first place, Chaucer allowed himself a good
deal more licence in matters of versification than his modern
editors will allow him: ' Current theories of Chaucer's
versification are based, not upon the text as found in the
MSS., or as established by critical processes, but upon the
artificial text made regular by all the devices at the disposal

[1] C. S. Lewis, ' The 15th Century Heroic Line ' in *Essays and Studies*
24 (1938), 28–41 (p. 33); cf. Fitzroy Pyle, ' The Pedigree of Lydgate's
Heroic Line ', *Hermathena* **25** (1937), 26–59 (suggests that the reversion
was not to semi-alliterative verse, but to pre-Chaucerian Alexandrines
and fourteeners).

[2] Pope, *Rape of the Lock*, iii, 1–4: scanned thus in an article in the
Edinburgh Review **27** (1816), 416.

of the scholar '.[1] Among the licences he clearly permitted
were trisyllabic feet at the beginning of a line and at the
caesura, and the omission of the unstressed syllable in the
same positions, usually with some rhetorical purpose.
Lydgate took these variants and elevated them into types.
They appear in Schick's analysis (ed. *TG*, pp. lvii–lix)
as Types E, B, D, and C respectively, and the truncated
forms, D (the ' headless ' line) and C (the Lydgate or broken-
backed line), are the characteristic marks of Lydgate's
versification, and of FL. Lydgate uses them indiscriminately, with or without rhetorical purpose: ' The reader
has the threefold tax of an emphatic variant unsupported
by a content deserving emphasis, and aggressively re-
current ' (Hammond, *Chaucer to Surrey*, p. 21; see also pp.
83–5).

In FL, as with the linked stanzas, the licences introduced
by Lydgate are further exploited, perhaps partly through lack
of technical resource. There are about eighty headless lines,
and this seems an unlikely place for scribal omission. In
favourable circumstances, where the first syllable of the line
bears rhetorical stress, and where the previous line is end-
stopped, the headless line is an effective variant (cf. *CT*,
III, 869–71), e.g.

> Some of oke, and some of other trees
> (269)
> Hond in hond, a knight and a lady
> (326)

Where these conditions are not fulfilled, the headless line
disrupts the flow of the stanza (e.g. 62, 65, 72, 76). There
are about forty examples of the Lydgate line, excluding reversal
of stress after the caesura, and including those doubtful lines
where a final -*e*, with hiatus, might provide the unstressed
syllable. Again such lines can be rhetorically effective (cf.
CT, III, 1647; VII, 951, 2345), e.g.

---

[1] *CT*, ed. Manly and Rickert (8 vols., 1940), ii, 40; see Hammond,
Bibliographical Manual, pp. 493–500; ' The 9-syllabled Pentameter Line
in some post-Chaucerian MSS ', *MP* 23 (1925–6), 129–52; Brusendorff,
op. cit., pp. 110ff.

A crown of gold, rich for any king

(172)

To love untrue in word, thought, ne dede

(486)

But more often they are not, e.g.

That well unneth a wight might it se

(46)

Three hensh-men, on him awaiting

(252)

Clear instances of trisyllabic feet, at any point in the line, are rare (e.g. 9, 102, 478, 553, 574). There are about forty other deficient lines, of which some may be corrupt (7, 8, 15, 25, 200, 255, etc.); some are corrected by the kind of pronunciation suggested above (p. 12), and some by emendation of -es.

This kind of analysis, of course, gives a very distorted picture of the versification, for it isolates the individual line, which in reality can never be considered as an entity, and neglects the essential continuity and flow of the verse. The poet of FL has a sense of this verse flow which Lydgate never had. In fact, apart from certain passages of description where the problems of syntax and metre are particularly acute, the verse of FL has a remarkable grace and fluency, attributable mainly to a systematic underweighting of the line, a complete freedom in matters of technique such as the placing of the caesura and reversal of stress (e.g. 6, 195, 472), and an addiction to *enjambement* of the freest possible kind, e.g.

He should not see if there were any wight
Within or no; but one within well might
Perceive all tho that yeden there without
In the field.

(72)

And on their heads, well
Dressed, were crownes of laurer grene.

(249)

It seems that these features have been imitated from Chaucer's octosyllabic verse, where he allows himself a vastly greater freedom than in decasyllabic: in the latter, for instance, as Ten Brink points out in a particularly fine passage of technical analysis (*Language and Metre of Chaucer* (1901), pp. 226–33), *enjambement* is always balanced by rhetorical emphasis or material weighting at the end of one line and the beginning of the next, and often disguised by inversion. Finer points of technique like this are neglected in FL (note the second example above). The lightness and freedom of the verse, and the run-on lines and stanzas, give to the movement of FL, at its best, a rare spirit and ease.

The metre of AL is altogether more regular. There are in all about eighty lines which are technically deficient, including headless lines (e.g. 243, 289, 460, 470), Lydgate lines (e.g. 112, 330, 613), and others (e.g. 475, 647, 693); though it should be observed that in over two-thirds of these lines the deficiencies are supplied in later MSS and in Thynne (e.g. 7, 19, 50, 105, 109). Consequently, a critical text like Skeat's is considerably smoother in metre than A, but there is very good reason to suppose that the greater ' correctness ' of later texts is due in most cases to scribal emendation. Certainly it is clear that many fifteenth-century scribes disliked headless and Lydgate lines and adjusted them whenever they could (Brusendorff, *op. cit.*, pp. 110–17). The handling of the verse in AL is assured, if monotonous. The author knows well how to economise in effort by the use of tags and tautological expressions, how to spin out a thought to the end of a stanza (103–5, 510f, 629f, 642–4), and how to find his rhymes the easy way (334–6, 351–5). He uses the licences of FL only rarely, and *enjambement* is rare. The end-stopped line is dominant, and there is less sense of movement in the verse, except in certain passages of dialogue.

Associated with the licence of versification in FL is a remarkable looseness of syntax. There are several aimless rambling sentences (1–14, 15–21, 64–77, 113–26, 141–68, 218–30, 239–50, 547–57); sequences of ideas follow one another with little attempt at subordination, and loosely paratactic constructions are frequent (151–4, 161–6, 229f, 510f, 581); participles are used as finite verbs (89, 173f, 211,

316f, 554), a characteristic of Lydgate's style, and sometimes the verb is omitted altogether (51f, 214f, 262f, 575); there are examples of anacoluthon (354–8, 540–3, 558–65) and of abrupt change of tense (536f).   Of course, some such freedom of syntax is characteristic of all ME verse, and precedent for the usages of FL can be found in Chaucer and, to an even greater extent, in Lydgate.   Habits of listening rather than reading permitted a much greater flexibility of syntax, and this flexibility survived long after private reading had replaced oral delivery.   Furthermore, English grammar had not yet been systematised on the model of Latin.   It would be possible to punctuate the grammatical confusion out of existence, and pretend that the sentence construction is complex but coherent, but to do so would misrepresent the realities.

There is in FL, furthermore, a good deal of inversion and distortion of normal syntax, usually governed by the exigencies of metre and rhyme.   Among these inversions are the placing of an object pronoun before its verb (46, 48, 62, 107, etc.) or of an auxiliary after its verb (44, 45, 50, 95, etc.), while the syntactical licence sometimes obscures the sense (e.g. 329, 338–40, 397–9).   Associated with this is a certain amateurish quality in the ordering of ideas and the handling of the narrative, a clumsiness usually disguised by the vigour and ease of the movement.   The mention of Flora, for instance, the lady of the flower, comes very much as an afterthought (379–82), just before she is needed in the narrative.   Similar awkward interpolations are introduced in descriptions (92f, 276f); certain lines are confused and ambiguous (338–40, 397–9, 574); while the description of the company of the flower and the exposition of the allegory of the leaf switch from ladies to knights and back again with disconcerting abruptness (327–35, 477–84).

In AL the sentences are more competently handled, though there are examples of distortion (130f, 447f, 479), of the loose use of the participle (425–7, 705–7), of anacoluthon (74–7), and of the confusion of direct and indirect speech characteristic of ME verse (15, 174f, 238, 641).   The handling of the narrative, on the other hand, is repetitive and uneconomical; the nature of the Court of Love allegory has much to do with this.

FL and AL show a marked contrast in their use of the tags and expletives which were the common stock of fifteenth-century poets. In so far as it is at all possible to isolate and identify such conventional expressions, it is clear that AL uses more than twice as many as FL (FL, 37; AL, 95). These tags, which are important in any evaluation of the style of ME verse, are of four main types, of which some examples may be given.

(a) Asseveration. Apart from single words like *certaine*, *trewly*, *soothly*, *iwis*, *forsoth*, this group includes many phrases, e.g. *out of doubt* (for references and parallels see 73n), *without dread* (152), *I you ensure* (60n), *withouten faile* (369; AL 188, 475, 537, 567, 646), *I trow* (62, 130, 201), *God wot* (186; AL 63, 631), *without lesyng* (AL 263), *wite ye wele* (AL 242, 451, 484), *wele ye wote* (AL 144), *wele I wote* (AL 166, 301, 687), *wote ye what* (AL 171, 246, 481, 542, 660), *this is no nay* (AL 306, 351, 521), *I dare wele say* (AL 353). FL has sixteen instances of such phrases, AL fifty-three.

(b) Opinion. E.g. *as I suppose* (20; AL 482), *as me thought* (36, 114, 349; AL 50), *as I would wene* (247), *to my dome* (306n), *by seeming* (229n), *as I cowth gesse* (AL 212). FL fifteen, AL seven.

(c) Adverbial intensives. E.g. *by manyfold* (96n), *in every (all) maner thing* (170, 550), *in every (no) maner wise* (AL 69n), *every dele* (AL 227, 703), *more and lasse* (AL 439), *yong and old* (AL 538n), *hie ne lowe* (AL 272). FL six, AL twenty-two.

(d) Brevity formulas and similar expressions. E.g. *without any more* (AL 209, 693), *to say yow in substaunce* (AL 335, 678), *to telle yow pleyne* (AL 170, 425, 598, 698), *to telle in wordis fewe* (AL 489). FL none, AL thirteen.

Apart from these tags, many other stereotyped phrases, less superfluous in character, are used in both poems. Examples will be found in the notes to the text (e.g. 14, 29, 43, 59, 82, 98, 144, etc.).

Medieval poets have often been rebuked for their habitual use of such clichés of expression. But it should be observed that the literary canons of the day were not opposed to such conventionality, and, furthermore, that pleonasm and tautology were peculiarly adapted to the conditions of oral delivery. 'These tags, more or less emptied of meaning through common use, and ridiculous by modern standards, have their importance in the economy of spoken verse, where a good voice carried them off. They helped out the composer, in need of a rime; the reciter on his feet, compelled to improvise; and the audience who, lacking the reader's privilege to linger over close-packed lines, welcomed familiar turns that by diluting the sense made it easier to receive.' [1] The study of fifteenth-century reading habits has made it clear that oral delivery was by *c.* 1450 more the exception than the rule, but naturally the old stylistic conventions would survive. The effect of these conventional turns of expression is to give an easy, conversational quality to the style, as in Chaucer, the texture of whose verse is so rich and firm and whose use of tags, though frequent, is so unobtrusive, that no one is distracted by them. Lydgate, however, uses tags with aggressive insistence and little tact, so that attention is drawn to, rather than away from them, and some real virtues of his style are obscured. The distinction between Chaucer and Lydgate is, on a smaller scale and to a lesser degree, the distinction between FL and AL.

The conditions of oral delivery and the precepts of rhetorical tradition coincided also in demanding from poetry a fixed technique of beginning and ending; the spring opening, as we have seen, was one such technique. The actual doctrines of the twelfth-century rhetoricians, which are the nearest we have to a summary of medieval poetic theory, are here, as in some other matters, not very enlightening. It is quite clear that there were many traditions of literary technique and convention which acted just as forcibly on the creative mind and which go unmentioned

---

[1] *14th Century Verse and Prose*, ed. K. Sisam (1921), p. xxxix. See further H. J. Chaytor, *From Script to Print* (1945); and Ruth Crosby's articles in *Speculum* **11** (1936), 88–110; **13** (1938), 413–32.

in Geoffrey of Vinsauf, Matthew of Vendôme, and the others. For the conclusion of a poem the rhetoricians suggest a *sententia* or *exemplum*, but make no particular mention (Matthew does quote, p. 191, an example from Ovid) of the modest *captatio benevolentiae*, the admission of inadequacy and request for indulgence, which was characteristic of the *peroratio* in classical rhetoric, and which, taken over into poetry, eventually led to the last stanza of FL. The affectation of humility and inadequacy was once intended to appeal to the vanity of a judge, but it went down very well at the end of a poem too, and not only at the end; Lydgate, for instance, trembles and quakes every time he approaches a difficult passage, and constantly bemoans the *rusticitas*, the rude and ' boistous ' nature of his style.

The modesty epilogue, as it may be called, was elaborately developed in the fifteenth century, especially in poems, such as those by Lydgate, addressed to a noble patron (see FL, 591n). A few lines in FL touch off all the echoes of the tradition, and the poet even manages to find room for a characteristic little individual detail (593). In AL, it will be noticed, the convention is not observed; in fact the ending of the poem, far from being humble, has a very self-satisfied air. This sorts well with the unusual, though not unprecedented opening, and the general indifference to tradition observable in the poem as a whole.

The submission formula is a *topos* of classical rhetoric, that is, it is one of the *loci communes* (' commonplaces ') from which material would be drawn for enriching the argument, one of the *argumentorum sedes*, or storehouses of trains of thought. There were many of these *topoi*, some of them particularly suited to the exordium and conclusion, many of them to epideictic or panegyric oratory, and with the collapse of the political foundation of forensic and deliberative oratory in the late Empire, and the more generalised application of epideictic oratory, they came to apply, with rhetorical doctrine in general, to literature. Formal literature in the Middle Ages relied on these *topoi* for the development and enrichment of its themes. They receive no mention in the rhetoricians, probably because they were taken for granted. The special character of FL, in fact, the 'ebullition of natural delight', the 'gusto', which Hazlitt eloquently praises (*Lectures on the English Poets, ed. cit.*, pp. 26–8), derives principally from the extended use of two *topoi* which Curtius calls the outdoing *topos* (*hyperoche*) and the inexpressibility *topos* (*European Literature and the Latin Middle Ages*, pp. 159–65).

The function of the outdoing *topos* is to affirm the surpassing nature of what is described.

(*a*) By asserting its superiority to anything experienced before, e.g.

> Thereto the herber was so fresh and cold,
> The wholsome savours eke so comforting
> That, as I demed, sith the beginning
> Of the world was never seen, or than,
> So pleasant a ground of none earthly man.

> (122–6)

(Cf. 60f, 86f, 129–31, 181f, 250, 306f; AL 514f. The notes offer further parallels to this and the other *topoi*.)

(*b*) By asserting its superiority to anything anywhere in the world (the 'India' *topos*), e.g.

> Though one would seeke all the world wide
> So rich a field coud not be espide
> On no coast.

> (74)

(Cf. AL 157f, 481–3 especially.)

(*c*) By asserting its power to please anyone, even one least likely to be pleased, e.g.

> There is no heart, I deme, in such dispaire,
> Ne with thoughts froward and contraire
> So overlaid, but it should soone have bote,
> If it had ones felt this savour soote.

> (84)

(Cf. 313–15, 432f.)

(*d*) By value comparisons (the ' Croesus ' *topos*; cf. *Conf. Am.*, iv, 1326), e.g.

> But for to speake of riches and of stones,
> And men and horse, I trow, the large wones
> Of Pretir John, ne all his tresory,
> Might not unneth have bought the tenth party.
>
> (203)

(Cf. 172, 215, 246–8, 254–6; AL 158.)

(*e*) By hyperbolic comparisons of other kinds, whether implied or expressed, e.g.

> Of men of armes comming such a rout
> As all the men on earth had ben assembled.
>
> (197)

(Cf. 57–9, 66–70, 100–4, 113–15, 119–21, 131–3, 192f, 199, 265f, 370f, 487–90; AL 166–8.)

(*f*) By assertions of a superiority barely within the compass of imagination, e.g. 524f; AL 163, 480.

(*g*) By comparisons based on negative formulae, e.g.

> And to my dome there never was indede
> Man that had seen halfe so faire a tre.
>
> (307)

(Cf. 229, 234, 427, 483; AL 50f, 67.)

(*h*) By general surpassing formulae, e.g. 63, 168; AL 452.

These *topoi*, it will be seen, are to a large extent based on comparative constructions (*such, so . . . that*),[1] and their tendency is to suffuse the description in a rich glow of idealisation, which, as a point of literary technique, derives ultimately from epideictic oratory. Matthew of Vendôme's theory of description, for instance, the most extended treatment of the subject in the Middle Ages, takes for granted that description is a form either of eulogy or of abuse, *ad praeconium* or *ad vituperium* (ed. Faral, p. 132). A medieval poet, presented with a subject for description,

---

[1] For a similar practice in Chaucer see C. Schaar, *The Golden Mirror* Lund, 1955), pp. 257–9, 427.

tends to put it in general terms, extolling its beauty or surpassing virtues, rather than to select details in order to present a realistic picture to the senses; he cherishes the ideal and universal rather than the actual and particular.

The inexpressibility *topos* is based on the common rhetorical figure of *occupatio* (the refusal to narrate), and is essentially an assertion of the poet's inability to do justice to his subject, and hence a form of eulogy, e.g.

> But to tell aright
> Their great beauty, it lieth not in my might,
> Ne their array; neverthelesse I shall
> Tell you a part, though I speake not of all.
>
> (140)

(Cf. 97; AL 512.)

This *topos* is often elaborately developed in medieval poetry (e.g. Machaut, *Remede de Fortune*, 808–22, *Dit dou Lyon*, 470–9; Lydgate, *Troy*, ii, 549–64, *RS*, 315–28), indicating clearly that it is eulogistic in function though a brevity formula in origin. Closer to the brevity formula is the apology for not enumerating or describing in full (e.g. 150f, 204f, 273; AL 467–9), though this too is a way of saying by implication that a full description would be beyond any poet's capabilities.

It is hardly necessary to point out that the above classification would not have been consciously made by medieval poets. Such *topoi* were part of a traditional stylistic apparatus, and were learnt by the poet of FL not from a rhetorical textbook but from the example and imitation of Chaucer, Lydgate, and the French poets. They were regarded as a means of heightening style and subject matter, though no doubt their very flexibility as a medium of thematic development endeared them to the poet in need of a rhyme (e.g. Pisan, *Dit de Poissy*, 402). They are rarely used by Hoccleve, and a great deal less often in AL than in FL.

Such *topoi* are only one aspect of an idealising tendency characteristic of FL and of medieval description in general. In early French courtly poetry, for instance, as Faral shows (*Les Sources latines des contes et romans courtois du moyen âge* (1913), pp. 307–88), descriptive passages are frequent, but

their purpose, whatever the subject, is to idealise rather than
to record reality, to excite admiration rather than to define.
Though the poets would often have drawn their material
from what they saw around them, their main sources are
books: the Bible, natural histories and encyclopaedias, and
Latin literature. The conventions of description of these
early poems are, through the medium of a common medieval
tradition, those also of FL: the enumeration of precious
stones, for instance (144–51), the effect of opulence associated
with the mention of the East (148, 202, 212), the attributes
of the terrestrial paradise garden (115).

The tendency towards idealisation is further illustrated
in the vocabulary of FL, where, instead of the search for the
mot juste enjoined by a later age, we find an extensive use of
idealising, non-specifying epithets, such as *bright* (239, 256,
260, etc.), *fair* (93, 304, 307, etc.), *fresh* (30, 52, 109, etc.),
pleasaunt (27, 49, 97, etc.), *rich* (75, 145, 152, etc.), *sweet*
(4, 15, 79, etc.), and *wholsome* (6, 10, 123, 409). Of these
7 words alone, with their adverbial derivatives, there are some
eighty instances in FL, against twenty in AL. The frequent
use of such words is no doubt partly due to the exigencies
of rhyme and metre, partly to a certain semantic relaxation
typical of all verse conditioned by the requirements of oral
delivery, and partly also to a rhetorical tradition in which
the epithet in itself was considered an ornament; but their
effective function in FL is, by their very iteration, to flood
the narrative ' dans la lumière idéale de l'allégorie '—a term
which Taine (*op. cit.*, i, 187) used as an expression of con-
demnation, but which recognises the special character of the
poem.

It is possible to look too deeply for the motive of such
idealisation: there is no need to assume, as some do, that the
senses of medieval poets were less acute, or more inhibited
than ours, or that they were prevented from observing detail
by the habit of symbolic interpretation, of systematically
drawing from every aspect of life the universal significance
and the universal principle. It seems to be rather a matter
of a particular literary technique and of the limitations
deliberately imposed in following that technique. When a

medieval courtly poet wanted to describe a beautiful woman, for instance, he would embark on a feature-by-feature description, perhaps embellishing it with a few details of his own, but rarely straying far from the familiar pattern; or, if he thought this convention a trifle tedious, he might say:

> For to tel hir gret semelines,
> Hir womanhed, hir port, & hir fairnes,
> It was a mervaile, hou ever that nature
> Coude in hir werkis make a creature
> So aungellike, so goodli on to se,
> So femynyn or passing of beaute.
>
> (*TG*, 265–70)

(Cf. AL 512–18.)

Whatever the case, he does not seem to have been impelled to use as his model a real, individual woman. Of course realism, in our sense, was by no means unknown in the Middle Ages. In popular literature, as might be expected, the formal tradition is not observed, and realistic description is frequent; furthermore, within the framework of the formal tradition itself, realism was accepted as a characteristic of the ' low ' style, as in comedy (in the Latin sense). There was thus ample precedent for Chaucer's practice, though his blending of the typical and the individual in the *Prologue* seems unique. However, in the fifteenth century we find this realism irrupting into formal, courtly literature. Sometimes it appears in an impatience with the elaborate description of a French original (e.g. *Partonope of Blois*, ed. EETS (E.S.) 109, ll. 6175–7); sometimes in a 'metaphysical' individuality of expression, such as we find throughout the poem called *How a Lover praiseth his Lady* (ed. E. P. Hammond, *MP* 21 (1923–4), 379–95), for instance, this conceit (ll. 346–7),

> Whos lyppys wyth chyld ben by maydenhede
> Swol and engreyned wyth rosys rede,

which owes only a hint to Geoffrey of Vinsauf's *Poetria Nova* (574–5). Sometimes it is not quite clear whether we are to take an epithet as conventional or realistic, as with Hawes's

F

cruddy (*Past. Pleas.*, 62), or *shene* in FL (270n). Whatever form it takes, a weakening of the older descriptive tradition is apparent; AL is a good example of the result. In FL the tradition of generalised eulogy and idealisation is preserved.

Several references have already been made to the ' rhetorical tradition ', and it remains now to elucidate further the importance of this tradition in FL. ' Rhetoric ', it has been said, ' is the greatest barrier between us and our ancestors. . . . Of the praise and censure which we allot to medieval and Elizabethan poets only the smallest part would have seemed relevant to those poets themselves ' (C. S. Lewis, *English Literature in the Sixteenth Century*, p. 61). This is true, especially of the fundamental distinction between the medieval view of poetry as a species of eloquence and the modern view of it as a form of self-expression, a transmutation of experience. Nevertheless, some distinctions must be made if the influence of the rhetorical tradition in the fifteenth century is to be properly assessed.

In the hundred years after his death Chaucer was praised, not for his acute observation of human nature, nor his sense of character and drama, nor his humour, but for the artifice of his style. For Lydgate and Hawes and their contemporaries he is the ' floure of rethoryk ', and Hoccleve declares that his death has ' despoiled this land of the swetnesse of rethorik '.[1] Both Lydgate and Hawes introduce elaborate accounts of rhetoric in their poems (*Fall*, vi, 3277–3500; *Past. Pleas.*, 652–1296); the name of ' Gaufred ' (Geoffrey of Vinsauf), the most famous of the medieval rhetoricians, is frequently mentioned, as Schick's note to *TG*, 110 shows (Chaucer's reference in *CT*, VII, 3347 is well known); an Epitaph on the Duke of Bedford, who died in 1495, demonstrates the wholesale transference of Latin rhetoric to English poetry, for not only does the poet use twenty different Latin metres, but he also explains in side-notes the various rhetorical devices that are employed (see

[1] Hoccleve, *Regement of Princes*, 2084f; cf. *Thebes*, 42; *Troy*, ii, 4699, iii, 553; *Fall*, i, 278; *Pilg.*, 19774; *KQ*, 1375; Dunbar's *Golden Targe* (*Poems*, ed. Mackenzie, 1932), 253–70; *Past. Pleas.*, 1164, 1168, 1374.

Berdan, *Early Tudor Poetry, 1485–1547*, pp. 129–33). In fifteenth-century poetry itself we find an elaborate stylistic artifice, as for example in the use of rhetorical ' colours ' like anaphora (*repetitio*),[1] oxymoron (e.g. *TG, Compleynt*, 495–521), and *annominatio*, or repetition with permutation and variation (e.g. *Fall*, ii, 4432–8). The aureation of fifteenth-century poetic diction is again largely attributable to the recommendations of the rhetoricians.

> Her redolente wordes of swete influence
> Degouted vapour moost aromatyke
> And made conversyon of my complacence,
> Her depured and her lusty rethoryke
> My courage reformed that was so lunatyke.[2]

That such ornament of style and diction is often factitious no one would deny; but a contrast with Chaucer's consummate use of rhetorical devices, the *sententiae* which open *PF*, for instance, or Troilus' apostrophe (*TC*, v, 540–53), shows that Lydgate and Hawes are responsible for this, not ' rhetoric ' itself.

In FL, however, there is remarkably little formalisation of style, and even less of the conscious artistry which marks Chaucer's style. What examples there are seem commonplace. There is some attempt to balance ideas one against the other, sometimes within the line, sometimes between lines, though the practice is of the simplest (e.g. 81–3, 122f, 156, 188f, 284f). There seems to be a more than accidental pleasure in the use of pairs of synonymous words (e.g. 5, 9, 14, 21, 26, 82), a feature also of Lydgate's and of Caxton's style. Such expressions may indicate an amplificatory ideal of style, though they may have more to do with the influence of alliterative verse. Repetition, of any of the traditional rhetorical kinds, is rare; the clearest examples are the simple

---

[1] E.g. *Past. Pleas.*, 2591–604, 2619–39, 4050–76, 5684–90; see the note in Hammond, *English Verse between Chaucer and Surrey*, pp. 533f (also pp. 452f on the colours in general).

[2] *Past. Pleas.*, 5264–8; see J. C. Mendenhall, *Aureate Terms* (University of Pennsylvania, 1919); V. L. Rubel, *Poetic Diction in the English Renaissance* (New York, 1941).

anaphora on *some . . . some* (158, 269–72, 284, 320). A line like

> So small, so thicke, so short, so fresh of hew,
> (52)

with its sequence of brief parallel sense units (cf. 337, 486), recalls the rhetorical figure of *articulus*. Of the *ornata difficultas*, that is, metaphor and associated figures, there is very little. The similes are brief and usually commonplace (29, 53, 59, 65, 66, 143, etc.), and the metaphors simple and undeveloped (e.g. 7, 100, 137, 192, 437, 553). In AL there is even less apparent formalisation of style, though there are some possible examples of play on words, or *annominatio* (34, 38, 457, 707): in fact, there is every tendency towards a colloquial idiom, revealed in the extensive use of popular idioms and exclamations, mostly in direct speech, but by no means confined to it (22–5, 63, 148, 243–5, 348–50); in a strong gnomic and proverbial element in the style (418–20, 576–8, 649–51, 665), rather different from the distinctive use of *sententiae* as a rhetorical ornament; and above all, in the poet's love of reproducing the rapid colloquial exchange of real dialogue (15–25, 95–102, 262–73, 277–87, 326–36, 358–364, 570–4, 680–92).

In neither FL nor AL is there much sign of the aureation characteristic of the main stream of formal verse in the fifteenth century. A certain pomposity marks the diction of AL in the frequent use of words like *contenuance, displesaunce, encombraunce*, etc., but such words are due less to an ideal of style than to the needs of rhyme. In FL the diction is restrained and departs little from the example of Chaucer, though, as in Chaucer, certain words (e.g. *exemplaire, honourable, marshall, occupacion*), now naturalised into ordinary English, may have been ' poetic ' in their day. Changes in the associations of words are also responsible for a certain illusion of simplicity given by the diction of FL, and, for that matter, of Chaucer: words like *plesaunt*, weakened and trivial in modern English, are used here with more of their original force.

It is always possible to find examples of rhetorical colours and rhetorical ornaments in a medieval poem like FL, but a discussion from such a point of view is not likely to yield much reward unless the poet has been deeply and pervasively influenced by the rhetorical tradition, as is the case with Chaucer. For a true rhetorician's treatment of FL we have only to turn to Dryden's paraphrase of the poem, and there to note the elaboration of metaphor (218, 321), the imagery of 'painting' (6, 46, 106), the personifications (5, 19, 50, 374, 437), the heightening of homely images in the interests of decorum (390), the persistent circumlocution (154, 210, 316), the repetition with variation (34), the constant functioning of amplification and ornamentation as ideals of style (see Tuve, *Seasons and Months*, p. 81).

There is no such elaborate artifice of style in FL, and in any case a detailed tabulation of rhetorical devices alone contributes little to the understanding of a poem. It is more valuable to have some appreciation of the traditions from which the poem sprang, the conventions of theme, arrangement, and imagery, the apparatus of style appropriate to a particular poetic genre.

The Flower and the Leaf is not a long poem, but this has been a long Introduction. The attempt to restore the losses of five hundred years is inevitably a lengthy process, but a necessary one if we are to understand the context in which a medieval poem stands, and more than ever necessary with *The Flower and the Leaf*, because of the richness of its heritage.

BIBLIOGRAPHY

Editions

FL was printed in all the editions of the collected works of Chaucer from 1598 to 1878, AL in all those from 1532 to 1810. Full accounts of these editions are given in E. P. Hammond's indispensable *Chaucer: a Bibliographical Manual* (New York, 1908), pp. 114–49. The following list is complete only to 1721.

> 1532   ed. Thynne; reprinted in 1542, 1552(?), and (with additions by Stow) 1561.
>
> 1598   ed. Speght. As Stow, with the addition of the *Isle of Ladies* and FL; revised ed. 1602, reprinted 1687.
>
> 1721   ed. Urry.
>
> 1845   Aldine ed.; revised by Morris 1866.
>
> 1854   ed. Bell, notes by J. M. Jephson; revised by Skeat 1878.

Other prints of FL in anthologies and miscellanies are listed in Hammond, p. 423; also modernisations and translations. Since its rejection from the canon, FL has been printed in limited editions by the Kelmscott Press (ed. F. S. Ellis, 1896) and the Essex House Press (ed. C. R. Ashbee, 1902), and by Skeat in *Chaucerian and Other Pieces*, vol. vii of the Oxford *Chaucer*, 1897 (FL, pp. 361–79; also AL, pp. 380–404). Textual notes by E. P. Hammond in *MLN* **40** (1925), 185–6. The literary history of the poem may be followed up through the allusions in C. F. E. Spurgeon, *500 Years of Chaucer Criticism and Allusion* (3 vols., 1925), e.g. i, 318, 366; ii, 29, 89, 101, 112, 124, 144, 169; part 3, 15, 29, 48, 124, and the note in Marsh (article cited below), p. 121.

Authorship and sources

Full references for the controversy about the authenticity of FL, and for Skeat's speculations as to the authorship of FL and AL, are given in Hammond, pp. 423–4. The only other articles on FL of any importance are by G. L. Marsh:

' The Authorship of FL ', *JEGP* 6 (1906–7), 373–94.
' Sources and Analogues of FL ', *MP* 4 (1906–7), 121–68, 281–328. Detailed, valuable.

Literary background

(i) *English Poems.* See list of Abbreviations.

(ii) *French Poems.*

Les Cent Ballades, ed. G. Raynaud, SATF (1905).

Chansons du XVe siècle, ed. G. Paris, SATF (1875).

COUVIN, WATRIQUET DE. *Dits*, ed. A. Scheler (Brussels, 1868).

DESCHAMPS, EUSTACHE. *Œuvres complètes*, ed. de Queux de Saint-Hilaire and G. Raynaud, 11 vols., SATF (1878–1903).

FROISSART, JEAN. *Œuvres*, ed. A. Scheler, 3 vols. (Brussels, 1870–2).

MACHAUT, GUILLAUME DE. *Œuvres*, ed. E. Hoepffner, 3 vols., SATF (1908–21).

MACHAUT, GUILLAUME DE. *Poésies lyriques*, ed. Chichmaref, 2 vols. (Paris, 1909).

MARGIVAL, NICOLE DE. *La Panthere d'Amors*, ed. H. A. Todd, SATF (1883).

ORLÉANS, CHARLES D'. *Poésies*, ed. P. Champion, 2 vols., CFMA (1923–7).

PISAN, CHRISTINE DE. *Œuvres poétiques*, ed. M. Roy, 3 vols., SATF (1886–96).

Recueil de poésies françaises des XVe et XVIe siècles, ed. A. de Montaiglon, 13 vols. (Paris, 1855–78).

Rondeaux et autres poésies du XVe siècle, ed. G. Raynaud, SATF (1889).

(iii) *Literary history and criticism*

See L. L. Tucker and A. R. Benham, *Bibliography of Fifteenth Century Literature, University of Washington Publications in Language and Literature*, vol. ii (1928).

BENNETT, H. S. 'The Author and his Public in the Fourteenth and Fifteenth Centuries', *Essays and Studies* **23** (1937), 7–24.

BENNETT, H. S. *Chaucer and the Fifteenth Century* (Oxford, 1947).

BERDAN, J. M. *Early Tudor Poetry 1485–1547* (New York, 1920).

BRUSENDORFF, AAGE. *The Chaucer Tradition* (Copenhagen, 1925).

CHAMPION, P. *Histoire poétique du quinzième siècle*, 2 vols. (Paris, 1923).

CHAYTOR, H. J. *From Script to Print* (Cambridge, 1945).

CROSBY, RUTH. 'Oral Delivery in the Middle Ages', *Speculum* **11** (1936), 88–110.

CURTIUS, E. R. *Europäische Literatur und lateinisches Mittelalter* (Bern, 1948). Quotations are from the English translation, *European Literature and the Latin Middle Ages* (1953). Inexhaustible.

FARAL, E. (ed.). *Les Arts poétiques du XIIe et du XIIIe siècle* (Paris, 1923). Fundamental.

HAMMOND, ELEANOR PRESCOTT. 'The 9-syllabled Pentameter line in some post-Chaucerian MSS.', *MP* **23** (1925–1926), 129–52.

HAMMOND, ELEANOR PRESCOTT (ed.). *English Verse between Chaucer and Surrey* (Duke University Press, N. Carolina, 1927). Comprehensive apparatus; a monument of scholarship.

KITTREDGE, G. L. 'Chaucer and some of his Friends', *MP* **1** (1903–4), 1–18. On the cult of the flower and the leaf.

LEWIS, C. S. *The Allegory of Love* (Oxford, 1936).

LEWIS, C. S. 'The Fifteenth Century Heroic Line', *Essays and Studies* **24** (1938), 28–41.

LEWIS, C. S. *English Literature in the sixteenth century, excluding Drama* (Oxford, 1954).

LICKLIDER, A. H.   *Chapters in the Metric of the Chaucerian Tradition* (Baltimore, 1910).

LOWES, J. L.   ' The Prologue to *LGW* as related to the French *Marguerite* Poems and the *Filostrato* ', *PMLA* **19** (1904), 593–683.

MENDENHALL, J. C.   *Aureate Terms* (University of Pennsylvania, 1919).

NEILSON, W. A.   ' The Origins and Sources of *The Court of Love* ', *Studies and Notes in Philology and Literature* **6** (Harvard, 1899).   For AL.

ROBERTSON, D. W.   ' The Doctrine of Charity in Medieval Literary Gardens ', *Speculum* **26** (1951), 24–49.   Unusual, informative.

RUBEL, V. L.   *Poetic Diction in the English Renaissance* (New York, 1941).

SICILIANO, ITALO.   *François Villon et les thèmes poétiques du moyen âge* (Paris, 1934).   Valuable illustrative material.

STEVENS, JOHN.   *Music and Poetry in the Early Tudor Court* (London, 1961).

SYPHERD, W. O.   *Studies in Chaucer's House of Fame*, Chaucer Society, 2nd series, no. 39 (1907).

TUVE, ROSEMOND.   *Seasons and Months: Studies in a Tradition of Middle English Poetry* (Paris, 1933).

The Floure and the Leafe

NOTE TO THE TEXT

THE text of FL is from Speght's edition of 1598 (Sp1), all variations from which, with the exception of the spelling conventions noted in the Introduction (p. 5) and the punctuation, are recorded in the textual notes. Additions to Sp1 are placed within square brackets in the text, and changes of Sp1 readings italicised, except that obvious misprints are silently corrected.

The text has been collated with Speght's edition of 1602 (Sp2), the 1687 reprint (Sp3), Urry (U), the Aldine edition and Morris's revision (M), Bell's edition and Skeat's revision, and Skeat's own edition (Sk), and a few of the more interesting readings recorded from those noted, in addition to the emendations incorporated in the text. References followed by a bracket in the textual notes are Sp1 readings or original emendations; references not followed by a bracket are emendations adopted from the later text indicated. Any reading noted for one edition will also be the reading of all the following editions earlier in date than any later edition noted.

THE FLOURE AND THE LEAFE

W HEN that Phebus his chaire of gold so hie
    Had whirled up the sterry sky aloft,
    And in the Boole was entred certainly;
When shoures sweet of raine discended [s]oft,
Causing the ground, fele times and oft,   5
Up for to give many an wholsome aire,
And every plaine was clothed faire

With new greene, and maketh small flours
To springen here and there in field & in mede—
So very good and wholsome be the shoures   10
That it renueth that was old and deede
In winter time, and out of every seede
Springeth the hearbe, so that every wight
Of this season wexeth glad and light.

And I, so glad of the season swete,   15
Was happed thus upon a certaine night:
As I lay in my bed, sleepe ful unmete
Was unto me; but why that I ne might
Rest, I ne wist, for there nas earthly wight,
As I suppose, had more hearts ease   20
Then I, for I nad sicknesse nor disease.

Wherefore I mervaile greatly of my selfe,
That I so long withouten sleepe lay;
And up I rose, three houres after twelfe,
About the springing of the day,   25
And on I put my geare and mine array,
And to a pleasaunt grove I gan passe,
Long or the bright sonne up risen was;

In which were okes great, streight as a line,
Under the which the grasse so fresh of hew   30
Was newly sprong; and an eight foot or nine
Every tree well fro his fellow grew,
With braunches brode, lade with leves new,
f366r That sprongen out ayen the sonne shene,
Some very red and some a glad light grene;   35

Which as me thought was right a plesaunt sight,
And eke the briddes song for to here
Would have rejoised any earthly wight.
And I, that couth not yet in no manere
Heare the nightingale of all the yere,   40
Full busily herkened with hart and with eare
If I her voice perceive coud any where.

And at the last a path of litle breade
I found, that greatly had not used be,
For it forgrowen was with grasse and weede   45
That well unneth a wight might it se.
Thou3t I, this path some whider goth, parde,
And so I followed, till it me brought
To right a pleasaunt herber, well ywrought,

That benched was, and with turfes new   50
Freshly turved, whereof the greene gras,
So small, so thicke, so short, so fresh of hew,
That most like unto green welwet it was.
The hegge also, that yede in compas
And closed in all the green herbere,   55
With sicamour was set and eglatere,

Wrethen in fere so wel and cunningly
That every branch and leafe grew by mesure,
Plain as a bord, of an height, by and by—
I see never thing, I you ensure,   60
So wel done; for he that tooke the cure
It to make, y trow, did all his peine
To make it passe all tho that men have seyne.

And shapen was this herber, roofe and all,
As a pretty parlour, and also   65
The hegge as thicke as a castel wall,
That who that list without to stond or go,
Though he would all day prien to and fro,
He should not see if there were any wight
Within or no; but one within well might   70

Perceive all tho that yeden there without
In the field, that was on every side
Covered with corne and grasse, that, out of doubt,
Though one would seeke all the world wide,
So rich a field coud not be espide   75
On no coast, as of the quantity,
For of all good thing there was plenty.

And I, that all this pleasaunt sight sie,
Thought sodainly I felt so sweet an aire
Of the eglentere, that certainly   80
There is no heart, I deme, in such dispaire,
Ne with thoughts froward and contraire
So overlaid, but it should soone have bote,
If it had ones felt this savour soote.

And as I stood and cast aside mine eie,   85
I was ware of the fairest medle tre
That ever yet in all my life I sie,
As ful of blosomes as it might be.
Therein a goldfinch leaping pretile
Fro bough to bough, and as him list he eet,   90
Here and there, of buds and floures sweet.

And to the herber side was joyning
This faire tree, of which I have you told.
And at the last the brid began to sing,
Whan he had eaten what he eat wold,   95
So passing sweetly that, by manifold,
It was more pleasaunt then I coud devise.
And when his song was ended in this wise,

The nightingale with so merry a note
Answered him that all the wood rong,   100
So sodainly that, as it were a sote,
I stood astonied; so was I with the song
Thorow ravished, that, till late and long,
I ne wist in what place I was, ne where;
And ayen, me thought, she song even by mine ere.

Wherefore I waited about busily   106
On every side, if I her might see;
And at the last I gan full well aspy
Where she sat in a fresh greene laurey tree,
On the further side, even right by me,   110
That gave so passing a delicious smell
According to the eglentere full well.

Whereof I had so inly great pleasure
That as me thought I surely ravished was
Into Paradise, where my desire   115
Was for to be, and no ferther passe
As for that day, and on the sote grasse
I sat me downe; for, as for mine entent,
The birds song was more convenient,

And more pleasaunt to me, by many fold,   120
Than meat or drinke, or any other thing.
Thereto the herber was so fresh and cold,
The wholsome savours eke so comforting
That, as I demed, sith the beginning
Of the world was never seen or than   125
So pleasant a ground of none earthly man.

And as I sat, the birds harkening thus,
Me thought that I heard voices sodainly,
The most sweetest and most delicious
f366v That ever any wight, I trow trewly,   130
Heard in their life, for the armony
And sweet accord was in so good musike
That the voice to angels most was like.

At the last, out of a grove even by,
That was right goodly and pleasant to sight,   135
I sie where there came singing lustily
A world of ladies; but to tell aright
Their great beauty, it lieth not in my might,
Ne their array; neverthelesse I shall
Tell you a part, though I speake not of all.   140

In surcotes white of veluet wele sitting
They were clad, and the semes echone,
As it were a maner garnishing,
Was set with emerauds, one and one,
By and by; but many a rich stone   145
Was set on the purfiles, out of dout,
Of colors, sleves, and traines round about,

As great pearles, round and orient,
Diamonds fine and rubies red,
And many another stone, of which I went   150
The names now; and everich on her head
A rich fret of gold, which, without dread,
Was full of stately rich stones set.
And every lady had a chapelet

On her head, of [leves] fresh and grene,   155
So wele wrought, and so mervelously,
That it was a noble sight to sene.
Some of laurer, and some ful pleasantly
Had chapelets of woodbind, and sadly
Some of Agnus castus were also   160
Chapelets fresh.   But there were many of tho

That daunced and eke song ful soberly;
But all they yede in maner of compace.
But one there yede in mid the company
Soole by her selfe, but all followed the pace   165
That she kept, whose heavenly figured face
So pleasaunt was, and her wele-shape person,
That of beauty she past hem everichon.

G

And more richly beseene, by manyfold,
She was also, in every maner thing;   170
On her head, ful pleasaunt to behold,
A crowne of gold, rich for any king;
A braunch of Agnus castus eke bearing
In her hand; and to my sight, trewly,
She lady was of the company.   175

And she began a roundell lustely,
That *Suse le foyle de vert moy* men call,
Seen & mon joly cuer en dormy.
And than the company answered all
With voice sweet entuned and so small,   180
That me thought it the sweetest melody
That ever I heard in my life, soothly.

And thus they came, dauncing and singing,
Into the middes of the mede echone,
Before the herber where I was sitting,   185
And, God wot, me thought I was wel bigone,
For than I might avise hem, one by one,
Who fairest was, who coud best dance or sing,
Or who most womanly was in all thing.

They had not daunced but a little throw   190
When that I heard, not fer of, sodainly,
So great a noise of thundering trumps blow
As though it should have departed the skie.
And after that, within a while, I sie,
From the same grove where the ladies come out,
Of men of armes comming such a rout   196

As all the men on earth had ben assembled
In that place, wele horsed for the nones,
Stering so fast that all the earth trembled.
But for to speake of riches and stones,   200
And men and horse, I trow, the large wones
Of Pretir John, ne all his tresory,
Might not unneth have bouȝt the tenth party.

Of their array who-so list heare more,
I shal rehearse, so as I can, a lite.   205
Out of the grove that I spake of before
I sie come first, all in their clokes white,
A company that were for their delite
Chapelets fresh of okes seriall
Newly sprong, and trumpets they were all.   210

On every trumpe hanging a broad banere
Of fine tartarium, were ful richely bete—
Every trumpet his lords armes *bere*;
About their necks, with great pearles set,
Colers brode; for cost they would not lete,   215
As it would seeme, for their scochones echone
Were set about with many a precious stone.

Their horse harneis was all white also.
And after them next, in one company,
Came [nine] kings of armes, and no mo,   220
In clokes of white cloth of gold, richly,
Chapelets of greene on their heads on hye.
The crowns that they on their scochones bere
Were set with pearle, ruby, and saphere,

And eke great diamonds many one;   225
But all their horse harneis and other geare
Was in a sute according, everichone,
As ye have heard the foresaid trumpets were.
And by seeming they were nothing to lere—
And there guiding they did so manerly.   230
And after hem cam a great company

Of herauds and pursevaunts eke
Arraied in clothes of white veluet;
And hardily, they were no thing to seke
How they on hem should the harneis set;   235
And every man had on a chapelet.
Scochones and eke horse harneis, in-dede,
They had in sute of hem that before hem yede.

f367r

Next after hem came in armour bright,
All save their heads, seemely knights nine;   240
And every claspe and naile, as to my sight,
Of their harneis were of red gold fine;
With cloth of gold and furred with ermine
Were the trappours of their stedes strong,
Wide and large, that to the ground did hong.   245

And every boose of bridle and paitrell
That they had was worth, as I would wene,
A thousand pound; and on their heads, well
Dressed, were crownes of laurer grene,
The best made that ever I had sene.   250
And every knight had after him riding
Three hensh-men, on him awaiting;

Of which ever *the* [on] on a short tronchoun
His lords helme bare, so richly dight
That the worst was worth the raunsoun   255
Of a king; the second a shield bright
Bare at his neck; the thred bare upright
A mighty spheare, ful sharpe ground and kene.
And every child ware, of leaves grene,

A fresh chapelet upon his haires bright;   260
And clokes white of fine veluet they were;
Their steeds trapped and raied right
Without difference, as their lords were.
And after hem, on many a fresh corsere,
There came of armed knights such a rout   265
That they besprad the large field about.

And all they were, after their degrees,
Chapelets new, made of laurer grene,
Some of oke, and some of other trees.
Some in their honds bare boughes shene,   270
Some of laurer, and some of okes kene,
Some of hauthorne, and some of woodbind,
And many mo which I had not in mind.

And so they came, their horse freshly stering
With bloody sownes of her trompes loud.   275
There sie I many an uncouth disguising
In the array of these knights proud.
And at the last, as evenly as they coud,
They took their places in middes of the mede,
And every knight turned his horse hede   280

To his fellow, and lightly laid a speare
In the rest, and so justes began
On every part about, here and there.
Some brake his spere, some drew down hors and
    man;
About the field astray the steeds ran;   285
And to behold their rule and governaunce,
I you ensure, it was a great pleasaunce.

And so the justes last an houre and more;
But tho that crowned were in laurer grene
Wan the prise—their dints were so sore   290
That there was none ayenst hem might sustene.
And the justing all was left of clene,
And fro their horse the nine alight anon,
And so did all the remnant everichon.

And forth they yede togider, twain and twain,   295
That to behold it was a worthy sight,
Toward the ladies on the green plain,
That song and daunced, as I said now right.
The ladies, as soone as they goodly might,
They brake of both the song and dance,   300
And yede to meet hem with full glad semblance.

And every lady tooke ful womanly
By the hond a knight, and forth they yede
Unto a faire laurer that stood fast by,
With leves lade, the boughes of great brede;   305
And to my dome there never was indede
Man that had seen halfe so faire a tre;
For underneath there might it wel have be

An hundred persons at their own plesance,
Shadowed fro the heat of Phebus bright,   310
So that they should have felt no grevance
Of raine ne haile, that hem hurt might.
The savour eke rejoice would any wight
That had be sicke or melancolius,
It was so very good and vertuous.   315

And with great reverence they enclining low
To the tree, so soot and faire of hew;
And after that, within a little throw,
They began to sing and daunce of new;
Some song of love, some plaining of untrew,   320
Environing the tree that stood upright,
And ever yede a lady and a knight.

f367v   And at the last I cast mine eie aside,
And was ware of a lusty company
That came roming out of the field wide,   325
Hond in hond, a knight and a lady;
The ladies all in surcotes, that richely
Purfiled were with many a rich stone;
And every knight of greene ware mantels on,

Embrouded well, so as the surcotes were.   330
And everich had a chapelet on her hed,
Which did right well upon the shining here,
Made of goodly floures, white and red.
The knights eke, that they in hond led,
In sute of hem ware chapelets everichone.   335
And before hem went minstrels many one,

As harpes, pipes, lutes, and sautry,
All in greene; and on their heads bare,
Of divers floures, made full craftely,
All in a sute, goodly chapelets they ware.   340
And so dauncing into the mede they fare,
In mid the which they found a tuft that was
All oversprad with floures in compas.

Whereto they enclined everichon
With great reverence, and that full humbly. 345
And at the last there began anon
A lady for to sing right womanly
A bargaret in praising the daisie;
For, as me thought, among her notes swete
She said *Si douce est la Margarete*. 350

Then they all answered her in fere
So passingly well and so pleasauntly
That it was a blisful noise to here.
But I not [how], it happed sodainly,
As about noone, the sonne so fervently 355
Waxe whote that the prety tender floures
Had lost the beauty of her fresh coloures,

Forshronke with heat; the ladies eke tobrent,
That they ne wist where they hem might bestow.
The knights swelt, for lack of shade nie shent. 360
And after that, within a little throw,
The wind began so sturdily to blow
That down goeth all the floures everichone
So that in all the mede there laft not one,

Save suche as succoured were among the leves 365
Fro every storme that might hem assaile,
Growing under hegges and thicke greves.
And after that there came a storme of haile
And raine in feare, so that, withouten faile,
The ladies ne the knights nade o threed 370
Dry on them, so dropping was her weed.

And whan the storm was cleane passed away,
Tho in white, that stood under the tre—
They felt nothing of the great affray
That they in greene without had in ybe— 375
To them they yede for routh and pite,
Them to comfort after their great disease,
So faine they were the helplesse for to ease.

Then I was ware how one of hem in grene
Had on a crown, rich and well sitting,   380
Wherfore I demed wel she was a quene,
And tho in greene on her were awaiting.
The ladies then in white that were coming
Toward them, and the knights in fere,
Began to comfort hem and make hem chere.   385

The queen in white, that was of great beauty,
Tooke by the hond the queen that was in grene
And said, ' Suster, I have right great pity
Of your annoy, and of the troublous tene
Wherein ye and your company have bene   390
So long, alas! and if that it you please
To go with me, I shall do you the ease

In all the pleasure that I can or may.'
Wherof the tother, humbly as she might,
Thanked her; for in right ill array   395
She was with storm and heat, I you behight.
And every lady then, anon right,
That were in white, one of them took in grene
By the hond; which when the knights had sene,

In like wise ech of them took a knight   400
Clad in grene, and forth with hem they fare
To an hegge, where they, anon right,
To make their justs they would not spare
Boughes to hew downe and eke trees square,
Wherwith they made hem stately fires great   405
To dry their clothes that were wringing weat.

And after that, of hearbs that there grew,
They made, for blisters of the sonne brenning,
Very good and wholsome ointments new,
Where that they yede the sick fast annointing.   410
And after that they yede about gadering
Pleasaunt salades, which they made hem eat
For to refresh their great unkindly heat.

The lady of the Leafe then began to pray
Her of the Floure (for so to my seeming 415
They should be, as by their array)
To soupe with her, and eke, for any thing,
That she should with her all her people bring.
And she ayen, in right goodly manere,
Thanketh her of her most friendly cheare, 420

f368r   Saying plainly that she would obay
With all her hart all her commaundement.
And then anon, without lenger delay,
The lady of the Leafe hath one ysent
For a palfray, after her intent, 425
Araied well and faire in harneis of gold,
For nothing lacked that to him long should.

And after that, to all her company
She made to purvey horse and every thing
That they needed; and then, full lustily, 430
Even by the herber where I was sitting,
They passed all, so pleasantly singing
That it would have comforted any wight.
But then I sie a passing wonder sight:

For then the nightingale, that all the day 435
Had in the laurer sete and did her might
The whol service to sing longing to May,
All sodainly gan to take her flight,
And to the lady of the Leafe forthright
She flew, and set her on her hond softly, 440
Which was a thing I marveled of greatly.

The goldfinch eke, that fro the medill tre
Was fled for heat into the bushes cold,
Unto the lady of the Flower gan fle,
And on hir hond he set him, as he wold, 445
And pleasantly his wings gan to fold;
And for to sing they pained hem both as sore
As they had do of all the day before.

And so these ladies rode forth a great pace,
And all the rout of knights eke in fere.   450
And I, that had sene all this wonder case,
Thought I would assay, in some manere,
To know fully the trouth of this matere,
And what they were that rode so pleasantly.
And when they were the herber passed by   455

I drest me forth, and happed to mete anon
Right a faire lady, I you ensure;
And she come riding by hir selfe alone,
All in white, with semblance ful demure.
I saluted her, and bad her good aventure   460
Must her befall, as I coud most humbly,
And she answered, ' My doughter, gramercy.'

' Madam,' quod I, ' if that I durst enquere
Of you, I would faine, of that company,
Wit what they be that past by this arbere ? '   465
And she ayen answered right friendly:
' My faire doughter, all tho that passed hereby
In white clothing, be servants everichone
Unto the Leafe, and I my selfe am one.

Se ye not her that crowned is,' quod she,   470
' All in white ? ' ' Madame,' quod I, ' yis.'
' That is Diane, goddes of chastity;
And for bicause that she a maiden is,
In her hond the braunch she bereth, this
That Agnus castus men call properly.   475
And all the ladies in her company

Which ye se of that hearb chaplets weare
Be such as han kepte alway her maidenhede.
And all they that of laurer chaplets beare
Be such as hardy were and wan by deed   480
Victorious name which never may be dede;
And all they were so worthy of ther hond,
In hir time, that none might hem withstond.

And tho that weare chapelets on ther hede
Of fresh woodbind, be such as never were   485
To love untrue in word, thought, ne dede,
But aye stedfast; ne for pleasance, ne fere,
Thogh that they shuld their harts all to-tere,
Would never flit, but ever were stedfast,
Till that their lives there asunder brast.'   490

' Now, faire madame,' quod I, ' yet I would pray
Your ladiship, if that it might be,
That I might know, by some maner way—
Sith that it hath liked your beaute
The trouth of these ladies for to tell me—   495
What that these knights be, in rich armour,
And what tho be in grene, and weare the flour,

And why that some did reverence to the tre
And some unto the plot of floures faire ? '
' With riȝt good will, my fair doghter,' quod she,
' Sith youre desire is good and debonaire.   501
Tho nine crowned be very exemplaire
Of all honour longing to chivalry,
And those, certaine, be called the Nine Worthy,

Which ye may se riding all before,   505
That in her time did many a noble dede,
And for their worthines ful oft have bore
The crowne of laurer leaves on their hede,
As ye may in your old bookes rede;
And how that he that was a conquerour   510
Had by laurer alway his most honour.

And tho that beare bowes in their hond
Of the precious laurer so notable,
Be such as were, I woll ye understond,
Noble knights of the Round Table,   515
And eke the Douseperis honourable;
Which they beare in signe of victory—
It is witnes of their dedes mightily.

f368v Eke there be knights old of the Garter,
That in her time did right worthily;   520
And the honour they did to the laurer
Is for [there-]by they have their laud wholly,
Their triumph eke and marshall glory;
Which unto them is more parfit riches
Then any wight imagine can or gesse.   525

For one leafe given of that noble tre
To any wight that hath done worthily,
And it be done so as it ought to be,
Is more honour then any thing earthly.
Witnes of Rome that founder was, truly,   530
Of all knighthood and deeds marvelous—
Record I take of Titus Livius.

And as for her that crowned is in greene,
It is Flora, of these floures goddesse.
And all that here on her awaiting beene,   535
It are such that loved idlenes
And not delite of no busines
But for to hunt and hauke, and pley in medes,
And many other such idle dedes.

And for the great delite and pleasaunce   540
They have to the floure, and so reverently
They unto it do such obeisaunce,
As ye may se.' ' Now, faire madame,' quod I,
' If I durst aske what is the cause and why
That knights have the signe of honour   545
Rather by the leafe than by the floure?'

' Sothly, doughter,' quod shee, ' this is the trouth:
For knights ever should be persevering
To seeke honour without feintise or slouth,
Fro wele to better, in all maner thing;   550
In signe of which, with leaves aye lasting
They be rewarded after their degree,
Whose lusty green May may not appaired be,

But aye keping their beauty fresh and greene,
For there nis storme that may hem deface, 555
Haile nor snow, wind nor frosts kene;
Wherfore they have this propertie and grace.
And for the floure within a little space
Woll be lost, so simple of nature
They be, that they no greevance may endure, 560

And every storme will blow them soone away,
Ne they last not but for a season—
That is the cause, the very trouth to say,
That they may not, by no way of reason,
Be put to no such occupacion.' 565
' Madame,' quod I, ' with all mine whole servise
I thanke you now, in my most humble wise;

For now I am acertained throughly
Of every thing I desired to know.'
' I am right glad that I have said, sothly, 570
Ought to your pleasure, if ye will me trow,'
Quod she ayen, ' but to whome doe ye owe
Your service? and which woll ye honour,
Tell me, I pray, this yeere, the Leafe or the
Flour?'

' Madame,' quod I, ' though I least worthy, 575
Unto the Leafe I owe mine observaunce.'
' That is,' quod she, ' right well done, certainly,
And I pray God to honour you avaunce,
And kepe you fro the wicked remembraunce
Of Male Bouch, and all his crueltie; 580
And all that good and well-condicioned be.

For here may I no lenger now abide;
I must follow the great company
That ye may see yonder before you ride.'
And forth, as I couth, most humbly, 585
I tooke my leve of her as she gan hie
After them, as fast as ever she might.
And I drow homeward, for it was nigh night,

And put all that I had seen in writing,
Under support of them that lust it to rede.   590
O little booke, thou art so unconning,
How darst thou put thy self in prees for drede?
It is wonder that thou wexest not rede,
Sith that thou wost ful lite who shall behold
Thy rude langage, full boistously unfold.   595

Explicit

The Assembly of Ladies

NOTE TO THE TEXT

THE text of AL is from MS Addit. 34360 (A), all variations from which, with the exception of the spelling conventions noted in the Introduction (p. 8), and the punctuation, are indicated in the textual notes. Additions to A are enclosed within square brackets in the text, and changes of A readings italicised. The three other texts, MS Trinity R.3.19 (Tr), MS Longleat 258 (L), and Thynne's edition of 1532 (Th), have been collated, and some of their readings adopted in preference to A. In addition to these, the textual notes record superior readings from the three other texts which have not been adopted, and also the more generally interesting variants. These three texts form a group against A and are usually quoted as a group (T). Such readings take no note of insignificant variations of spelling; where there is variation, the spelling of Tr is silently adopted. The two main lacunae in A (33, 519–32) are supplied from Tr. References followed by a bracket in the textual notes are A readings or original emendations; references not followed by a bracket are usually emendations adopted from the text indicated.

THE ASSEMBLY OF LADIES

f37ʳ

IN Septembre, at fallyng of the leef,
  The fressh season was al to-gydre done
  And of the corn was gadred in the sheef;
In a gardyn, abowte tweyne after none,
There were ladyes walkyng, as was ther wone,   5
Foure in nombre, as to my mynde doth falle,
And I the fift, symplest of alle.

Of gentil wymmen foure ther were also,
Disportyng hem everiche after theyr guyse,
In crosse aleys walkyng be two and two,   10
And som alone after theyr fant*asyes*.
Thus occupied we were in dyvers wise,
And yit in trowth we were nat alone:
Theyr were knyghtis and squyers many one.

' Wherof I serve? ' on of hem asked me.   15
I seyde ageyne, as it fil in my thought:
' To walke aboute the mase, in certeynte,
As a womman that nothyng rought.'

f37ᵛ

He asked me ageyn whom I sought
And of my coloure why I was so pale.   20
' Forsoth,' quod I, ' and therby lith a tale.'

' That must me wite,' quod he, ' and that anon;
Telle on, late se, and make no taryeng.'
' Abide,' quod I, ' ye be an hasti one;
I lete yow wite it is no litle thyng;   25
But for because ye have a grete longyng
In yowre desire this procese for to here
I shal yow telle the playne of this matiere.

It happed thus that in [an] after none
My felawship and I, bi one assent,   30
Whan al oure other busynesse was done,
To passe oure tyme in to this mase we went
[And toke oure weyes yche aftyr other entent:]
Som went inward and went they had gon oute,
Som stode amyddis and loked al aboute;   35

And soth to sey som were ful fer behynde
And right anon as ferforth as the best;
Other there were, so mased in theyr mynde,
Al weys were goode for hem, both est and west.
Thus went they furth and had but litel rest,   40
And som theyr corage dide theym so assaile
For verray wrath they stept over the rayle.

And as they sought hem self thus to and fro
I gate my self a litel avauntage;
Al for-weryed, I myght no further go,   45
Though I had wonne right grete for my viage;
So com I forth in to a streyte passage,
Whiche brought me to an herber feyre and grene
Made with benchis ful craftily and clene;

That, as me thought, myght no creature   50
Devise a bettir by proporcioun.
f38r   Save it was closed wele, I yow ensure,
With masonry of compas environ
Ful secretly, with steyres goyng down
In myddes the place, a tornyng whele, sertayne, 55
And upon that a pot of margoleyne;

With margarites growyng in ordynaunce
To shewe hem self as folk went to and fro,
That to behold it was a grete plesaunce;
And how they were accompanyed with mo,   60
Ne m'oublie-mies & sovenez also;
The poore penses ne were nat disloged there—
No, no, God wote, theyr place was every where.

The floore beneth was paved faire and smoth
With stones square of many dyvers hewe   65
So wele joyned that, for to sey the soth,
Al semed on, who that non other knewe.
And underneth the streames, newe and newe,
As silver newe bright spryngyng in such wise
That whens it com ye cowde it nat devise.   70

A litel while thus was I alone
Beholdyng wele this delectable place;
My felawshyp were comyng everichone
So must me nede abide as for a space,
Remembryng of many dyvers cace   75
Of tyme past, musyng with sighes depe,
I set me downe and ther fil in slepe.

And as I slept me thought ther com to me
A gentil womman metely of stature;
Of grete worship she semed for to be,   80
Atired wele, nat hye but bi mesure,
Hir contenaunce ful sad and ful demure,
f38v   Hir colours blewe, al that she had upon;
Theyr com no mo but hir silf alon.

Hir gowne was wele enbrowdid, certaynly,   85
With sovenez aftir hir owne devise;
On the purfil hir word, by and by,
Bien loialment, as I cowde me avise.
Than prayd I hir in every maner wise
That of hir name I myght have remembraunce.   90
She sayde she was callid Perseveraunce.

So furthermore to speke than was I bold:
Where she dwelt I prayed hir for to say.
And she ageyne ful curteisly me told:
' My dwellyng is and hath be many a day   95
With a lady.'   ' What lady, I yow pray? '
' Of grete astate, thus warne I yow,' quod she.
' What calle ye hir? '   ' Hir name is Loiau*l*te.'

'In what office stand ye, or in what degre?'
Quod I to hir, 'that wold I wit ful fayne.'   100
'I am,' quod she, 'unworthy though I be,
Of hir chamber hir ussher in certayne;
This rodde I bere as for a tokene playne,
Lyke as ye knowe the rule in suche service
Perteyneng unto the same office.   105

She charged me be hir comaundement
To warne yow and youre felawes everichone
That ye shuld come there as she is present
For a counsaile, whiche shuld be anone,
Or seven dayes bien comen and gone.   110
And more she badde that I shuld sey
Excuse ther myght be none nor delay.

Another thyng was nygh forgete behynd
f 39r   Whiche in no wise I wold nat but ye knewe—
Remembre it wele and bere it in your mynde: 115
Al youre felawes and ye must com in blewe,
Everiche yowre matier for to sewe,
With more, whiche I pray yow thynk upon,
Yowre wordes on yowre slevis everichon.

And be nat ye abasshed in no wise,   120
As many as bien in suche an high presence;
Make youre request as ye can best devise
And she gladly wil yeve yow audience.
Ther is no grief nor no maner offence
Wherin ye fele your hert is displeased   125
But with hir help right sone ye shul bien eased.'

'I am right glad,' quod I, 'ye telle me this;
But ther is none of us that knowith the way.'
'And of your wey,' quod she, 'ye shul nat mys;
Ye shul have one to guyde yow day be day   130
Of my felawes—I can no better say—
Suche on as shal telle yow the wey ful right;
And Diligence this gentil womman hight,

A womman of right famous governaunce
And wele cherisshed, I sey yow for certeyne;   135
Hir felawship shal do yow grete plesaunce,
Hir porte is suche, hir maner is terewe and playne;
She with glad chiere wil do hir busy peyne
To bryng yow there.   Farwele, now have I done.'
' Abide,' quod I, ' ye may nat go so soone.'   140

' Whi so ? ' quod she, ' and I have fer to go
To yeve warnyng in many dyvers place
To youre felawes and so to other moo,
And wele ye wote I have but litel space.'
f39v   ' Yit,' quod I, ' ye must telle me this cace,   145
If we shal any men unto us calle? '
' Nat one,' quod she, ' may come among yow alle.'

' Nat one? ' quod I, ' ey, benedicite!
What have they don?   I pray yow, telle me that.'
' Now, be my lif, I trowe but wele,' quod she,   150
' But evere I can beleve ther is somwhat,
And for to sey yow trowth, more can I nat;
In questions nothyng may I be large,
I medle me no further than is my charge.'

' Than thus,' quod I, ' do me til undrestond   155
What place is there this lady is dwellyng? '
' Forsoth,' quod she, ' and on sought al a lond,
Feirer is none, though it were fore a kyng;
Devised wele, and that in every thyng;
The toures high ful plesaunt shul ye fynde,   160
With fanes fressh tournyng with every wynde;

The chambres [and] parlours both of oo sort,
With [bay] wyndowes goodely as can be thought,
As for daunsyng and other wise disport;
The galaries right wonderfully wrought;   165
That wele I wote, yef ye were thider brought
And toke good hede therof in ever[y] wise,
Ye wold it thynk a verray paradise.'

'What hight this place?' quod I, 'now sey me
   that.'
'Plesaunt Regard,' quod she, 'to telle yow pleyne.'
'Of verray trouth?' quod I, 'and wote ye what,   171
It may wele be callid so sertayne.
But furthermore this wold I wite ful fayne,
What shal I do as soone as I com there
And after whom that I may best enquere?'   175

f4or   'A gentilwomman, porter at the yaate,
There shal ye fynde; hir name is Contenaunce.
If so happe ye com erly or late,
Of hir were goode to have som aqueyntaunce;
She can telle how ye shal yow best avaunce   180
And how to come to this ladyes presence;
To hir wordis I rede yow yeve credence.

Now is it tyme that I part yow fro,
For in goode soth I have grete busynesse.'
'I wote right wele,' quod I, 'that that is soo,   185
And I thanke yow of youre grete gentilnesse;
Yowre comfort hath yeve me suche hardynesse
That now I shal be bold withouten faile
To do after youre avise and counsaile.'

Thus parted she and I left al alone.   190
With that I sawe, as I behielde aside,
A womman come, a verray goodely oon,
And furth withal as I had hir aspied
Me thought anon that it shuld be the guyde;
And of hir name anon I did enquere.   195
Ful wommanly she yave this answere:

'I am,' quod she, 'a symple creature
Sent from the court; my name is Diligence.
As soone as I myght com, I yow ensure,
I taried nat after I had licence,   200
And now that I am com to yowre presence,
Looke what servise that I can do or may
Comaunde me, I can no further say.'

I thanked hir and prayed hir to come nere
Because I wold se how she were arrayed.   205
f40v Hir gowne was bliew, dressed in goode manere,
With hir devise, hir worde also, that sayde
Taunt que je puis; and I was wele apayed,
For than wist I without any more
It was ful triew that I had herd afore.   210

' Though we toke now before a lite space
It were ful goode,' quod she, ' as I cowth gesse.'
' How fer,' quod I, ' have we unto that place? '
' A dayes journey,' quod she, ' but litel lesse,
Wherfor I rede that we onward dresse,   215
For I suppose oure felawship is past
And for nothyng I wold that we were last.'

Than parted we at spryngyng of the day
And furth we wente a soft and esy pase,
Til at the last we were on oure journay
So fer onward that we myght se the place.   220
' Nowe lete us rest,' quod I, ' a litel space,
And say we as devoutly as we can
A Pater Noster for seynt Julyan.'

' With al myn hert,' quod she, ' I gre me wele;   225
Moche better shul we spede whan we have done.'
Than taryed we and sayde it every dele.
And whan the day was fer gon after none
We sawe a place, and thider come we sone,
Whiche rounde about was closid with a wal   230
Semyng to me ful like an hospital.

There fonde I oon had brought al myn array,
A gentilwomman of myn acqueyntaunce.
' I have mervaile,' quod I, ' what maner wey
Ye had knowlache of al this governaunce? '   235
' Yis, yis,' quod she, ' I herd Perseveraunce,
How she warned youre felawes everichone,
And what array that ye shal have upon.'

41r ' Now, for my love,' quod I, ' I yow pray,
Sith ye have take upon yow al this peyne,   240
That ye wold helpe me on [with] myne array,
For wite ye wele I wold be go ful fayne.'
' Al this prayer nedith nat certeyne,'
Quod she ageyne; ' com of, and hie yow soone,
And ye shal se how wele it shal be done.'   245

' But this I dowte me gretely, wote ye what,
That my felaws bien passed by and gone.'
' I waraunt yow,' quod she, ' that ar they nat,
For here they shul assemble everichon.
Natwithstandyng, I counseil yow anone   250
Make ye redy and tarye ye no more;
It is non harme though ye be there afore.'

So than I dressid me in myn array
And asked hir if it were wele or noo.
' It is,' quod she, ' right wele unto my pay;   255
Ye dare nat care to what place so ever ye goo.'
And while that she and I debated soo
Com Diligence, and sawe me al in bliew:
' Suster,' quod she, ' right wele broke ye your
      niewe.'

Than went we forth and met [at] aventure   260
A yong womman, an officer semyng.
' What is your name,' quod I, ' goode creature? '
' Discrecioun,' quod she, ' without lesyng.'
' And where,' quod I, ' is yowre abidyng? '
' I have,' quod she, ' this office of purchace,   265
Chief purviour that longith to this place.'

' Faire love,' quod I, ' in al youre ordynaunce,
What is hir name that is the herbegyer? '
' Forsoth,' quod she, ' hir name is Aqueyntaunce,
A womman of right graciouse maner.'   270
Than thus quod I, ' What straungiers have ye
      here? '
f41v ' But fewe,' quod she, ' of hie degre ne lowe;
Ye bien the first, as ferforth as I knowe.'

Thus with talis we com streyght to the yaate;
This yong womman departed was and gone.   275
Com Diligence and knokked fast therate.
' Who is without? ' quod Contenaunce anone.
' Triewly,' quod she, ' faire suster, here is one.'
' Whiche oon? ' quod she; and ther-withal she
          lough:
' I, Diligence, ye knowe me wele inough! '   280

Than opened she the gate and in we goo.
With wordis feyre she sayde ful gentily:
' Ye ben welcom, iwis; bien ye no mo? '
' No,' quod she, ' save this womman and I.'
' Now than,' quod she, ' I pray yow hertily,   285
Take my chambre as for a while to rest
To yowre felawes bien comen, I hold it for the
          best.'

I thanked hir and furth we gon echeon
Til hir chambre without wordes mo.
Come Diligence and toke hir leve anon;   290
' Where ever yow list,' quod I, ' nowe may ye goo,
And I thank yow right hertily also
Of yowre laboure, [for] whiche God do yow mede;
I can nomore, but Jhesu be yowre spede.'

Than Contenaunce asked me anone: 295
' Yowre felawship, where bien they now? ' quod she.
' Forsoth,' quod I, ' they bien comyng echeone,
But in certeyne I knowe nat where they be.
At this wyndow whan they come ye may se;
Here wil I stande awaityng ever among,   300
For wele I wote they wil nat now be long.'

Thus as I stode musyng ful busily
I thought to take heede of *hir* array.
f42r Hir gowne was bliew, this wote I verily,
Of goode facion and furred wele with gray;   305
Upon hir sleve hir worde, this is no nay,
The whiche saide thus, as my penne can endite,
A moy que je voy, writen with lettres white.

Than ferforth as she com streyght unto me,
' Yowre [worde],' quod she, ' fayne wold I that I
            knewe.'   310
' *Forsoth*,' quod I, ' ye shal wele know and se:
And for my word, I have none, this is trewe;
It is inough that my clothyng be blew
As here before I had comaundement,
And so to do I am right wele content.   315

But telle me this, I pray yow hertily,
The stiward here, sey me, what is hir name? '
' She hight Largesse, I say yow surely,
A faire lady and right of nobil fame;
Whan ye hir se ye wil report the same.   320
And undir hir, to bid yow welcom alle,
There is Bealchiere, the marchal of the halle.

Now al this while that ye here tary stille
Yowre owne matiers ye may wele have in mynde;
But telle me this, have ye brought any bille? '   325
' Ye, ye,' quod I, ' or ellis I were behynde;
Where is ther on, telle me, that I may fynde
To whom I may shewe my matiers playne? '
' Surely,' quod she, ' unto the chambrelayne.'

' The chambrelayn,' quod I, ' say ye trewe? '   330
' Ye verily,' quod she, ' be myn advise,
Be nat aferd but lowly til hir shewe.'
' It shal be don,' quod I, ' as ye devise,
But me must knowe hir name in every wyse.'

f42v

' Triewly,' quod she, ' to telle yow in substaunce,
Without feyneng, hir name is Remembraunce.   336

The secretarye yit may nat be forgete,
For she may do right moche in every thyng;
Wherfor I rede whan ye have with hir met
Yowre matier hole telle hir withoute feyneng;   340
Ye shal hir fynde ful goode and ful lovyng.'
' Telle me hir name,' quod I, ' of gentillesse.'
' Be my goode soth,' quod she, ' Avisenesse.'

'That name,' quod I, 'for hir is passyng goode,
For every bille and cedule she must se.   345
Now, goode,' quod I, 'com stonde where I stoode;
My felawes bien comyng, yonder they be.'
'Is it a jape, or say ye soth?' quod she.
'In jape? nay, nay! I say it for certeyne;
Se how they come togyder tweyne and tweyne.'   350

'Ye say ful soth,' quod she, 'it is no nay;
I se comyng a goodely company.'
'They bien,' quod I, 'suche folk, I dare wele say,
That list to love, thynk it ful verily;
And my faire love, I pray yow feithfully,   355
At any tyme whan they upon yow cal,
That ye wil be goode frend to theym al.'

'Of my frendship,' quod she, 'they shul nat mys,
As for ther case to put therto my payne.'
'God yield it yow,' quod I; 'but telle me this: 360
How shal we knowe whiche is the chambrelayne?'
'That shal ye wele knowe by hir worde, certayne.'
'What is hir worde, suster, I pray yow say?'
'*Plus ne purroy*, thus writeth she alway.'

43ʳ

Thus as we stoode to-gydre, she and I,   365
At the yate my felawes were echon.
So mette I theym, as me thought was goodely,
And bad hem welcom al by one and oon.
Than forth com Contenaunce anon:
'Ful hertily, feyre sustres al,' quod she,   370
'Ye bien right welcom to this contre.

I counseile yow to take a litel rest
In my chambre, if it be youre plesaunce.
Whan ye bien there me thynk it for the best
That I gon in and cal Perseveraunce   375
Because she is oon of youre acqueyntaunce,
And she also wil telle [yow] every thyng
How ye shal be rulyd of your comyng.'

My felawes al and I, be oon avise,
Were wele agreed to do as she sayde.   380
Than we began to dresse us in oure guyse
That folk shuld se us nat unpurvayde,
And wageours among us there we layde
Whiche of us atired were goodeliest
And whiche of us al preysed shuld be best.   385

The porter than brought Perseveraunce;
She welcomd us in ful curteys manere:
' Thynk ye nat long,' quod she, ' youre attendaunce;
I wil go speke unto the herbergier
That she may purvey for youre loggyng here,   390
Than wil I gon to the chambrelayne
To speke for yow, and come anon agayne.'

And whan she departed and was agone
We sawe folkes comyng without the wal,
f43v   So grete people that nombre couthe we none.   395
Ladyes they were and gentil wymmen al
Clothed in bliew everiche, her wordes withal;
But for to knowe theyr wordis *or* devise
They com so thycke we myght in no wise.

With that anon come Perseveraunce   400
And wher I stoode she com streight to me:
' Ye bien,' quod she, ' of myn old acqueyntaunce,
Yow to enquere the bolder dare I be
What worde they bere eche after theyr degre;
I pray yow telle it me in secrete wise   405
And I shal kepe it close on warantise.'

' We bien,' quod I, ' fyve ladies al in feere,
And gentil wymmen foure in company;
Whan they begynne to opyn theyr matiere
There shal ye knowe her wordis, by and by.   410
But as for me I have none verily
And so I told to Countenaunce here afore;
Al myn array is bliew, what nedith more? '

' Now,' quod she, ' I wil go in agayne,
That ye may know what ye shal do.'   415
' Forsoth,' quod I, ' yif ye wil take the peyne,
Ye dide right moche for us, yif ye did so;
The rather spede the sonner may we go.
Grete cost alwey there is in taryeng,
And long to sue it is a wery thyng.'   420

Than parted she and come agayne anon:
' Ye must,' quod she, ' com to the chambrelayne.'
' We bien,' quod I, ' now redy, everichone,
To folowe yow whan ever yow list, certeyne.
We have none eloquence, to telle yow pleyne,   425
Besechyng yow we may be so excused
Oure triewe meanyng that it be nat refused.'

Than went we forth after Perseveraunce.
To se the prease it was a wonder case;
There for to passe it was grete combraunce,   430
The people stoode so thykk in every place.
' Now stonde ye stille,' quod she, ' a litel space,
And for yowre ease somwhat shal I assay
Yif I can make yow any better way.'

And furth she goth among hem everychon,   435
Makyng a wey that we myght thurgh passe
More at oure ease, and whan she had don
She bekened us to com there as she was,
So after hir we folowed more and lasse.
She brought us streight unto the chambrelayne;
There left she us and than she went agayne.   441

We salwed hir as reson wold it soo,
Ful humbly besechyng hir goodenesse,
In oure matiers that we had for to doo,
That she wold be goode lady and maystresse.   445
' Ye bien welcom,' quod she, ' in sothfastnesse,
And so what I can do yow for to please
I am redy, that may be for youre ease.'

f 44r

We folowed hir unto the chambre doore:
' Suster,' quod she, ' come in ye after me.'   450
But wite ye wele, there was a paved floore,
The goodeliest that any wight myght see;
And furthermore aboute than loked we
On eche a corner and upon every wal,
The whiche is made of berel and cristal;   455

f44v

Wheron was graven of storyes many oon:
First how Phillis of wommanly pite
Deyd pitously for the love of Demephon;
Next after was the story of Thesbe,
How she slowe hir self under a tre;   460
Yit sawe I more [how] in pitous case
For Antony was slayne Cleopatrace;

That other syde was how *Me*lusene
Untriewly was disceyved in hir bayne;
Ther was also Anelada the quene   465
Upon Arcite how sore she did complayne;
Al these storyes wer graven ther certayne
And many mo than I reherce yow here—
It were to long to telle yow al in feere.

And bicause the wallis shone so bright   470
With fyne umple they were al over-spredde
To that entent folk shuld nat hurt theyr sight,
And thurgh that the storyes myght be redde.
Than further I went as I was ledde
And there I sawe without any faile   475
A chayer set with ful riche apparaile;

And fyve stages it was set from the grounde,
Of cassidony ful curiously wrought,
With foure pomels of gold and verray rounde
Set with saphirs as fyne as myght be thought.   480
Wote ye what, yif it were thurgh sought
As I suppose from this contre til Ynde,
Another suche it were hard to fynde.

For wete ye wele, I was ful nere that,
So as I durst beholdyng by and by.   485
Above ther was a riche cloth of state
Wrought with the nedil ful straungely,
f45^r Hir worde theron, and thus it sayde triewly:
A Endurer, to telle in wordis fewe,
With grete lettres, the better for to shewe.   490

Thus as we stoode a doore opened anon;
A gentil womman semely of stature,
Beryng a mace, com out, hir self alone—
Triewly, me thought, a goodely creature.
She spak nothyng to lowde, I yow ensure,   495
Nor hastily, but bi goodely warnyng:
' Make roome,' quod she, ' my lady is comyng.'

With that anon I saw Perseveraunce
How she hield up the tappet in hir hande.
I sawe also in right goode ordynaunce   500
This grete lady withyn the tappet gan stande,
Comyng outward, I wil ye undrestande,
And after hir a noble company,
I cowde nat telle the nombre sikerly.

Of theyr names I wold nothyng enquere   505
Further than suche as we wold sue unto,
Sauf oo lady whiche was the chaunceler—
Attemperaunce, sothly, hir name was soo—
For us must with hir have moche to doo
In oure matiers and alwey more and more.   510
And so furth to telle yow furthermore:

Of this lady hir beauties to discryve
My konnyng is to symple verily,
For never yit the dayes of al my live
So inly fayre I have none sene triewly,   515
In hir astate assured utterly;
Ther lakked naught, I dare yow wele ensure,
That longged to a goodely creature.

[*f62r*] [And furthermore to speke of hyr aray
         I shall yow tell the maner of hyr goune: 520
         Of cloth of gold full ryche, hyt ys no nay,
         The colour blew of a ryght good fassion,
         In taberd wyse, the slevys hangyng don;
         And what purfyll ther was and in what wyse
         So as I can I shall hyt yow devyse.   525

[*f62v*] Aftyr a sort the coler and the vent,
         Lyke as ermyn ys made in purfelyng,
         With gret perles full fyne and oryent
         They were couchyd all aftyr oon worchyng,
         With dyamondes in stede of pouderyng;   530
         The slevys and purfyllys of assyse,
         They were made lyke in every wyse;]

f45v   Abowte hir nekke a s*er*pe of fayre rubies
         In white floures of right fyne enemayle;
         Upon hir hede sette in the fresshest wise   535
         A cercle with grete balays of entaile;
         That in ernest to speke, withouten faile,
         For yong and old and every maner age
         It was a world to loke on hir visage.

         This comyng to sit in hir astate,   540
         In hir presence we knelid downe echeon
         Presentyng up oure billis and, wote ye what,
         Ful humbly she toke hem by oon and oon.
         Whan we had don than com they al anon
         And dide the same iche after in theyr manere,   545
         Knelyng attones and risyng al in feere.

         Whan this was don, and she sette in hir place,
         The chambrelayne she dide unto hir cal,
         And she goodely comyng til hir a-pace
         Of hir intent knowyng nothyng at al: 550
         ' Voyde bak the prease,' quod she, ' unto the wal;
         Make larger rome, but loke ye do nat tarye,
         And take these billes unto the secretarye.'

The chambrelayne dide hir comaundement
And com ageyne as she was bode to doo;   555
The secretarie there beyng present
The billes were delyvered til hir also,
Nat only oures but many another moo.
Than this lady with gode avise ageyne
Anone withal callid hir chambrelayne.   560

' We wil,' quod she, ' the first thyng that ye doo,
The secretary make hir come anon
With hir billes, and thus we wille also,
f46r   In oure presence she rede hem everychone
That we may take goode avise theron   565
Of the ladyes whiche bien of oure counsaile.
Looke this be don without any faile.'

The chambrelayn whan she wist hir entent
Anon she dide the secretary calle:
' Lete yowre billes,' quod she, ' be here present;
My lady [it] wil.' ' Madame,' quod she, ' I shal.'
' In hir presence she wil ye rede hem al.'
' With goode wil I am redy,' quod she,   572
' At hir plesure whan she comaundith me.'

And upon that was made an ordynaunce   575
They that com first theyr billes to be redde.
Ful gently than seyde Perseveraunce:
' Reason it wold that they were sonnest spedde.'
Anon withal upon a tappet spredde
The secretary layde hem downe everichon;   580
Oure billes first she red oon by oon.

The first lady, beryng in hir devise
Sanz que jamais, thus wrote she in hir bille:
Compleyneng sore and in ful pitous wise
Of promesse made with feithful hert and wil   585
And so broken ayenst al maner skille,
Without desert alweys in hir party,
In this matier desiryng remedy.

I

Hir next felawes word was in this wise—
Une sans chaungier; and thus she did compleyne:
Though she had bien gwerdoned for hir service,
Yit nothyng, as she takith it, pleyne,   592
Wherfor she cowde in no wise restreyne
But in this case sue until hir presence,
As reason wold, to have recompence.   595

So furthermore to speke of other tweyne:
Oon of hem wrote after hir fantasye
Oncques puis lever, and for to telle yow pleyne,
Hir compleynt was grevous verily
For as she sayde ther was grete reason why,   600
And as I can remembre that matiere
I shal yow telle the processe al in fere.

Hir bille was made compleyneng in her guyse
That of hir joye, comfort and gladnesse
Was no suerte, for in no maner wise   605
She fonde therin no poynt of stabilnesse,
Now ill nov wele, out of al sikernesse;
Ful humble desiryng of her grace
Som remedy to shewe in this case.

Hir felaw made hir bille, and thus she sayde   610
In pleyneng wise: there as she lovid best,
Whethir she were wroth or ill apayde,
She myght nat se whan she wold faynest,
And wroth was she in verray ernest
To telle hir worde, and forsoth, as I wote,   615
Entierment vostre right thus she wrote.

And upon that she [made] a grete request,
With hert and wil and al that myght be done,
As until hir that myght redresse it best,
For in hir mynde thus myght she fynde it sone 620
The remedy of that whiche was hir bone;
Rehersyng that she had seyd before,
Besechyng hir it myght be so no more.

f46v

And in like wise as they had don before
The gentil wymmen of oure company   625
Put up their billes; and for to telle yow more,
f47r One of hem wrote *C'est sanz dire*, verily;
Of hir compleynt also the cause why
Withyn hir bille she put it in writyng,
And what it saide ye shul have knowlachyng.   630

It sayde, God wote, and that ful pitously,
Like as she was disposed in hir hert,
No mysfortune that she toke grevously,
Al on til hir it was the joy or smert;
Somtyme no thank for al hir desert;   635
Other comfort she wayted non comyng,
And so used [it] greved hir nothyng;

Desiryng hir and lowly hir besechyng
That she for hir wold se a bettir way,
As she that had bien al hir dayes livyng
Stadefast and triewe and so wil be alway.   640
Of hir felaw somwhat shal I yow say,
Whos bille was redde next after forth withal,
And what it ment reherce yow I shal.

En dieu est she wrote in hir devise,   645
And thus she sayde, without any faile:
Hir trowth myght be take in no wise
Like as she thought, wherfor she had mervaile,
For trowth somtyme was wont to take availe
In eche matiere, but now al that is goo—   650
The more pite that it is suffred soo.

Moche more ther was wherof she shuld compleyne
But she thought it to grete encombraunce
So moche to write, and therfor, in certayne,
In God and hir she put hir affiaunce,   655
As in hir worde is made a remembraunce,
Besechyng hir that she wold in that case
f47v Shewe til hir the favour of hir grace.

The thridde she wrote rehersyng hir grevaunce,
Yee, wote ye what, a pitous thyng to here,   660
For as me thought she felt grete displesaunce—
One myght wele perceyve bi hir chiere,
And no wonder, it sat hir passyng neere;
Yit loth she was to put it in writyng,
But neede wil have his cours in every thyng.   665

Sejour ensure this was hir worde certeyne,
And thus she wrote but in a litel space:
There she loved hir labour was in vayne
For he was sette al in another place;
Ful humble desiryng in that cace   670
Som goode comfort hir sorow to appese
That she myght live more at hertis ease.

The fourth surely, me thought, she liked wele,
As in hir port and in hir havyng,
And *Bien monest*, as ferre as I cowth feele,   675
That was hir worde, til hir wele belongyng;
Wherfor til her she prayde above al thyng,
Ful hertily, to say yow in substaunce,
That she wold sende hir goode contenuaunce.

' Ye have rehersed me these billis alle,   680
But now late se somwhat of youre entente.'
' It may so happe peraventure ye shal.'
' Now, I pray yow, while I am here present.'
' Ye shal, parde, have knowlache what I ment;
But thus I say in trowth, and make no fable,   685
The case it silf is inly lamentable,

And wele I wote that ye wil thynk the same
Like as I say whan ye han herd my bil.'
' Now, goode, telle on, I hate yow, be seynt Jame.'
f48r   ' Abide a while, it is nat yit my wil;   690
Yet must ye wite, bi reason and bi skil,
Sith ye knowe al that hath be done afore.'
And thus it sayde, without any more:

'Nothyng so lief [as] death to come to me
For fynal end of my sorwes and peyne;   695
What shuld I more desire, as seme ye—
And ye knewe al aforne it for certeyne
I wote ye wold; and for to telle yow pleyne,
Without hir help that hath al thyng in cure
I can nat thynk that it may long endure;   700

And for my trouth, preved it hath bien wele—
To sey the soth, it can be no more—
Of ful long tyme, and suffred every dele
In pacience and kept it al in store;
Of hir goodenesse besechyng hir therfor   705
That I myght have my thank in suche wise
As my desert deservith of justice.'

Whan these billes were redde everichone
This lady toke goode avisement,
And hem til aunswere, eche on by oon,   710
She thought it to moche in hir entent,
Wherfor she yaf in comaundement
In hir presence to come both oon and al
To yeve hem there hir answere in general.

What did she than, suppose yow, verily?   715
She spak hir silf and seyde in this manere:
'We have wele sen youre billis by and by
And som of hem ful pitous for to here.
We wil therfor ye knowen this al in feere:
Withyn short tyme oure court of parlement   720
Here shal be holde in oure paleys present,

And in al this wherein ye fynde yow greved
There shal ye fynde an open remedy,
In suche wise as ye shul be releved
Of al that ye reherce heere triewly.   725
As of the date ye shal knowe verily,
Than ye may have a space in your comyng,
For Diligence shall bryng it yow bi writyng.'

We thanked hir in oure most humble wise,
Oure felawship echon bi on assent,   730
Submyttyng us lowly til hir servise,
For as us thought we had oure travel spent
In suche wise as we hielde us content.
Than eche of us toke other by the sleve,
And furth withal, as we shuld take oure leve.   735

Al sodainly the water sprang anone
In my visage and therwithal I woke.
' Wher am I now ? ' thought I, ' al this is goon,'
Al amased; and up I gan to looke.
With that anon I went and made this booke,   740
Thus symply rehersyng the substaunce
Because it shuld nat out of remembraunce.

' Now verily your dreame is passyng goode
And worthy to be had in remembraunce,
For though I stande her[e] as longe as I stoode 745
It shuld to me be none encombraunce,
I toke therin so inly [grete] plesaunce.
But tel me now what ye the booke do cal,
For me must wite.'   ' With right goode wil ye shal:

As for this booke, to sey yow verray right   750
_f49r_ And of the name to tel the certeynte,
" La semble de Dames ", thus it hight;
How thynk ye that the name is ? '   ' Goode, parde! '
' Now go, farewele, for they cal after me,
My felawes al, and I must after sone.'   755
Rede wele my dreame, for now my tale is done.

TEXTUAL NOTES

THE FLOWER AND THE LEAF

4 soft *U*
37 for to *Sp*2; *Sp*1 fort
53 welwet] *Sp*1 wel wot I; *U* woll wot I
62 y trow] *Sp*1 ytrow
105 ayen] *M* ay
109 laurey] *Sp*2 laurer
131 their] *Sk* his
141 In *Sk*; *Sp*1 The
142 clad] *Sp*2 in clad; *Sk* y-clad
150 went] *Sk* want
155 leves *Sk*; *Sp*1, 2 omit; *U* braunchis; *M* floures(!)
213 bere *U*; *Sp*1 here
238 hem yede *Sp*2; *Sp*1 him yede
246 boose] *Sp*2 bosse
253 ever the on on] *Sp*1 euery on; *U* every first on; *Sk* the first upon
258 spheare] *Sp*2 sphere; *Sp*3 spere
271 kene] *U only* bene
274 horse] *Sp*1 horses
293 nine *U*; *Sp*1 ninth
296 worthy *Sp*2; *Sp*1, *Sk* worldly
300 the *Sp*2; *Sp*1 they
308 there might it] *U* it there might
316 enclining] *U* enclinid
350 douce est *Sp*1 (*gloss*); *Sp*1 (*text*) douset &
354 how *U*
461 Must] *Sp*2, *Sk* Might; *U* Mote
471 yis *M*; *Sp*1 yes
478 alway] *Sk* ay
480 and wan by deed] *Sp*1 and manly indeed; *U* in manly dede; *Sk* and wan indede
518 It is] *U* As
522 for thereby] *Sp*1 forby; *U* for by it
541 and] *Sk omits*
553 May] *U omits*
563 is the *Sp*2; *Sp*1 if their

THE ASSEMBLY OF LADIES

8 foure] *Th* fayre
11 fantasyes] *A*, *L* fantise; *Tr* fantasy; *Th* fantasyse
29 an *T*
33 *supplied from T* (other *Tr*, *L*; *Th* our)
50 me *T*; *A* my
53 masonry *T*; *A* mesure
55 a] *T* with
57 With *T*; *A* Was
61 *Tr* Ne momblynes and souenes also; *L*, *Th* Ne momblysnesse and
    souenesse also
64 beneth] *T* and benche
86 sovenez] *T* stones
88 loialment] *T* et loyalment
98 Loiaulte *L*; *A* Loiauute(?); *Tr*, *Th* Loyalte
111 more] *T* furthermore
121 many as *A* (as *inserted above*); *T* many
124–5 *transposed in A*
149 they] *T* I
153 be] *T* be to
162 and *T*
163 bay *T*
167 every *T*; *A* euer
214 *A* litel h lesse(?)
225 quod . . . wele] *T* I assent with good wyll
235 governaunce] *T* ordenaunce
241 with *T*
245 how wele] *T* anon
248 waraunt] *T* warne
260 at *T*
278 she] *T* I
281 *A* Than she opened she
293 for *T*
298–9 *T* But where they ar I know no certaynte/Without I may theym
    at thys wyndow se
303 hir *T*; *A* theyr
308 *A T*; *A* O
309 ferforth as] *T* forth withal
310 worde *T*
311 Forsoth *T*; *A* Ferforth.—se *T*; *A* she
345 se *T*; *A* she
359 case] *T* ease
377 yow *T*
382 se us] *T* say we were

386 than] *T* came and
398 or] *A* al; *T* or theyr
415 know] *T* haue knowlege
418 we *T*; *A* ye
430 There *T*; *A* They
450 Suster] *T* Systers
455 is] *T* was
461 how *T*
463 how Melusene] *A* how Enclusene; *T* Hawes the shene
479 foure] *A* iiij
491 as *T*; *A* al
496 bi] *T* with
519–32 *supplied from Tr (and so L, Th)*
533 serpe] *A, T* sorte
534 In *T*; *A* Of
571 it *T*
572 ye . . . al] *Tr* yow there call; *L, Th* ye theim calle
580–1 *transposed in A*
589 felawes] *T* folowyng hyr
592 as . . . pleyne] *T* lyke as she that toke the playn (*Th* payne)
598 lever *T*; *A* leur
612 ill] *Tr* euyll; *L, Th* wele
615 and forsoth] *T* as ferforth
617 made *T*
628 *not in Tr; L, Th* And her mater hole to specyfy (*L in later hand*)
636 wayted] *T* wanted
637 used it *T*; *A* it used
639 se] *T* seke
666 Sejour] *T* Soyes
674 havyng] *T* behauyng
693 it] *T* it is
694 as *T*
697 knewe *L, Th*; *A, Tr* knowe
702 it can be] *T* I can say
720 court *T*; *A* comfort
745 here *T*; *A* her
747 grete *T*
748 now *T*; *A* how

NOTES

THE FLOWER AND THE LEAF

1–14. In courtly love-allegory the convention of the spring opening is generally observed (see Introduction, p. 48). There is no single ' source ' for this passage (a few of the more interesting parallels are noted below), but the poet is evidently trying, though without much success, to imitate the balance and poise of the opening sentence of the Prologue to the *Canterbury Tales* (' Whan . . . Whan . . . Thanne . . .'). For some further typical examples of spring description in English see *BD*, 402–15; *LGW*, 125ff; *RR*, 49–70; *BK*, 1–63; *RS*, 87–180; *Troy*, i, 3907–39, ii, 3319–55; *Secrees*, 1296–337; *KQ*, 134–47.

1–3. The astronomical periphrasis, as a poetic means of indicating date or time, was another conventional feature. See Introduction, p. 48, and, for further references to the device, Hammond, *English Verse between Chaucer and Surrey*, p. 527; Curtius, *European Literature and the Latin Middle Ages*, pp. 275–6; *TG*, ed. Schick, pp. cxxii–iii; C. Schaar, *The Golden Mirror*, pp. 475–8. The lines in *FL* are imitated from *CT*, V, 671–2: ' Appollo whirleth up his chaar so hye,/Til that the god Mercurius hous, the slye '. Further imitations of Chaucer's lines occur in Orleans 2455f: ' Whan fresshe Phebus day of seynt valentyne/ Had whirlid up his golden chare aloft '; also *Troy*, i, 626; Lydgate, *Serpent of Division* (ed. MacCracken, 1911), p. 55; *GL*, 1436. The more pious members of a medieval audience would be familiar from their Books of Hours with the picture of Phoebus passing across a starry sky in his golden chariot. The lines refer, of course, not to the rising of the sun, but to its northward course through the zodiac after the vernal equinox which, in Chaucer's time, occurred on 12 March. After passing through Aries the sun entered Taurus (' the Boole ') on 12 April.

Certainly, if it is not merely a tag, may indicate that the sun was *well* into its course through Taurus, which fits a May-day setting (cf. 437).

4. shoures sweet. *CT*, I, 1: ' shoures soote '.

5f. The smell of earth after spring showers. A neat touch of observation which enriches the conventional pattern by varying the more usual detail, illustrated in *Troy*, i, 3921f: ' And the bawme vapoureth up alofte/In-to the eyre of the erbes softe '; also *Night.*, II, 39f.

7f. This image, of spring ' clothing ' the earth with a fresh garment of green, was very common: cf. *RR*, 63–70; *TC*, iii, 353; *LGW*, 129; *BK*, 51; *Troy*, ii, 3343; *RS*, 96; and especially *TC*, i, 156f (' Aperill, whan clothed is the mede/With newe grene '); *Troy*, i, 3931f: ' And Flora had with newe grene ageyne/ Hir lyuere schad up-on euery playn '.

was clothed may be parallel to *discended*, or intended to be subordinate to *causing* (i.e. ' to be clothed ').

8. maketh may be sing. (subj. *raine*) or pl. (subj. *shoures*); loosely parallel to *discended* or to *causing* (with a rel. pron. understood, see 212n). Analysis is futile with these loose sentences; the sense is clear enough.

10–12. The deeply symbolic image of spring giving new life to the barren death of winter was again a common one, e.g. *RR*, 57–62; *BD*, 410–15; *TC*, ii, 52, iii, 352; *LGW*, 125–8; *KQ*, 134–47; the idea is elaborately developed in *Pilg.*, 3449–92, and Froissart, *Prison Amoureuse*, 2252–88.

very good. *very* is not used as an adverbial intensive by Chaucer, but the development is well under way here. Clear-cut examples (see Glossary) are not common until late in the fifteenth century. Lydgate's usage (e.g. *Fall*, ix, 1692, 2219) is transitional; cf. *AL*, 192n.

11. **That it renueth.** *it* is apparently subj., standing for *shoures* (*of raine*).

14. **glad and light.** One of Lydgate's favourite phrases, e.g. *TG*, 1216; *RS*, 188; *Troy*, i, 2760, 3206, ii, 2998, 3345, etc.

17f. ' The prospect of sleeping was very remote ' (see *OED*, s.v. *unmeet*, 3). According to the usual convention, the poet goes to sleep at this point, and the dream begins; or else he wakes up and goes out on purpose to ' doon his observaunce to May ', to hear the birds sing (*FL*, 40), or to seek solace for his mistress's cruelty. The description of the poet's sleeplessness here owes something to *BD*, 1–43 (from Froissart; cf. *CN*, 42), though there the sleeplessness is due to love-sickness (cf. *FL*, 21).

20. **hearts ease.** Cf. *AL*, 672; *CT*, IV, 434 (some MSS); *TC*, v, 1740; *Fall*, i, 552, ii, 3700, iv, 674; etc.

21. The lack of any sort of ' complaint ' is unusual, though cf. Froissart, *L'Espinette Amoureuse*, 352: ' Je n'oc doubtance ne esmai ' (in a passage closely parallel to *FL*).

24. **three houres after twelfe.** This seems extraordinarily early to us, but it does serve to indicate how strictly the medieval day was governed by the sun: the early-morning festivals in honour of May were no hollow rites.

25. **springing of the day.** Cf. *AL*, 218; *Troy*, i, 1197; Orleans, 2265; etc.

27–126. The descriptions that follow are full of echoes of Chaucer, Lydgate, and other English and French poets; only the closest parallels are noted below.

29ff. Cf. *RR*, 1391–4:

> These trees were set, that I devyse,
> Oon from another, in assyse,
> Fyve fadome or sixe, I trowe so;
> But they were hye and great also;

BD, 419f (imitated from *RR*): ' And every tree stood by hymselve/Fro other wel ten foot or twelve '; Machaut, *Dit dou Lyon*, 192–6. **streight as a line** refers, of course, to the rows of oak trees. The simile is common: see *TC*, ii, 1461; *Troy*, ii, 6739; *Night.*, II, 234 (and Glauning's note).

31. **an eight foot.** For this use of the indef. article with cardinals see *CT*, III, 600, VI, 771.

34. **ayen the sonne shene.** Cf. *CT*, I, 1509, V, 53; *TC*, ii, 920; *Troy*, i, 1268, ii, 591. Usually applied to birds singing. Compare line 28. Perhaps the sun, though risen, is not yet ' up risen '; but the apparent contradiction is due rather to the lack of ' realistic ' visualisation, characteristic of medieval nature description.

35. **Some very red.** ' The young leaves of the oak, when they first burst from the bud, are of a red, cinereous colour ' (Bell). This touch of observation drew forth praise from no less a naturalist than Gilbert White himself (*Letters*, ed. Holt-White (2 vols., 1901), ii, 78).

37. *RR*, 100f: ' For out of toun me list to gon/The song of briddes forto here.' The use of ' for to here ' as a rhyming tag (cf. *AL*, 27, 718) is frequent in Chaucer, e.g. *HF*, 180, 189, 862, 1518, etc. For the *topos* in the next line cf. Machaut, *Dit dou Vergier*, 20–6:

> Pour oïr la melodie
> Des oisillons qui ens estoient. . . .
> N'onques homs vivans n'ot tant d'ire
> Que, s'il peüst leur chant oïr,
> Qu'il ne s'en deüst resjoïr. . . .

39–42. Cf. *CN*, 51–5:

> And then I thoghte, anon as it was day,
> I wolde go som whider to assay
> If that I might a nightingale here;
> For yet had I non herd of al this yere,
> And hit was tho the thridde night of May.

It was considered a good omen, foretelling success in love, to hear the nightingale before the cuckoo upon the advent of both with spring (see *CN*, 46–50, and Milton's sonnet).

43–6. A conventional detail. Cf. *RR*, 729–31; *BD*, 398–401:

> Doun by a floury grene wente
> Ful thikke of gras, ful softe and swete,
> With floures fele, faire under fete,
> And litel used, hyt semed thus;

Machaut, *Dit dou Vergier*, 13f: ' Si trouvay une sentelette/Pleinne de rousée et d'erbette '; *Dit dou Lyon*, 185f: ' une sente po battue/Pleinne d'erbe poignant et drue '; *Jugement dou Roy de Behaingne*, 43; *Remede de Fortune*, 831; *BK*, 38; *AL*, 47. The narrow and little-trodden path was necessary for the closely guarded privacy of the arbour.

45. **forgrowen.** The intensive prefix *for-* (v. *OED*) was especially common with past participles: cf. 358, *AL* 45.

49. **herber.** OF *herbier*, a grassy place, a herb garden (Lat. *herbarium*). When first introduced in English the word could be used of a lawn, or flower garden, or orchard, but here it has its full modern meaning: ' A bower or shady retreat, of which the sides and roof are formed by trees and shrubs closely planted or intertwined ' (*OED*). The spelling *arbere* (465), which is rare before 1500, and probably scribal, is due to the normal change of *er* to *ar* (cf. *carve*, *starve*, etc.), and perhaps also to a supposed connection with Lat. *arbor*, tree. No fifteenth-century garden was complete without its arbour, a shady bower tucked away in a corner of the garden, carefully screened and not easy to find, the ideal place for melancholy meditation upon the cruelty of one's mistress (*BK*), or for a courtly conversation secure from all curious ears—except those of the poet (*BDM*). Turf-topped ' benches ' were very popular; they were of earth, supported by planks or wattle fencing, or, later in the century, by masonry. Cf. *LGW*, 97f (*G*): ' And in a lytel herber that I have,/Ybenched newe with turves, fresshe ygrave . . .'; *CT*, IV, 2235: ' a bench of turves, fressh and grene '; *TC*, ii, 822, 1705; *Churl*

and Bird, 51; *AL*, 48; *Pearl* (ed. Gordon, 1953), 38; *KQ*, 213; Crisp, *Medieval Gardens* (2 vols., 1924), i, 73–5, 81–3, ii, figs. 114–32, 149–62. Wordsworth's plan for a winter garden for Lady Beaumont included an arbour explicitly modelled on the one in *FL*, ' a little parlour of verdure ', with a mossed seat all around, and walls and ceiling of evergreen foliage (*Letters 1806–1820*, ed. de Selincourt, i, 96).

51. A verb, ' was ', is to be understood at the end of the line.

52. This kind of turf was greatly admired, especially in English gardens, as is brought out by Chaucer's elaboration of his French original in *RR*, e.g. 128: ' The medewe softe, swote and grene ' (*Rom.*, 122: ' La praerie grant e bele '); 1419f: ' the grass, as thicke yset/And softe as any veluet ' (1393: ' l'erbe bassete e drue '); 1425f: ' the sote grene gras/As fayre, as thicke, as myster was ' (1398: ' tant d'erbe '). Cf. *LGW*, 118.

53. **welwet.** The emendation suggested by E. P. Hammond in *MLN* **40** (1925), 185f. She explains that a careless scribe must have written *wot* for a partly separated second syllable, and a text-meddler inserted *I*, with the common tag *wot I* in mind. This is Speght's reading; to make sense of it, Urry changed *wel* to *woll*, ' wool ', an emendation which all subsequent editors adopted. This comparison is not found elsewhere, and Saintsbury commented on its ' infelicity ' (*CHEL*, ii, 219). Grass was often compared with velvet, however (e.g. *RR*, 1420; *BK*, 80; *Troy*, ii, 2450), and spellings like *welwet*, *ueluet* are common in the fifteenth century (e.g. *Troy*, ii, 715, 2450, iii, 5342; *Fall*, vi, 3482; *Thebes*, 1441).

54–9. In a medieval garden, pattern and precision, proportion and symmetry, the control exerted by art over nature, were the qualities admired (see Introduction, p. 50). So here the hedge was praised for the cunning with which it imitates a wooden fence. See 29n, and cf. Froissart, *Le Joli Mois de May*, 25–33:

> Au regarder pris le vregié,
> Que tout autour on ot vregié
> De rainselés
> Espessement et dur margiet
> Et ouniement arrengié;
> Au veoir les
> Ce sambloit des arbrisselés
> Qu'on les euïst au compas fais
> Et entailliés.

(The garden was exactly marked out, and bounded by a thick, firm hedge, evenly cut; the shrubs looked as if they had been trimmed to a precise pattern.)

56. **sicamour.** Two trees go by this name in English: one is a kind of fig tree (*ficus sycomorus*, the *sycomore* of the Bible, Luke 19:4), native to the Levant, and not grown outdoors in England; the other is a large shady tree like the plane (*acer pseudoplatanus*, the usual modern sense), naturalised in England since the sixteenth century (see the Royal Horticultural Society's *Dictionary of Gardening* (1951), pp. 23, 820, and the references there). The reference here is purely literary.

eglatere. The usual form is *eglentere* (80), but record elsewhere of *egletyn*, *eggletyne* (v. *OED*, *MED*) discourages emendation.

57. The close-knit screen of branches and leaves (as also in *RR*, 1395–1400; *BD*, 424–6) was desirable both for privacy and for shade (the

latter more important in a French garden). These secluded nooks provided the secrecy which was at once essential to the proper conduct of fashionable love affairs and also extremely difficult to obtain in a courtly household.

59. by and by. The basic sense of this phrase is ' in succession ': this meaning of *by* can be clearly seen in the phrase *one by one*. *By and by* was not used temporally until the late fifteenth century. See Glossary, and cf. *CT*, I, 1011, 4143; *LGW*, 304; *RR*, 4581; Hammond, Glossary, s.v.

60. I you ensure. Cf. 287, 457; *AL*, 52, 199, 495, 517. A very common tag, e.g. *PF*, 448; *RS*, 295, 897, 1299, 1366, etc.; Orleans, 3168, 5248, 5371, etc.

60-3. For this *topos* of eulogy cf. *CT*, V, 909-12; Machaut, *Dit de la Rose* (ed. Tarbé, *Poètes de Champagne*, iii, 65), 23f: ' Je ne vi haye ne haiette/Si bien ne si proprement faitte '.

62f. peine/seyne. The unusual spelling and pronunciation of the latter (' seen ') are from an Anglian p.p. *gesegen*, ME *seʒen, seien*.

65. prety. Not used by Chaucer, and not generally common until late in the fifteenth century, though frequent in Charles of Orleans (*praty*, *pratile*).

parlour: Lat. *parlatorium*, the room in a monastery set aside for conversation. In fourteenth-century houses the *parlour* was a small room set apart from the great hall for private conversation; the word came to be applied to any small sitting-room. Cf. *TC*, ii, 82; *P.Pl.*, B, x, 97.

66ff. Cf. *KQ*, 213-17:

> Ane herbere grene, with wandis long and small
> Railit about; and so with treis set
> Was all the place, and hawthorn hegis knet,
> That lyf was none walking there forby
> That myght within scarse ony wight aspye;

BDM, 187f: ' The leves were so thik, withouten fayle,/That thorough-out might no man me espy '; *Lancelot of the Laik*, ed. EETS (O.S.) 6, ll. 53-6.

73. out of doubt. Cf. 146; *CT*, I, 487, 1141, 3561, 3987, etc.

74. For this *topos* cf. *CT*, VII, 2298-302: ' I seye, so worshipful a creature. . . ./Was noon, though al this world men sholde seke '; *LGW*, 244f; *CT*, I, 2587-9.

76. on no coast. Cf. *CT*, III, 922: ' But he ne koude arryven in no coost . . .'; *Thebes*, 2450; *Pilg.*, 14901.

79f. *Troy*, i, 1210f: ' And hony-souklis amonge the buschis grene/ Enbamed hadde enviroun al the Eyr '. The sweet scents of a garden were not only pleasant, but hygienic also, since it was believed that the plague was spread by ' bad air ' (e.g. *Past. Pleas.*, 1981; Cavendish, *Metrical Visions*, 119; and the note in Hammond). In his *Dietary* Lydgate advises: ' Walk in gardeyns sote of ther savour ' (37).

80-4. A frequent *topos*, e.g. Machaut, *Dit dou Vergier*, 55-8:

> Plein de si trés bonne odour
> Que nuls n'en aroit la savour,
> Tant fust ses cuers desconfortez,
> Qu'il ne fust tous reconfortez;

Watriquet de Couvin, *Dis de la Fontaine d'Amours*, 30f: ' N'est hons, tant eüst de douleur,/Qu'a l'oudeur ne fust alegiez '; *RS*, 5605–12 (not of odours, but closely parallel):

> Ther melodye was in all
> So heuenly and celestiall
> That ther nys hert, I dar expresse,
> Oppressed so with hevynesse
> Nor in sorwe so y-bounde,
> That he sholde ther ha founde
> Comfort hys sorowe to apese
> To a-sette his hert at ese;

Eye and Heart, 33; *Pilg.*, 408; *Chansons du XVe siècle*, ed. G. Paris, LXX.

82. froward and contraire. This phrase, first used in *RR*, 5411, is common in Lydgate: *Thebes*, 3178; *Troy*, i, 2202; *Fall*, i, 1892; (*contrarie*) vi, 3535, vii, 1601, viii, 99, ix, 142, 1063.

85f. A phrase of transition, similarly used in 324, 379, and in *CT*, I, 896: ' He was war, as he caste his eye aside . . .'; *HF*, 1407f: ' Tho was I war, loo, atte laste,/As I myne eyen gan up caste . . .'; cf. *RS*, 996; *Orleans*, 5086; *KQ*, 241, 274, 725.

86. The medlar is a tree of stunted appearance, with low-hanging branches and a small and round fruit, fit to eat only when decaying. This last characteristic lent it a symbolic aptness which was recognised by Chaucer (*CT*, I, 3871, where it is given its picturesque popular name) and Shakespeare (*Romeo and Juliet*, II, i, 35; *As You Like It*, III, ii, 125) as well as this poet (see Introduction, p. 35).

92. joynyng. The rhyme here indicates a stress on the second syllable (cf. 89 above).

96. by manifold. Cf. 120, 169; a phrase used by Gower and Hoccleve (*OED*) though not by Chaucer.

passing. Used by Chaucer as an adjective or participle, but never as an adverb, though this usage was well established by 1400 (e.g. *RS*, 1097, 1216, 1411, 1538, etc.). See Glossary.

98. in this wise. Cf. *CT*, I, 1446, 2187, II, 350, 793, etc. These tags in *wise* (cf. 400, 567) are much less common in *FL* than in *AL* (see *AL*, 69n).

99. merry, ' sweet, pleasant ' in ME, not ' merry '.

100. that all the wood rong. This detail was popular both in English and in French, e.g. *Troy*, i, 3933–5:

> And ny3tyngales, that al the wode rong,
> Ful amorously welcomed in hir song
> The lusty sesoun.

See Hammond's note to *Churl and Bird*, 75.

101. as it were a sote, ' (like) a fool, as it were ', ' as if I were a fool '. Cf. 143. For the development of the phrase *as it were* see *OED* s.v. *as*, 9; *MED*, s.v. *as*, 2(a).

103. late and long. This phrase, though not used by Chaucer, appears in *Conf. Am.*, i, 1645, and *P.Pl.*, A, vi, 6.

105. ayen. No emendation is needed. The poet is recalled from reverie by the recurring memory of the nightingale's song.

106. waited. See Glossary.

109. The nightingale and the laurel are associated to suit the allegory (cf. *Night.*, I, 63); the bird usually sat in a hawthorn tree (*CN*, 287, *CL*, 1355), with her breast against the thorn, which increased the poignancy of her song.

laurey: Lat. *laureus*, adj. This form is quite common in the fifteenth century, especially in compound with *tree* (*OED*).

110. further. Comparative of *fore*: the sense is ' more forward ', i.e. on the nearer side, the one facing into the arbour.

113. Cf. *AL*, 747 (T); *Troy*, v, 2142: ' For unto hym was inly gret plesaunce '; *Fall*, i, 3974: ' That he hadde so inli gret plesaunce/Off my repair '.

114f. Cf. *Troy*, ii, 2481f: ' That me sempte tho in myn avis,/I was ravished in-to paradys ' (by Mercury's pipes). The image of the garden as ' le paradis terrestre ' was a customary one, e.g. *RR*, 648; Machaut, *Dit dou Vergier*, 66; *La Fonteinne Amoureuse*, 1369.

118. sat. *Set* is far more common in this context, as Skeat points out, but there is evidence for a reflexive use of *sit* (*OED*, s.v. 30b), even as early as Chaucer (*LGW*, 2721).

121. meat or drinke. A common tag; note its use in a similar context in *LGW*, 177.

124f. A frequent *topos* of eulogy, e.g. *CT*, I, 2102 (' That nevere, sithen that the world bigan . . .'), V, 930, VII, 2111, IX, 120; *HF*, 100; *LGW*, 229; *Troy*, ii, 588, 5099, 5251, etc.

128. Cf. *Eye and Heart*, 41–3:

> And in chasing not fer oute of my way
> I harde womannys voix wondre clere
> More swetter harde I neuer to my pay;

Margival, *La Panthere d'Amors*, 152–6.

129–33. Cf. *PF*, 191 (' With voys of aungel in here armonye '); *BD*, 307f (' Was never herd so swete a steven/But hyt had be a thyng of heven '); *HF*, 1395f. These descriptions were often imitated in the fifteenth century, e.g. *Churl and Bird*, 71–3; *Past. Pleas.*, 342f; *GL*, 274–7.

131. their. Modern ' correct ' usage demands *his*, but Chaucer and his followers often use a plural verb or second adjective or pronoun after a sing. indefinite or distributive adjective or pronoun (e.g. *any*, *every*).

136f. With this, the first sight of the company of the leaf, compare closely parallel passages in Deschamps, *Lay de Franchise*, 93–5; Froissart, *Paradys D'Amour*, 957–66; also Machaut, *Dit dou Vergier*, 157; *Conf. Am.*, iv, 1305–7.

137. A world of ladies (Dryden: ' a fair assembly of the female kind '). Cf. *TC*, iii, 1721: ' a world of folk ' (as in *KQ*, 571); *Conf. Am.*, viii, 2456–8: ' With him cam al the world at ones/Of gentil folk that whilom were/Lovers '; *Isle of Ladies*, 435f: ' At once there tho men might seen/A world of ladies fall on kneen '.

137f. Cf. *CT*, V, 34f: ' But for to telle yow al hir beautee/It lyth nat in my tonge '.

141. surcotes. Rich, sleeveless over-garments, particularly characteristic of the late fourteenth century. In the fifteenth century the sleeve openings became so large that eventually the upper part of the garment consisted only of narrow strips of material up to the shoulders. See M. G. Houston, *Medieval Costume in England and France* (1939), pp. 9f, 44, 106, etc.

142. **semes.** In the richest clothes, ornamental strips of material, sometimes studded with precious stones, were inserted in or laid over the seams. Cf. *Pierce the Ploughman's Crede*, ed. EETS (O.S.) 30, ll. 552f: ' Þei ben y-sewed wiþ whiȝt silk & semes full queynte,/Y-stongen wiþ stiches þat stareþ as siluer '.

144. ' The seams were studded with emeralds, one after another in rows, the rows side by side '. **one and one.** Cf. *CT*, I, 679; *AL*, 368, 543, 581, 710.

145–51. The borders of the costliest garments were sometimes ornamented with precious stones in this fashion. Some sense of the brilliance and splendour of such decoration can be obtained from the paintings of, for example, Jan van Eyck (ed. L. Baldass, Phaidon, 1952, figs. 62–5, 113, 116, 120, 129); cf. M. J. Friedländer, *From Van Eyck to Bruegel* (Phaidon, 1956), figs. 44, 45, 66, 164; *AL*, 526n. The ornamentation could be extended to cover the whole garment: ' And all þo robes ben orfrayed all abouten & dubbed full of precious stones & of grete oryent perles full richely ' (Mandeville's *Travels*, ed. EETS (O.S.) 153–4, vol. i, p. 153; cf. *FL*, 148); cf. *CT*, I, 2161–4, VII, 2468–70; *Pearl*, 197–204, 217–19; *Eye and Heart*, 430–5; *FL*, 328n.

148. **orient.** Originally ' a pearl from the Indian seas, as distinguished from those of less beauty found in European mussels ' (*OED*), but a vague epithet in the fifteenth century (' of supreme excellence '), drawing its sense from the splendours associated with the East. Cf. *AL*, 528; *LGW*, 221; *P.Pl.*, B, ii, 14; *Assembly of Gods*, 308; *GL*, 485, 932.

150. Evidently an echo of *PF*, 287: ' And many a mayde of which the name I wante '. There is no other instance of *went* for *want*, but according to Dobson (*English Pronunciation 1500–1700*, pp. 548f) there was a tendency to pronounce short *a* (not yet, of course, rounded to *o* after *w*) as *e* in the vulgar speech of London, and elsewhere, at least as early as the sixteenth century.

152. **fret.** A rich network of gold lace set with precious stones, fashionable at the beginning and end of the fifteenth century, though in the middle of the century a far more elaborate headdress was the fashion. Cf. *LGW*, 215; *KQ*, 317–21:

> . . . hir goldin haire and rich atyre
> In fret-wise couchit were with perllis quhite
> And grete balas lemyng as the fyre,
> With mony ane emeraut and faire saphire;
> And on hir hede a chaplet fresch of hewe.

157. **to sene.** The old inflected infinitive with *-e*, preserved also by Chaucer for the sake of rhyme: *LGW*, 224, 1034, 2425, etc.

160. **Agnus castus.** During the Greek festivals in honour of Demeter (Ceres), to make themselves prolific, women sat on branches of ἄγνος on the ground, and during that day avoided sexual intercourse. The association of the plant with continence, and confusion with another word ἁγνός, ' chaste ', led to the belief that the branches themselves could make women chaste. The plant and its symbolism spread over Europe, the Latin *castus*, ' chaste ' was added to its name, and there

K

was further association with *agnus*, ' lamb ', the Christian symbol of chastity. The plant itself resembles the willow, to which a similar virtue was ascribed (as in Desdemona's song). It was the strong smell of the dried leaves which was supposed to be the prophylactic agent, whence one of its popular names, ' monk's pepper '. See Bartholomew Anglicus, *De Proprietatibus Rerum* (ed. Batman, 1582), xvii, 15; Pliny, *Natural History*, xxiv, 38, 59; Gubernatis, *Mythologie des Plantes*, ii, 4–7; *Agnus Castus: a Middle English Herbal*, ed. G. Brodin (Upsala, 1950), p. 207. For the significance of laurel and woodbine see Introduction, p. 34, and *FL*, 485n.

were. The strong form of the preterite (also *ware* 259, etc.) is rare before 1500. Chaucer uses *wered*. This rare change of a weak to a strong verb was due to analogy with verbs of the *bear, swear, tear* class.

162. **soberly.** An important qualification, for dancing could easily be associated with unchaste love if carried on as in *RR*, 743ff or *PF*, 232–5.

163. *CT*, I, 1889 (' in manere of compas '); *Troy*, iii, 1016. See 176n.

164–8. In *BD* 817–30 occurs a similar description—a company of ladies of whom one stands out, far surpassing the others. Cf. *Panthere d'Amors*, 225.

176. **roundell.** The original form of the *roundell* was the *rondet de carole*, popular as early as the twelfth century in France as a dance song. The form was designed for performance by a soloist and a chorus, with the chorus repeating one or two of the opening lines as a refrain (*FL*, 179), thus: *aAabAB*. The soloist also led the dance (*FL*, 165), sometimes as the head of a chain, sometimes at the centre of a circle (*FL*, 163). The dancing was frequently held out of doors without musical accompaniment, and was closely associated with the May festivals (Arcite sings a *roundel* when he goes out ' to doon his observaunce to May ', *CT*, I, 1510–12). For descriptions of these dances, often with snatches of song quoted, see esp. *Les Tournois de Chauvenci* (ed. H. Delmotte, Paris, 1835), 2370, 3093ff, 4341ff; *Guillaume de Dole* (ed. SATF, 1893), 507ff, 2355ff, etc.; and for further information, Jeanroy, *Origines*, pp. 392ff; J. Bédier in *RDM* 1896 (iii, 146–72), 1906 (i, 398–424); G. Reese, *Music in the Middle Ages* (1940), pp. 222f. The literary form, *rondel* or *rondeau*, dates from the fourteenth century. It was still written to music, but not for dancing, and developed a bewildering complexity of forms, though all were based on the above pattern (see *Rondeaux*, ed. Raynaud, pp. xxxiv–li). The commonest form has 13–14 lines, as in Chaucer's *Merciles Beaute*. The *roundell* in *FL* is clearly an old-fashioned dance song (see 183).

177f. Lines or refrains from well-known songs were often quoted in medieval poems (cf. 350) to give an air of topicality. See *Guillaume de Dole*, Introduction, pp. lxxxix ff; *CT*, VII, 2879; *Fortune*, 7; *Comp. d'Amours*, 24; *PF*, 677 (some MSS); *CN*, 250, 289; *Past. Pleas.*, 371, 1584. The lines quoted here are a corrupt version of the opening lines of a fifteenth-century French song, printed from a Bayeux MS by A. Gasté in *Chansons normandes du XVe siècle* (Caen, 1866), p. 135.

> Dessoubz la branche d'ung verd moy,
> S'est mon jolli cueur endormy,
> En attendant le mien amy
> Qui me debvoit revenir voir.

(Beneath the green may branch, my joyful heart went to sleep while I waited for my lover to come back to see me.) It is the song of a woman, describing how she is waiting for her lover, and affirming the constancy of her love; it has an evident appropriateness at this point in *FL*. *Branche* has been changed to *feuille* to make the song fit more closely the allegory of the leaf; *moy* was a dialect variant of *mai*, the word applied to branches of spring greenery (Godefroy's *Dictionnaire*, s.v.). In form the song is closer to the *bergerette* (see 348n) than the *rondel*, the rhyme scheme being *abba/cbcb/abba*; no refrain is indicated in the edition cited. The first line of the song, and the version of it in *FL*, observe a lyric convention of frequent occurrence, by which the *jeux d'amour* take place in the secrecy of the greenwood, ' soubz la feuille du bois ramé '. See *Guillaume de Dole*, 295, 521, 2505, 3415, 5416; *Chansons*, ed. Paris, VI, CXXI, CXXX, etc. Attempts to explain the form *seen* & in *FL* (e.g. as *sien*, ' hers ', *son*, ' her ', *sied*, ' sit ') are not convincing; it seems to be a hopeless corruption.

180. **small.** Used by Chaucer of voices pitched high (*CT*, I, 688, 3360; *Rosemounde*, 11). It probably has that sense here, though, since it is used as a term of praise, it may also mean ' fine, delicate '.

186. **bigone.** Literally ' gone about, surrounded ', whence ' provided ' (see Glossary); often used by Chaucer, usually with *wel* (*TC*, ii, 294, 597; *PF*, 171, etc.) as here, or *wo* (*TC*, iii, 117, 1530, iv, 464, etc.); cf. MnE *woebegone*.

188f. Skeat compares *AL*, 384f. A far closer parallel is *CT*, I, 2201f: ' What ladyes fairest been or best daunsynge,/Or which of hem kan dauncen best and synge '.

190–277. The description that follows is particularly indebted to the last part of the *Knight's Tale*; and cf. *Anelida*, 29–35.

192. **thundering trumps.** Cf. *CT*, I, 2174: ' a trompe thonderynge '. There is a very similar irruption in Deschamps's *Lay de Franchise*: ' Mais d'un grant bruit yssant d'une valée/Ou il ot gens qui venoient jouster ' (145f).

193. **departed.** For the stressed prefix see G. J. Tamson, ' Word-Stress in English ', *Morsbach Studien zur englischen Philologie*, iii (Halle, 1898), pp. 96, 126.

198. **for the nones.** Originally *for þan anes* ,where *þan* is the dat. of the def. art. The phrase has a meaning here, but was often used as a rhyming tag, e.g. *CT*, I, 545, 879, 1423.

201. **large wones**, ' spacious dwellings, palace apartments '. Cf. *CT*, III, 2105; *Sir Orfeo* (ed. Bliss, 1954), 365f: ' Wiþ-in þer wer wide wones/Al of precious stones '.

202. **Pretir John.** Prester John, the fabulous medieval Christian monarch of Asia. He is first mentioned in the twelfth century, and thereafter the legends showed a steady accretion, partly by association with the stories of the Mongol conquerors. His kingdom was transferred in the fifteenth century from India and Asia to Ethiopia, where a Nestorian Christian king may well have reigned before the Asian myth gained currency, and where a Christian kingdom was discovered by the Portuguese. The name ' Prester John ' (cf. priest, Lat. *presbyter*, Fr. *prêtre*) was understood both as an individual and a generic title, and speculations as to its origin displayed a wealth of fertile invention; but all the legends agree on the enormous extent and unlimited wealth of his kingdom, which became the storehouse of all that was richest and most extravagant in the medieval conception of the splendours of the

East. The medieval legends of Prester John appear in Mandeville's *Travels* (i, 179ff, ii, 132, 143) and *De Prop. Rerum* (xviii, 45). See *Encyclopaedia Britannica*, art. ' Prester John '; *Marco Polo's Travels*, ed. H. Yule (2 vols., 1903), i, 226–44. Forms like *Pretir*, without *s*, are recorded elsewhere (see *OED*), and are perhaps due to the influence of Italian *prete Gianni*, and possible confusion with ME *pretor*, ' praetor '.

203f. Some editions run on to a colon after *array*.

203f. **unneth** is itself negative (from OE *unēaþe*, not easily), but, narrowed in syntactical usage to mean ' hardly, scarcely ', it is here, as often in ME (though rarely in Chaucer), supported by another negative. See *OED*, s.v. *uneath*, *adv.* lc, and compare vulgar MnE ' I couldn't hardly . . .'.

209. **okes seriall**. Taken from the *Knight's Tale*, where Emely is described as wearing ' A coroune of a grene ook cerial ' (*CT*, I, 2290); this, in its turn, is from Boccaccio's *Teseida*: ' E coronò di quercia cereale ' (vii, 74; see Skeat's *Chaucer*, v, 87). In Chaucer and Boccaccio the crown of ' ook cerial ' is worn by Emely and therefore associated with the service of Diana, which, presumably, is the reason for introducing it here. Also, the ' cereal oak ' was commonly identified with the evergreen or holm-oak (*ilex*), as by Francis Thynne in his *Animadversions* of 1599 (pp. 47–50). If the poet thought it was an evergreen, his symbolism would be even more precise, since the ilex was renowned for its strength and durability (*De Prop. Rerum*, xvii, 83). The original Italian name, in point of fact, evidently derives from *cerrus* (adj. *cerreus*), the name given by Pliny to one of the six varieties of oak he distinguishes (*Natural History*, xvi, 8, 19), called in English the Turkey or bitter oak (*quercus cerrus*), a deciduous tree, common in Piedmont and the Apennines, but not introduced into England until 1735.

212. **tartarium.** This is the medieval Latin form; the more usual forms in ME are *tartar*, *tartarin* (OFr *tartaire*, *tartarien*). It was a term used for all rich stuffs of Oriental origin, probably brought from China by way of Tartary, whence the name. They were admired both for the fineness of the material, probably a kind of silk or taffeta, and for the brilliancy of colour and design, a brilliancy often enhanced by weaving with gold thread and enriching with gold spangles (i.e. *bete*). See P. Toynbee, ' Tartar Cloths ', *Romania* **29** (1900), 559–64; also, e.g., *P.Pl*, B, xv, 224; Mandeville, i, 24, 116, 152, 153, etc. *Tartarium* is not to be identified with ' clooth of Tars ' (*CT*, I, 2160; *Gawain and the Green Knight*, 571; *P.Pl.*, B, xv, 163, etc.) from Tharsia (Turkestan).

were, ' (which) were . . .' A relative pronoun is omitted, as often in ME, e.g. *CT*, I, 529 (and Robinson's note).

bete. The original meaning, ' beaten ', referred to the hammering of gold into a fine foil for purposes of decoration (OFr *or battu*), but the extension of sense to cover other forms of adornment with gold (damascening, embroidering, etc.) was already well under way in the fourteenth century (e.g. *CT*, I, 979; *TC*, ii, 1229; *RR*, 837; *Gawain*, 78, 1833, 2028; see O. F. Emerson in *Philological Quarterly* **2** (1923), 85–9), and in the fifteenth century the meaning ' embroidered with gold thread ' was more or less established (e.g. *Fall*, v, 1028, vi, 1829, viii, 1432, 1961), though in *Troy* (e.g. i, 4071, ii, 726, 5634, iii, 495) Bergen proposes ' painted '.

220. **kings of armes.** Heralds in royal employ (now three only in England: Garter, Clarenceux, Norroy), who presided over the Colleges of Heralds. Their presence would dignify only the most distinguished

occasions (in France the term had a wider application). Miss Hammond conjectured that this line was deficient because of the omission of *nine*; the scribe probably left a space for *ix*, intending to rubricate it later (*MLN* **40** (1925), 186). Each king of arms would attend one of the Nine Worthies (240). Such an emendation makes sense of **and no mo.**

224. Skeat compares *AL*, 480, but again Chaucer provides a closer parallel, *CT*, VII, 2468f: ' Of rubies, saphires, and of peerles white/ Were all his clothes brouded up and doun '.

229. ' They had nothing to learn '. A similar idiom still exists: ' I am yet to learn . . .' (as in *TC*, v, 161).

by seeming. Cf. 415; *BD*, 944; *CT*, VII, 648; OFr *par semblant, a mon semblant.*

lere. The verbs *leren*, ' teach ' and *lernen*, ' learn ' were often confused in ME; cf. modern vulgar use of ' learn '.

232. A herald would be attached to every important noble household; a pursuivant was a probationary herald. A manual on jousting in MS Lansdowne 285 (ed. in *Archaeologia* **17** (1814), 290–6) describes how the heralds, ' beryng sheeldes of devise ', must enter first to announce the combat, followed by the knights, whose helmets and spears are borne by their servants so that the knights may make obeisance to the ladies before they do battle. In the tournament itself, the job of the heralds was to announce the champions as they entered the lists and proclaim their nobility and prowess, to scrutinise carefully the conduct of the fight, and to take note of the knights' exploits; and finally to bring their report to the judge.

233. **veluet.** Trisyllabic, as in Chaucer.

234. ' They had no need to go and find out. . . .' Cf. Orleans, 196: ' Good hope as loo was no thing to seche/For penne and papir had he found anoon '.

238. Each bore the livery and coat of arms of his lord, like the kings of arms and trumpeters before them.

240. Cf. *CT*, I, 2180 (' Al armed, save hir heddes, in al hir gere '), V, 90; *TC*, ii, 625.

242. **red gold.** The epithet was conventional in ME, but perhaps not without reason, for medieval gold is said to have been frequently alloyed with copper. See *Early Middle English Texts*, ed. Dickins and Wilson (1951), p. 176 (*Havelok*, 47n).

245. **did hong.** *Do* is used as an auxiliary by Chaucer only in interrogative constructions; the general weakening to auxiliary usage is a feature of fifteenth-century English (e.g. 572; *AL*, 6n; *Troy*, Prol., 6, 234, i, 436, 466, 545, etc.), though the independent and causative uses continued.

246. **boose.** The spelling is well attested: *CT*, I, 3266 (all MSS), *Thebes*, 85.

paitrell. Originally the breast-piece of a horse in armour, often richly ornamented, and retained for ornament after its defensive use had passed away. In his sermon Chaucer's Parson condemns just the elaborate trappings described here (*CT*, X, 433).

248. **worth a thousand pound.** (Note the pl.) This topic of comparison, often used emphatically (not for . . .), was not uncommon, e.g. Orleans, 672, 5944; *GL*, 1143 (' The claspis and bullyons were worth a

thousande pounde '). Chaucer's usage is less inflationary: *CT*, V, 683 (' twenty pound '); *RR*, 501 (' an hundred pound ').

249. Cf. *CT*, I, 2875 (' Eek on his heed a coroune of laurer grene '), I, 2175.

252. **hensh-men.** EME *heng(e)st-man*, ' groom ', ' attendant upon a horse ', which was elevated to ' groom-in-waiting ' in the fourteenth century (cf. the history of *marshal*; see *AL*, 322n). Henry, Earl of Derby, took two *henksmen* in his retinue on his expeditions to Prussia and Palestine in 1392–3, and from about this time the henchmen, young men of rank, formed a regular part of the retinue of kings and queens, rising in number from three under Henry VI to seven under Richard III. In the fifteenth and sixteenth centuries nobles and knights also had henchmen, usually three, squires or pages of honour who rode behind them in processions, progresses, marches. This sense of *henchman* died out in the seventeenth century, but in the eighteenth the word began to be used of a Highland chief's right-hand man, the origin of the modern sense. See *OED*; Skeat, *A Student's Pastime*, pp. 217, 221, 342–5.

253. ' Of which, in each case, the first, on a short spear-shaft. . . .' One must suppose that *the* was written *þe*, printed *ye*, and perhaps abbreviated (small *e* over *y*), and thus became attached to *ever*. The omission of an *on* is easily understood. The use of *the one* for the first of three is rare, but does occur in *RS*, 3632. The other emendations are desperate.

255. For this value formula cf. *Churl and Bird*, 229–31.

> That thou hast lost so passyng gret richesse,
> Which myht suffise bi valew in rekenyng
> To pay the raunsom of a myhty kyng.

See *OED*.

257. **neck.** Urry and other editors emend to ' back ', but the meaning is that the shields were supported by straps (*guiges*) passing round the neck.

258. **spheare.** An inverted spelling. ' Sphere ' is commonly spelt *spere, speare* in the fifteenth century (*Fall*, i, 598, 800, 803, 3109, etc.), and *sphere* is quoted as a homophone for *spear* in Dobson (*op. cit.*, p. 1010).
　ful sharpe ground. Cf. *CT*, I, 2549, VII, 883; *TC*, iv, 43; *Troy*, iii, 764, 1573, 2449, 5156, etc. (an epic formula in Lydgate).

259. **child**, ' young man ', a frequent sense in ME; e.g. *CT*, I, 3325, VII, 810, 2155. See *MED*, s.v. 5, 6.

263. **Without difference.** *Difference*, as a technical term in heraldry, is the alteration of a coat of arms to distinguish a junior member or branch of a family from the chief line (*OED*), and the phrase ' without difference ' occurs frequently in this sense. An heraldic allusion here is probable: the henchmen would naturally display the same coat of arms as their lords.

269. **oke.** An emblem of strength, endurance, and victory (*Coriolanus*, II, ii, 103), sacred to Jupiter among the Romans, for whom the oaken (' civic ') crown was *militum virtutis insigne clarissimum* (Pliny, *Natural History*, xvi, 3, 7; cf. *Fall*, iv, 304; *De Prop. Rerum*, xvii, 134).

270. **shene:** (< OE *sciene*, ' beautiful ') often confused with *shine*. It seems to have its original meaning here, as often in Chaucer, unless it be taken as a ' realistic ' epithet, ' shiny, glistening (with dew) '.

271. kene. By hypallage, the quality of those who bear the oak is here transferred to the oak itself.

273. ' And many others which I did not remember '; or perhaps, by association of the phrase *have mind of* (' give heed to '), ' And many others which I did not (have time to) notice '.

274. horse. The plural elsewhere is *horse*; *horses* (Speght), which also upsets the metre, is scribal.

275. Cf. *CT*, I, 2511–2 (' Pypes, trompes, nakers, clariounes,/That in the bataille blowen blody sounes '); *Lancelot of the Laik*, 1035 (the ' bludy sown ' of bugles).

276. disguising. See Glossary. The word was often used of fashions of dress so extravagant as to be morally censurable, e.g. *CT*, X, 414, 417, 425; *Knight of La Tour Laundry* (ed. EETS (O.S.) 33), pp. 62, 82. The pejorative sense faded during the fifteenth century. The poet is evidently echoing Chaucer: ' Ther maystow seen devisynge of harneys/ So unkouth and so riche . . .' (*CT*, I, 2496–7). The word had another application in the fifteenth century, to describe courtly mummings or pageants, of which this procession of the Nine Worthies and their retinue would be a good example.

278. evenly. Although the meadow was not prepared for jousting, the knights made the best of it: the opposing ranks were drawn up in as regular a formation as possible. The *justes* here described are the comparatively harmless *justes of peas* (OFr *joutes a plaisance*), fought with the pointless lance or coronel, as opposed to the *joutes a outrance* fought against the heathen (as by Chaucer's Knight) or in war. Tournaments were very popular in the fifteenth century, though in their ornamental and stylised ceremonial they were fundamentally different from the legalised war of the thirteenth century (see N. Denholm-Young, ' The Tournament in the 13th century ', *Studies in Medieval History presented to F. M. Powicke* (1948), pp. 240–68). Single combat was the rule, and the old-fashioned mêlée had been replaced by a better organised and less exhausting form of *combat a la foule*, more like a series of simultaneous single combats or jousts (see *FL*, 280f). These tourneys were sometimes associated with May-day festivities, and held, not in the prepared lists, but on open fields. There are elaborate accounts of the great *fêtes de tournoi* in *Les Tournois de Chauvenci*; *Guillaume de Dole*, 2067–958; Pisan, *Duc des Vrais Amans*, 635–1281; the *Knight's Tale*. See *Chaucer's World*, ed. E. Rickert (1948), pp. 207–17; *Mediaeval England*, ed. A. L. Poole (1958), pp. 621–4.

280. horse. Perhaps part of a compound expression, as in *horse-harneis*, but a gen. sg. *horse* does occur in the fifteenth century (Wyld, *op. cit.*, p. 316). Chaucer uses *horses* (*TC*, i, 223).

282. rest. A contrivance fitted to the right side of the cuirass to receive the butt end of the lance when charging, in order to prevent it being driven back upon impact. See *OED*; Jusserand, *Les Sports dans l'ancienne France* (1901), pp. 104f, 115f.

284. ' One . . . another. . . .' Cf. *TC*, iv, 45: ' They fighte and bringen hors and man to grounde '.

285. steeds, i.e. the riderless horses.

286. Cf. *RR*, 4958: ' In good reule and in governaunce '.

289. The nine knights mentioned above (240).

295f. Cf. *Troy*, iii, 237: ' And forþe he rod, so like a manly knyȝt/þat to beholde it was a noble siȝt '; the latter line is repeated in *Troy*, iv, 3453.

twain and twain. Cf. *AL*, 350; *CT*, I, 898: ' tweye and tweye '. It is one of Lydgate's favourite phrases: *RS*, 5235; *Troy*, ii, 4117, 6792; *Fall*, i, 6387; ' togydre tweine and tweine ' occurs in *RS*, 5537; *Troy*, i, 1314, ii, 691; *Fall*, v, 891.

296. **worthy.** Some scribes were in the habit of writing *wordy* for *worthy*, for instance the scribe of the *Trentale Sancti Gregorii* in MS Cotton Caligula A.II (*Political, Religious and Love Poems*, ed. EETS (O.S.) 15, pp. 114ff, ll. 8, 80, 172). The change of *wordy* to *wordly*, a very common spelling for *worldly* in fifteenth-century MSS, is a small one, and one quite within the capabilities of the fifteenth-century scribe or the sixteenth-century printer. This would account for the presence of *worldly* in Speght. It is just conceivable that *worldly* is a unique extension of the substantival sense, ' delight, marvel ', of *world* (e.g. *AL*, 539), meaning ' marvellous '.

299. The ladies did not wish to show an indecorous haste. This is not mere coyness, but part of the author's conception of proper feminine behaviour. Or it may be that they did not want to stop the dance in the middle of a figure or the song in the middle of a stanza.

304. **laurer.** The tree described here is clearly the great bay-laurel (*laurus nobilis*) which, in its Mediterranean homeland, grows to a height of sixty feet, and is renowned for the fragrance of its scent. It is first recorded in England in 1562. The common laurel (*prunus laurocerasus*), though examples up to forty feet high have been known, is really a shrub, and in any case was not introduced into England until the seventeenth century (see *Dictionary of Gardening*, pp. 1134, 1697).

306. **to my dome.** Cf. *PF*, 480; *RR*, 901; *Comp. d'Amours*, 52.

308. Urry's emendation, adopted by all subsequent editors, sounds better to us, but the impersonal construction with *it* is frequent in ME (e.g. *Gawain and the Green Knight*, 280, 1251).

308–10. Cf. *Le Mariage des Sept Arts* (ed. A. Långfors, CFMA, 1923). In a dream, the poet goes out into the fields.

> Enmi ot un pint verdoiant
> Si grant que par desous, en l'ombre,
> Tant de gent que n'en sai le nombre
> Mout bien aombrer s'i peüssent,
> Que ja point de soleil n'eüssent,
> Nis ce fust en plain esté.
>
> (10–15)

(In the middle was a green pine tree, so large that underneath, in its shade, innumerable folk might well have found shelter from the rays of the sun, even in high summer.)

He then sees a group of beautiful ladies, who turn out to be the Seven Liberal Arts. A passage from the French prose romance *Perceforest*, quoted by Miss Seaton (*Sir Richard Roos*, p. 324), is very similar, though the further comparisons she draws, to prove that the romance was known to the author of *FL*, are of little significance.

314. **melancolius.** Usually ' enraged, angry ' in the fifteenth century (e.g. *Troy*, ii, 1388, 8202, iii, 1277, 5390), though the sense was often weakened to ' irascible ' (e.g. *Fall*, iv, 1361, vi, 1097), which is possibly the meaning here, though ' melancholy ' is more apt (cf. *HF*, 30).

316. **enclining.** Editions from 1687 onwards make this finite (*enclined*), but it is no part of an editor's job to correct a lady's grammar.

318. **within a little throw.** Cf. 190, 361; *Fall*, i, 4448, ii, 3534, 3557, iii, 2670, etc.

320. The themes of most medieval courtly love-poetry; in the later Middle Ages, at least, the latter predominates, the tradition of the *Complainte Amoureuse* of faithless or unrequited love. The tradition extends from Ovid's *Heroides* to Shakespeare's *Lover's Complaint* and further, and there are countless examples of the genre in Chaucer and the French poets. In *RR* the *complaynte* is considered an essential accomplishment of the lover (2325–8).

untrew is also used as a noun in a variant of *LGW*, 1890.

321. **environing,** ' standing round ' (*MED*), or, better, ' walking round ' (*yede*, 322 suggests this; cf. *RR*, 526).

328. **Purfiled.** The *purfil* was the hem of a garment; but *purfiled* was often extended to apply to garments studded all over with gems or other ornaments (Skeat, *Chaucer*, v, 23), which may be its sense here; see 145n.

329. **ware mantels on.** This construction (cf. MnE ' had a mantle on ') is found also in *BD*, 1217; for *were* (*up*)*on* cf. *CT*, III, 559, 1018.

331–3. This refers, of course, to the ladies of the company.

336. Minstrels played a large part in the May festivities, and tend to be associated, in literature at least, with light love (cf. *RS* 5564–612).

337. **sautry.** The psaltery differed from the harp in having a sounding-board behind and parallel with the strings; in this it resembled the dulcimer, though the strings were plucked, not hammered. For illustrations see Plates IX, XII, in K. Geiringer, *Musical Instruments* (ed. W. F. H. Blandford, 1943).

339. Hawes may have remembered this line: ' With many dragons of meruaylous lykenes/ Of dyuers floures made full craftely ' (*Past. Pleas.*, 2014f).

342. **tuft.** ME *toft*, ' hillock ' (cf. *tuffet*), not MnE *tuft*.

344. This detail, like the theme of the daisy in general, and the idea of a song in its praise, is taken from the Prologue to *LGW*, where Chaucer goes out on a May morning to worship the daisy, ' to doon it alle reverence ', and kneels to greet it as it opens (115–17).

348. **bargaret.** OFr *bergerette*, a pastoral song: ' sorte de poésie rustique, chant du berger qui se chantait le jour de Pâques ' (Godefroy). In the fifteenth century the word developed, like *roundell* (176n), a more precise literary signification: it was used for a variation of the *rondeau* where the second section (or *baton*) had no refrain, a different pair of rhymes, and often a totally different form from the other two sections. The simplest form was: *abba/cdcd/abbaR*, where *R* indicates the repetition of the first line or two lines (see *Rondeaux*, ed. Raynaud, pp. li–liv). The reference in *FL* is one of only three quoted in *OED*, and by far the earliest.

in praising, ' in praise of '. Cf. *LGW*, 189, 248, 416: ' in preysing of '.

350. **margarete.** A fruitful symbol in the Middle Ages, since it was the French for a pearl as well as a daisy, and also a woman's name (see *Pearl*, ed. Gordon, pp. xxvii ff). The reference here is to the

common wild field-daisy, properly called in French the *pâquerette*. The quotation, if it is not made up, is probably from the refrain of some popular French pastoral.

354. But I not how. Cf. Froissart, *L'Espinette Amoureuse*, 396: ' Ne sçai comment, mès droit là vi. . . .' Urry's emendation has been generally adopted.

355. The construction is ambiguous. *As* may be a conj. introducing ' the sonne . . . whote', with ' that the prety tender floures ' etc., subordinate to *happed*; or it may be pleonastic (as often in ME), with ' the sonne . . . whote' subordinate to *happed*, and ' that the prety tender floures ' etc., as its consequent.

356. whote. The development of prothetic *w-* before *hō-* was common in the fifteenth century: it represents a ' strong rounded on-glide ' (Wyld, p. 306) which became an independent consonant. The sound was lost in the sixteenth century in standard English, though occasionally the spelling was kept (*whole*, *whore*). See A. Kihlbom, *Fifteenth Century English* (Uppsala, 1926), pp. 162–8.

358. tobrent. *to-* as a verbal prefix usually means ' to pieces ' (488; *CT*, VI, 474, VII, 2025). Here it is merely an intensive.

359. ' They didn't know what to do with themselves.'

368. The allegory of uncontrolled passion here (see Introduction, p. 33), with hot sun followed by hail and rain, is quite unforced. Hail and very warm weather are explicitly associated in *De Prop. Rerum*, xi, 10; cf. *Troy*, i, 212: ' And as the sonne is hoot a-fore þise schoures '.

370. threed had often enough been used as a synecdoche for ' clothing ' (cf. use of ' stitch '), but never before in this context. See *Anglia* **15** (1893), 119.

393. can or may. Often used as a rhyming tag by Chaucer, e.g. *CT*, IV, 816, VII, 354, 460, etc.

394. the tother. Originally *pet other*. Another instance of wrong division; see 198n.

395. ill. Chaucer uses this adj. only when he is imitating N dialect (*CT*, I, 4045, 4089, 4174, 4184); it occurs also eight times in *RR*, fragments B and C. It was naturalised into literary standard English in the fifteenth century.

403. to make their justs. ' In order to joust with them afterwards ' (Skeat). But the jousting definitely ended some time ago (292), and there is no further mention of any. Some fifteenth-century instances of *justis* (e.g. *Generydes*, 6921, *La Tour Laundry*, p. 110, l. 17) suggest that it may have been used rather more vaguely, of courtly pastimes in general, though it is most unlikely to have lost altogether its connection with jousting. A variant *Iustes*, *Iuste* for *Lust* in *CT*, I, 1932, which occurs in some good MSS, would, in its context, support this more generalised sense; if, however, it is merely a mechanical scribal error, as Manly says (ed. of *CT*, 8 vols., 1940, iii, 431), it might suggest emendation in *FL* to *lustes*, the sense being ' to carry out their wishes ' (cf. *Troy*, i, 2679).

404. square, ' to square, to make square by cutting ' (Skeat), a well-known technical term for the trimming of felled trees and logs. This may seem a superfluous labour since they were only to be burnt anyway, but probably the sense of the verb had weakened to ' cut down ', and in any case it is a rhyming word. On the other hand, *square* could be an adj., 'stout, sturdy'; *OED* gives no examples of this sense applied to anything but the human form, but Lydgate often uses *round* and *square* together of stones, towers, etc. (e.g. *Thebes*, 2211; *Troy*, ii, 548, 6273; *Pilg.*, 19487; cf. *Isopes Fabules*, 937: 'a bryge sqware'), which suggests some more generalised meaning for the latter (though Bergen glosses 'four-cornered, but rounded ').

406. wringing weat. This appears to be the first occurrence of this idiom.

407. Pliny and all subsequent natural historians, up to the seventeenth century at least, were mainly concerned with the 'virtues ' of plants, their natural and symbolical properties. Most people in the Middle Ages, therefore, would have known straightaway what herbs to gather to make a sunburn lotion. John Gerard's *Herball* (1597) mentions whiteroot (Solomon's seal), kale-seed, Galen's moonwort, and linseed, amongst others.

412. salades. The word would be applied to most vegetables eaten uncooked, though particularly to those used in a 'salad '; the reference here is illuminated by *Secrees*, 1375f: 'Ageyn heetys whan men distempryd be/ Folkys gadre purslane and letuse that be clene '. Normally, the Books of Nurture warned against eating green salads and raw fruits; it seemed to be regarded as a dangerous fad (*Manners and Meals*, ed. EETS (O.S.) 32, pp. 124, 266). Lettuce was also a traditional antaphrodisiac: ' In men this hearb withstandeth moving of Venus. . . . Also the seede of all manner Lettuce chasteth in sleepe, dreames of lecherie ' (*De Prop. Rerum*, xvii, 92).

435–48. For the allegorical significance of the birds, see Introduction, pp. 35–6.

436. did her might. Cf. *RR*, 78f: 'Than doth the nyghtyngale hir myght/To make noyse and syngen blythe '.

437. service. This conceit, that the song of birds in spring was a 'service ' in honour of God, or Nature, or Love, was very popular with medieval poets. Cf. *CN*, 69–71:

> They were so joyful of the dayes light
> That they begonne of May to don hir houres!
> They coude that servyce al by rote;

RR, 669–72, 713; *BD*, 302; *PF*, 676; *RS*, 460; Dunbar, *Golden Targe*, 10, 21; *Thrissill and Rois*, 5. Sometimes the idea was elaborately developed, with close parody and quotation of the Mass, e.g. Jean de Condé, *La Messe des Oisiaus*; *CL*, 1352–428; *The Birds' Matins*, ed. MacCracken, *Archiv* **130** (1913), 310.

447. Cf. *RR*, 106–8:

> The smale foules song harknyng,
> That peyned hem, ful many peyre,
> To synge on bowes blosmed feyre;

BD, 318; Machaut, *Dit dou Vergier*, 33; *Fonteinne Amoureuse*, 1358; Watriquet de Couvin, *Mireoirs as Dames*, 47. The birds strove to do proper honour to the season. The popular idea was that they competed with one another (*FL*, 100), an idea that finds frequent expression in medieval poetry, e.g. *RR*, 667; Machaut, *Remede de Fortune*, 2983; Froissart, *L'Espinette Amoureuse*, 361; see Pliny, *Natural History*, x, 43, 83.

456. happed. This ' chance ' meeting was very necessary in an allegorical dream or vision poem of this kind: someone had to explain the meaning of what had gone before.

458. by hir selfe alone. Skeat compares *AL*, 84, but the tag is common. See *CT*, I, 3543, VI, 841; *KQ*, 491; *Thebes*, 1152, 1823, 2315, etc.

459. demure. Not used by Chaucer, but very popular with later poets, e.g. *BDM*, 777 (' Fals semblaunce hath a visage ful demure '); *AL*, 82; *RR*, 4627; *GL*, 854, 861, 886, 975; *CL*, 653.

460. The second **her**, which Jephson and subsequent editors omit, indicates a blending of two idioms, one of salutation, the other wishing good luck.

461. Must: *moste*, pret. subj., ' might '. A scribe with a tendency to modernise spelling has here confounded the subjunctive with the usual *moste*, ' must '.

471. yis. *Yes* and *no* were the emphatic forms of *yea* and *nay*, and were used in answer to questions in negative form. The distinction died out after 1500. Cf. *AL*, 63.

479–83. Some of the ladies certainly wore chaplets of laurel (158), but the description that follows could fit only Amazons. The author, with a customary lack of system, has here slipped in a reference to the knights (268).

480f. As Speght's text stands, line 481 is quite disconnected; perhaps the original mistake arose when *wan by* was misread *manly*, and the *in* of *indeed* was a later rationalisation. The phrase *by deed* (' by feats of arms ') is not common, but its adoption goes further towards explaining the presence of *manly* in Speght than the neater *wan indeed*.

482. worthy of ther hond, ' of the deeds of their hand ', i.e. deeds of valour, prowess. Cf. *CT*, II, 579 (' That was ful wys, and worthy of his hond '), I, 2103; *Thebes*, 2266.

485. ' The woodbind is a good emblem of faithful attachment; for it winds itself so firmly round some stronger tree that it becomes indissolubly fixed in the bark ' (Bell). It is used with the same significance in Lydgate, *Floure of Curtesye*, 261; cf. *TC*, iii, 1231. For Pliny it was an antaphrodisiac (*Natural History*, xxv, 33, 70).

490. The sense is clear, the expression perhaps a little unusual, with *lives* replacing *harts* (488). Cf. MnE ' a broken life '.

494. beaute. Used as a form of address; cf. ' your Grace ', ' your Honour '; *AL*, 443n, 594, 705. This usage is a feature of Lydgate's style. See *RS*, ed. Sieper, ii, 51.

501. debonaire: *de bonne aire*, ' of good and gentle disposition ', almost invariably of persons; here it means ' polite, virtuous '.

502. very exemplaire. *exemplaire* was a favourite word of Lydgate's, e.g. *TG*, 294, 752; *Fall*, i, 924, ii, 3393, viii, 79, 2383; *Minor Poems*, ii, 380 (' verray exemplayre '). Cf. Deschamps, ' vray exemplaire ' (SATF, vol. x, p. xxviii).

504. the Nine Worthy. Joshua, David, and Judas Maccabeus; Hector, Alexander, and Julius Caesar; Arthur, Charlemagne, and Godfrey of Boulogne: three Jews, three Pagans, and three Christians. The Nine Worthies, as such, first appear in *Les Vœux du Paon*, a popular Alexander romance of the early fourteenth century by Jacques de Longuyon, but there had long been a tendency towards the grouping of such names in the *Ubi sunt* formula as examples of the transience of earthly glory. The Nine Worthies were a popular subject for representation in pictures, tapestries, and ornaments, and were further portrayed in pageants and tableaux, especially at May festivals, and in mumming plays (as in *Love's Labour's Lost*; the names there have changed considerably). It should come as no surprise to find this miscellaneous collection of heroes united in the image of the chivalric ideal, though the modern historical imagination balks at the idea of Joshua, for instance, as a medieval knight: the Middle Ages made sense of the past by consistently interpreting it in the light of their own culture. Nor was the choice of *Nine* Worthies arbitrary: nine was the most profoundly symbolic of all numbers, since its root was the Trinity. See especially *The Parlement of the Thre Ages*, 300–583; Gollancz's edition (*Select Early English Poems*, ii, 1915) provides full illustrative material, and there are further references in the EETS edition (O.S. 246, 1959) by M. Y. Offord, pp. xl–xlii, xlv. The Nine appear frequently in late medieval literature as types of nobility, as illustrous examples for the present, and as a *topos* for the power of death, e.g. Deschamps, Poems 12, 239, 403; Machaut, *Dit dou Lyon*, 1315–20; Pisan, *Cent Balades*, XCII; *Assembly of Gods*, 463–9; *Morte Arthure* (ed. EETS (O.S.) 8), 3406–46; Lydgate, *Minor Poems*, ii, 811, 830; *Past. Pleas.*, 5523–85.

507–11. ' In great worship and praising Conquerors were sometime crowned with Garlandes of boughes of the Laurell tree. . . . It was had in worship in Triumphes and victorie ' (*De Prop. Rerum*, xvii, 48); cf. *CT*, I, 1027; *Troy*, ii, 874.

512. **bowes.** Not ' bows ', but ' boughs '. Dryden fell into the trap.

516. **Douseperis.** *Les douze pers*, the twelve peers of France, Charlemagne's paladins, said to be attached to his person as being the bravest in his realm: Roland, Oliver, Ogier the Dane, Guy of Burgundy, etc. (the names vary in different sources; see G. Paris, *Histoire poétique de Charlemagne* (Paris, 1905), pp. 416–20, 507). In history the term was applied also to the twelve great temporal and spiritual peers of France. In England *douzepers* was used as one word (even in the sing., *doucepere*, *Faerie Queene*, III, x, 31), often vaguely, of any illustrious knights (e.g. *Morte Arthure*, 66). The knights of the Round Table and the *douzepers* were closely associated by virtue of the juxtaposition of Arthur and Charlemagne in the Nine Worthies.

517. **Which.** Antecedent *laurer* (513). The syntax is awkward.

519. **knights old of the Garter.** *old*, ' former ', i.e. ' knights of old '. This expression, and ' in her time ' (520), suggest that the Order was already of some antiquity, and consequently imply a date late in the fifteenth century for *FL* (see *NQ*, 5th series, **2** (1874), 44; *Academy* **13** (1878), 9). The Order of the Garter was established in 1349, the garter, with its motto, having been the device of Edward III and his companions at the great Eltham tournament in the previous year. To explain the origin of the device, tradition has it that, when the Countess of Salisbury's garter fell off while he was dancing with her, the King picked it up and, with the words ' Honi soit qui mal y pense ', tied it on his own leg. The Order fell into comparative decay in the fifteenth century and its former glories were only partially restored by Edward IV. See Hoccleve, *Balade au treshonourable conpaignie du Garter* (*Minor Poems*, ed. EETS (E.S.) 61, i, 42); Lydgate, *Legend of St George*

(*Minor Poems*, i, 145), where he declares that the Order was founded
' siþen goon ful yoore '.

522. for thereby. Speght's *forby* is meaningless: the sense demands
' because by it '. The adverb *forby* refers only to place (' aside, past,
besides '), while *forþy*, though an adverb of reason, is merely con-
junctive (' for this reason, therefore '). I have adopted this emendation
instead of the usual one because of its greater harmony, and because it
seems, through an intermediate error, *for forby* (*for-* is a very possible
misreading of *þer-*), more easily explicable.

523. triumph. Both ' victory ' in the abstract, and ceremonial victory
procession, in which the conqueror rode crowned with laurel (*Anel.*, 43).

marshall. This is a very late fifteenth-century phonetic spelling,
probably scribal (cf. Cavendish, *Metrical Visions*, in Hammond, 1121:
' marsheall '). In Chaucer *marcial* is trisyllabic (*TC*, iv, 1669), and this
pronunciation, and spelling, seem to be needed here.

530f. ' Take witness (of him) of Rome, who was the founder. . . .'
The reference is to Julius Caesar (Dryden names him), who was regarded
with great veneration in the Middle Ages, and considered the very
father of chivalry: see *CT*, VII, 2681, 2683; *Fall*, vi, 2871–919. In the
French historical romances based on his life, and especially in *Les Faits
des Romains*, he is portrayed as a model of chivalric and courtly behaviour (see L. Petit de Julleville, *Histoire de la langue et de la littérature
française* (8 vols., Paris, 1896–9), i, 225–9; P. Meyer in *Romania* 14
(1885), 1–36), and a reputable scholar of the Renaissance quotes an
account of the actual institution of knighthood and heralds by Julius
Caesar before Carthage (see Claude Fauchet, *Origines des chevaliers,
armoiries et heraux*, Bk. I, ch. 3, in *Œuvres* (Paris, 1610), f. 518). He
gives as his source a manuscript dating from the reign of Charles VII,
and the tradition certainly has every air of being medieval. With
reference to the laurel, we may note that it was to Caesar that the
Senate granted the right to wear a laurel crown at all times, a privilege
which he treasured greatly—not least, as Suetonius rather maliciously
points out, because he was bald (*De Vita Caesarum*, i, 45).

532. Record I take of. A phrase often used by Lydgate, e.g. *Troy*, iv,
276, 2980, 4526, 5892, etc.

Titus Livius. Livy (59 B.C.–A.D. 17) was considered the greatest of
the Roman historians, and an unimpeachable ' auctoritee '. Chaucer
often refers to him as such, but there is no evidence that he had read
him (see Lounsbury, *Studies in Chaucer*, ii, 278–84; *PF*, ed. Brewer, p.
113), and to Lydgate he was little more than a name (Hammond, p. 93).
The details in *FL* were common knowledge, here dignified with the
cloak of (supposed) authority; in fact Livy's history extends only to
167 B.C., the rest, down to his own time and including Julius Caesar,
existing only in bald summaries, or *periochae*, which contain no comment
or panegyric and no reference to the laurel (Bks. 103–16 concern
Caesar). Chaucer, when dealing with the story of Julius Caesar, refers
to Lucan, Suetonius, and Valerius Maximus (*CT*, VII, 2719), and to
Lucan again in *HF*, 1499; *CT*, II, 400, but not to Livy.

533. ' And as for her in green, that is crowned . . .'.

534. *Churl and Bird*, 26: ' Of floures all Flora, goddes and quene '; cf.
BD, 402; *LGW*, 171; *RS*, 921; *Troy*, i, 1294, 3931, ii, 3340, iv, 6953, etc.
Flora usually appears in descriptions of spring, clothing the earth with
flowers. She was the Roman goddess of springtime and flowers, and

her festival, the *Floralia*, lasting from 28 April to 3 May, was tradition-
ally characterised by licentious display.

536. **It are such.** An example of the agreement of the verb *to be* with
its complement rather than its subject (as in *HF*, 1323; *LGW*, 1506;
BDM, 531). Cf. ' It am nat I ' (*CT*, I, 1460).

536. **idlenes.** Commonly referred to as ' moder of all vices ' (*CT*, VIII,
1; *Conf. Am.*, iv, 1086; *Fall*, i, 4685, ii, 2249, etc.), and associated by
moralists with lechery, whence its peculiar aptness as the name of the
portress of the Garden of Love (*RR*, 593). It is contrasted by Gower
with the knightly deeds that men should perform in the service of Love
(*Conf. Am.*, iv, 1610, 2036).

537. **delite.** Morris and subsequent editors insert *had* afterwards, but
it is quite possible to take *delite* as a verb: the abrupt change of tense
is a feature of ME syntax.

538. **hunt and hauke.** Cf. *CT*, IV, 81; *Thebes*, 1618; *Fall*, ix, 1070;
Beryn, 2346; *Generydes*, 932; and in alliterative poetry.

541. The omission of **and** (as in Skeat) satisfies modern grammar, but
misrepresents fifteenth-century poetic usage.

549. *BD*, 1100: ' Withoute feynynge outher slouthe ', repeated in
Suffolk, B, xix, 4; *RR*, 1971 (' Withoute feynyng or feyntise '), 2947
(' withoute feyntise '); cf. *BDM*, 385, 528; *KQ*, 991; *Beryn*, 1487.

550. **Fro wele to better.** OFr *de bien en mieulx* (later a motto of Charles
V), translated by Lydgate ' Fro good to beter ' (*Fall*, Prol., 20), a phrase
he repeats in *Pilg.*, 23696 and *St Edmund* (see Hammond, p. 438). *De
mieulx en mieulx*, another French idiom which may have influenced *FL*,
was even more common (e.g. *Cent Ballades*, LI, 33; Deschamps, *Lay
Amoureux*, 206; Pisan, *Rond.* XXXV; *Chansons*, ed. Paris, CXV, 27),
and was also used as a motto, in England, by the Pastons, and in *TG*, 310
(see MacCracken in *PMLA* **23** (1908), 128–40).

553. Urry's emendation, adopted by most subsequent editors, is
officious, since one of the rare ' rhetorical ' commas in Sp1 deliberately
separates *May* and *may*. Furthermore, the author is evidently imitating
PF, 129f: ' Thorgh me men gon unto the welle of grace/There grene
and lusty May shal evere endure '.

554. **keping.** Another loosely related participle.

562. Cf. Orleans, 2259f: ' Ther nys leef nor flowre that doth endewre/
But a sesoun as sowne doth in a belle '.

565. I.e. no such occupation (function) as to symbolise perseverance
and fidelity.

567. Skeat compares *AL*, 729, but the line is part of a stock salutation
at the beginning of letters (e.g. *Paston Letters*, ed. Gairdner (1896),
nos. 60, 234, 275, 313, etc.), and appears frequently in poetry, e.g.
Chaucer, *Balade of Complaint*, 15; *Fall*, i, 4291, 7010, ii, 1954; Orleans,
1181, 5608, 6317.

571. *CT*, I, 1571: ' So that I koude doon aught to youre plesaunce '.

574. **this yeere.** Limits *honour*, of course, not *tell*. In the courtly cult
of the flower and the leaf the choice was made on the first of May,
according to Charles of Orleans (Introduction, p. 24), and was binding
for the ensuing year.

580. **Male Bouch,** ' Slander ', one of the allegorical personifications of *RR* (' Wykked-Tonge ', 3027). The main target for *Malebouche* seems, from Lydgate's description (*TG*, 153; and stanza 3a in MSS *G, S*, ed. Schick, p. 14), to have been the reputation of women. Further references occur in *Conf. Am.*, ii, 389; *Floure of Curtesye*, 84; *BK*, 260; *Pilg.*, 13269 (applied to Jean de Meun himself); *BDM*, 741; etc.

581. **well-condicioned,** ' well-disposed, good-natured '. The sense of the line is: ' And may God also preserve from Slander all who are good and courteous '.

588. The reference to night coming on may be not so much a ' realistic ' indication of the time compassed by the poem as a relic of a pastoral convention of conclusion observed by Theocritus, Virgil, and Spenser, amongst others (Curtius, *op. cit.*, p. 91).

589. **put . . . in writing.** Cf. *AL*, 629, 664; *Assembly of Gods*, 2061; Orleans, 1718; *OED*, s.v. *put* 16(b).

590. **Under support of,** ' in the hope of the patronage of, trusting to the goodwill of ': a very common phrase of supplication or submission at the beginning or end of a poem, especially in Lydgate, e.g. *Fall*, i, 468: ' Undir support off all that shal it reede,/Upon Bochas riht thus I will proceede '; *Seynt Margarete*, 76 (*Minor Poems*, i, 176); *Troy*, iv, 1222, v, 173; *De Profundis*, 21 (*Minor Poems*, i, 78); *Testament*, 209 (*Minor Poems*, i, 337).

591. **thou.** The 2 sg. is not used between the ladies, but only here, in good-natured contempt, as an affectionate diminutive for the ' little booke '.

591-5. Some of the detail here is fresh, though the passage is inspired by a literary convention of great antiquity (see Introduction, p. 68, and, for further discussion, Curtius, *op. cit.*, pp. 83-5, 132-3, 411-12; J. S. P. Tatlock, ' The Epilog of Chaucer's Troilus ', *MP* **18** (1921), 625-59). In the fifteenth century the most elaborate submission formulas were reserved for ' commanded ' works, prepared at the request of some powerful patron (see Hammond, p. 392); the examples in Lydgate are prolonged and effusive. The full modesty epilogue has an initial command, ' Go, little boke ' (retained even at the end of the *Troy-Book* and the vast *Fall of Princes*); an apology for the author's inadequacy, for his ' rude langage ' and ' rurall termes '; a request for the reader to make corrections and improvements where he thinks fit; an assertion that all lies ' under support of ' the patience and tolerance of the reader, and that the author would never have presumed to trespass so far had it not been for his patron's insistence; and a final commendation of the poem, with all its faults, to the mercy of the reader. It will be seen which elements in *FL* are conventional, which not. Chaucer draws on the tradition once only, in the noble and moving epilogue to *Troilus*; but the fifteenth century, with the increasing importance of patrons, is profuse in examples, e.g. Lydgate, *Churl and Bird, Danse Macabre, Fall, Troy, TG, BK, Pilg.*, 164-84 (at the end of Lydgate's introduction); *BDM, KQ, GL, CL, Past. Pleas.*, Dunbar's *Golden Targe*. Caxton follows the convention closely in his Prologues and Epilogues.

592. **put in prees.** The phrase is a very common one (e.g. *PF*, 603; *Troy*, ii, 8577, iii, 1924, 2444, 2592, etc.) and does not of course refer to a printing-press. The sense is: ' How can you be so bold, for very shame, as to thrust yourself forward into the competing throng? '

595. boistously. Often used by Lydgate of his style, in affected humility, or of the unlettered, or of those who decry rhetoric; frequently it is conjoined with *rude* or *rurall*. See *Troy*, ii, 928, iii, 4238, v, 3466; *Fall*, vi, 3281, vii, 888; and cf. *Past. Pleas.*, 1202, 1215.

THE ASSEMBLY OF LADIES

1–3. The autumn opening is rare compared with the spring opening, but seems to have been developed by a few English poets for rather sad and sober poems, like *AL*, to which it is more appropriate. So Hoccleve begins his *Complaint* (*Minor Poems*, i, 95):

> After that hervest inned had his sheves,
> And that the broune season of Myhelmesse
> Was come, and gan the trees robbe of ther leves . . .

and continues with a sad contemplation of the transience of life and his own unhappy lot. George Ashby uses a similar opening in *A Prisoner's Reflections* (ed. EETS (E.S.) 76), and it appears in French at the beginning of hopeless love plaints, though more often as a mere variation in the *pastourelle*. See Tuve, *Seasons and Months*, pp. 108–10, and Helen E. Sandison, *The ' Chanson d'Aventure ' in Middle English*, Bryn Mawr College Monographs, vol. xii (1913), pp. 26–9. This respect for classical decorum is shown also with the midwinter opening, as in *TG* and the *Testament of Cresseid*; in the latter Henryson actually announces the rhetorical precept he is observing: ' Ane doolie sessoun to ane cairfull dyte/Suld correspond, and be equivalent ' (ed. G. G. Smith, 1908).

4–11. A similar description of ladies walking and disporting themselves in a garden with *aleyes* appears in *TC*, ii, 813–26.

5. as was ther wone. Cf. *CT*, I, 1040, 1064; *TC*, v, 647.

6. doth. For the auxiliary usage cf. 41, 195, 466, 548, 552, 569, 590, 748; and see *FL*, 245n.

8. foure. Cf. 408. This reading is most important, because it makes clear the sequence of ' complaints ' at the end of the poem: first, the four ' ladyes ' present their petitions, or rather have them read (582–623), then the four ' gentil wymmen ' (624–79), and finally the authoress (694–707). All the MSS have *foure*. Thynne changed it to *fayre*, presumably because lines 10–11 obviously refer to more than four, but we must assume that there the authoress has in mind all nine of the *felawship*. Skeat adopted Thynne's reading, apparently under the impression that only five ladies were involved in the petitioning, the first four offering their complaints (582–623) and then the same four having their petitions read (624–79); see his note to l. 87. The social distinction between *ladyes* and *gentil wymmen* was not sharp enough to prevent them taking part in the same pastimes and amusements, but the distinction did exist: ' Noble princesses and ladyes of estate,/And gentilwomen lower of degre ' (Lydgate, *Seynt Margarete*, 519f, in *Minor Poems*, i, 192); ' Ladyes of euery londe. . . ./Wythe gentyll wymmen of lower degre ' (*Parl. of Love*, 5–7, in *Political, Religious and Love Poems*, ed. Furnivall, p. 76).

10. crosse aleys. These paths are often mentioned in medieval garden descriptions, usually bordered with a low rail (*AL*, 42) and covered with sand, e.g. *TC*, ii, 820–22; *CT*, IV, 2324; *Churl and Bird*, 50; *GL*, 648.

However, *crosse* implies a formal symmetry which was fashionable in gardens only from the late fifteenth century onwards.

11. **fantasyes.** *fantise* (MS) does occur as a spelling of *feintise*, ' weakness ' in e.g. *Cursor Mundi*, Prol., 55 (ed. EETS (O.S.) 57, etc., App III, p. 1652), but this meaning is not possible here. In any case the phrase *after theyr fantasyes* was a stereotyped one (e.g. 597; *CT*, III, 190, V, 205). However, the Laud MS of *Cursor Mundi*, Prol., 55, has *fantasy*, while *fantasyes* occurs in *Guy of Warwick*, 3204 (fifteenth-century version, ed. Zupitza), where the sense demands *fantise*. This confusion of *fantise* and *fantasy(es)* accounts for the MS reading here. As for the rhyme *fantasyes/wise*, with elision of *e* in the plural ending, cf. 533, *rubies/wise*; *Guy*, 3204, *fantasyes/servyse*; *Gen.*, 4676, *fantesyce/cervice*.

14. Cf. *Gen.*, 646: ' Ther wer knyghtes and Squyers many on,/Hym self walkeng in his disporteng place '; also 3089, ' With knyghtes and with Sqyers many on '.

Theyr. The spelling indicates the falling together of *eir/air* and *er* (see Dobson, pp. 775–6).

15. **Wherof I serve.** For this expression (' What am I doing? ') cf. *CT*, IX, 339; *RR*, 703; the mixture of direct and indirect speech is common, and defies logical punctuation. John Stevens (*op. cit.*, p. 180) suggests that the question refers to some kind of allegiance in a courtly pastime.

18. Cf. *CT*, IV, 685: ' He wente his wey, as hym no thyng ne roghte '; *TC*, iv, 948; *Gen.*, 50. She attempts at first to evade his questions by pretending there is nothing in particular on her mind.

21. **therby lith a tale.** This earlier form of the Shakespearian ' Thereby hangs a tale ' (*As You Like It*, II, vii, 28; *Taming of the Shrew*, IV, i, 60, etc.) seems to be the first recorded occurrence of the idiom; it appears also in *GL*, 1178 (written 1523).

22. **must me wite.** This impersonal use of *must* with personal object, ' it is necessary for (me) to ' (also 74, 334, 509, 749), is not found in *FL*, and is rare in Chaucer (*CT*, VIII, 946; *RR*, 1473). It seems to be a peculiar usage of the original best preserved in A; the other texts read *ye* for *me* in 334 (a markedly inferior reading), *nedeth* for *must* in 509, and *we* (Tr), *I* (Th) for *me* in 749 (L *me*). See *OED*, s.v. *must*, *v*¹, 10.

23. **Telle on, late se.** Apparently imitated from *Pilg.*, 11217, 20011, 21515, 23977.

30. **felawship.** Frequently used in ME of an organised society of persons, a religious brotherhood or sisterhood, etc., but it means here simply ' a company of friends '.

32. **mase.** Mazes and labyrinths, known in ancient times, do not reappear in gardens until the late Middle Ages, though in churches they had long been worked into pavements to symbolise the toils of sin, and also cut in the turf outside, perhaps to be followed on hands and knees as a penance, with prayers repeated at fixed stations (Crisp, *Medieval Gardens*, i, 70–2). Mazes became very popular with the increasing formalisation of Tudor gardens, as at Hampton Court and Hatfield; at first the paths were separated only by raised flower-beds, low hedges, or rails, which could easily be stepped over (42), though later the barriers became more formidable. See W. H. Matthews, *Mazes and Labyrinths* (1922).

34. **and went.** For *wende(n)*, ' thought '. The unusual spelling, which appears in all MSS, suggests that a pun is intended.

36f. ' And to say true, some were a long way behind, and suddenly found themselves as far forward as the best '.

39. est and west. I.e. ' whatever direction they went '; for the tag see *CT*, I, 2601, V, 459, VI, 396; *BD*, 88; etc.

42. They grew so frustrated that they stepped over the rail which, perhaps together with a low hedge, separated the paths of the maze.

46. ' Though I had gained very considerably through my venture (journey) ', i.e. through persevering with her walk along the paths of the maze while her companions lost their patience. *grete* is better taken as an adverb (see *OED*, s.v. *great*, B, I) than as an absolute use of the adjective, ' a great (distance) '.

47. streyte passage. Cf. *CT*, VII, 1445 (Harley MS); *Thebes*, 2155; *Troy*, v, 1439; *Pilg.*, 4528, 24745. In Chaucer and Lydgate *passage* is commonly used in an abstract sense; its meaning here is a later development.

48. herber. See *FL*, 49n.

52. Save, ' safe(ly) '; not an uncommon spelling in late ME.

53. masonry. Arbours in late fifteenth-century gardens were often walled for special privacy. The reading of A, *mesure*, makes poor sense.

of compas environ. *LGW*, 300: ' And with that word, a-compas environ,/ They setten hem ful softely adoun '; cf. *RR*, 526.

55. tornyng whele. Skeat reads *with* (as T) for *a*, and associates *tornyng whele* with *turn-pike*, used in Scotland of spiral or winding stairs (*OED*). He suggests that the ' steyres goyng down . . . with tornyng whele ' are spiral stairs leading down in the middle of the arbour, which was built on a mount. Certainly, from the end of the fifteenth century, arbours were often built on mounts, sometimes in the middle of mazes (see A. Amherst, *History of Gardening in England*, 1895, pp. 76–8, 112–16; F. Crisp, *Medieval Gardens*, i, 84–9, ii, figs. 108–12; M. L. Gothein, *History of Garden Art*, 2 vols., 1928, i, 420, 438, 447), but the spiral steps would hardly emerge in the middle of the arbour, and the mount would surely have been mentioned in the approach to the arbour (47f). Furthermore, the association of ' turning-wheel ' and ' turn-pike ' is quite arbitrary.

The lay-out of the arbour is not as clear as it might be, but the *steyres* and the *whele* are probably distinct features; the former are wide steps leading down to a sunken part of the arbour, while *tornyng whele* has the accepted sense (*OED*, s.v.) of ' a turn-stile gate ', such as was commonly placed at the entrance to a convent. The pot of marjoram would be set on the flat top of the gatepost. However, *tornyng whele* may be merely a fanciful name for a stone disk on a stand (like a sun-dial), used for displays of potted flowers (*OED*, s.v. *wheel*, sign. 8); or the reference may be to one of the ingenious contrivances popular in late fifteenth-century gardens, perhaps a revolving water-driven ' machine '.

56. margoleyne, marjoram, a flower closely associated with the rites of love, as in *L'Amant rendu Cordelier* (ed. SATF, 1881), 1400, and a symbol of virtue and honour, supposed to preserve true love from the attempts of seducers (Gubernatis, ii, 220).

61. Ne m'oublie-mies, ' forget-me-nots ' (*myosotis*), flowers by their name symbolic of constancy in love, and also of unrequited love:

Charles d'Orléans, *Rondeaux*, No. 24 (ed. Champion, ii, 304); *Le Verger d'Amour* (ed. Montaiglon, *Recueil de poésies*, ix, 283). The misreadings of the later MSS led to the establishment in Speght's glossary of a ghost-word ('momblishnesse: taulke') which survived in dictionaries (Bailey, 1731, even supplied an etymology) until the time of the old *Century* (see *OED*, Supplement, p. 335).

sovenez, pl., 'remember-me' (*veronica chamoedrys*), a name by which Skeat said the flower was still known in Yorkshire and Scotland; it is usually called the germander speedwell. Cf. Orleans, 5019: 'soven'. In the booksellers' reprint of Thynne *souenesse* became *sonenesse*, which appears in Speght's glossary ('sonenesse: noise') and in Bailey.

62. penses, 'pansies' (*viola tricolor*), also called 'heart's ease', 'love-in-idleness' (*A Midsummer Night's Dream*, II, i, 168). The Anglicised form of Fr. *pensée*, 'thought' is seen as early as Charles of Orleans (5020, 'pancy'). It is worth noting that all the flowers mentioned here were emblems of serious, constant love, while the pansy and the forget-me-not were further used in illumination as religious emblems (Joan Evans, *Pattern*, i, 63).

63. No, no. See *FL*, 471n. This repetition of *no, yis*, etc., for emphasis (cf. 236, 326, 349) is a very characteristic feature of the style of Charles of Orleans's English poems (e.g. 1286, 1390, 4643, 4776, 4781, 5092).

64f. The arbour was paved with decorated tiles laid in a pattern (also 451). Cf. *TC*, ii, 82, 'a paved parlour'; *CT*, III, 2105; *Past. Pleas.*, 3235, 5236.

68. streames. This was not a fountain in the modern sense. The jets of water issued from a natural spring-head (ingeniously concealed, 70), and were led through conduits about the garden, in this case on one side of the arbour and below floor-level (**underneth**). Cf. *Churl and Bird*, 52–6.

> Sote herbis with condittes at the hond,
> That wellid up ageyn the sonne shene,
> Lich siluer stremys, as any cristal cleene
> The burbly wawis in ther vp boylyng
> Round as berel, ther bemys out shewyng;

RR, 1413; *RS*, 5720; *GL*, 652; see Crisp, *Medieval Gardens*, vol. i, fig. 103, vol. ii, figs. 203–15.

newe and newe. A common phrase, e.g. *CT*, VI, 929; *TC*, iii, 116; *TG*, 759; *Thebes*, 4116; *RS*, 308.

69. in such wise. Cf. 706, 724, 733; *CT*, II, 153, III, 110, etc. These tags in *wise*, usually rhyming, are very common in *AL*, and are collected here, with a few specimen references from Chaucer to indicate their conventional nature: *in this wise*, 589 (see *FL*, 98n); *in no wise*, 114, 120, 399, 593, 647 (*CT*, II, 796, V, 705); *in every wise*, 167, 334, 532 (*CT*, II, 1098, IV, 695); *in every* (*no*) *maner wise*, 89, 605 (*CT*, III, 1898, IV, 605); *in dyvers wise*, 12 (*CT*, X, 564; *TC*, i, 61); *in secrete wise*, 405 (*CT*, IV, 1937, VI, 143).

82. demure. See *FL*, 459n; the combination 'sad and demure' was particularly favoured by Lydgate, e.g. *Troy*, i, 1320, 1572, iv, 5171, etc.

83. blewe. The wearing of blue is emphasised throughout the poem (116, 206, 304, etc.) because blue was the colour of truth and fidelity, especially as opposed to green: 'In stede off bleu, which stedfast is and cleene,/She loued chaunges off many dyuers greene' (*Fall*, i, 6446f). *CL*, 246–9 recalls both this feature and the general theme of *AL*.

'Lo! yonder folk', quod she, 'that knele in blew,
They were the colour ay, and ever shall,
In sign they were, and ever will be trew
Withouten chaunge.'

Cf. 'true blue', 'True blue will never stain'. The symbolism of colours, especially in dress, was very strong in the Middle Ages. For comment and further references see Introduction, p. 37.

85–8. Her gown was embroidered with *sovenez*, the flower which she had taken, appropriately enough (see 61, 62n), as her emblem or device, and her motto was stitched on the hem, probably the hem of the wide, hanging sleeve (see 119). Cf. Orleans, 5016–20:

The lynyng of hit was with nedille wrought
So playne so thikke so smothe so pratily
With litille litille flowris soft
The soven and the daisy
But most of pancy myght y spy

(further resemblances here to *AL*, 487, 61–2). There is abundant testimony to the practice of embroidering garments with devices, especially flowers and mottoes, in the later Middle Ages (e.g. Fairholt's *Costume*, ed. Dillon (1885), i, 123; Houston, *Medieval Costume*, p. 135; Joan Evans, *Pattern*, i, 96f, 102). Charles of Orleans carried the idea to its limit by having a gown sewn with pearls, which on the sleeves formed the words and music of a song (Evans, i, 145). This kind of ornamentation, coupled with the significance of colour and the influence of heraldry, meant that dress had a rich symbolic language of its own. These devices and mottoes are not, however, to be confused with coats of arms, family crests, and family mottoes, since the former are essentially personal, and are not used for identification but as an ingenious form of mystification. The mottoes are cryptic, usually amatory, often obscure: *Rien ne m'est plus*, *Vostre rien* (in reply to the first), *Sejour de dueil*, *Fors vous seulle* (quoted by Champion, *Histoire poétique du quinzième siècle* (2 vols., 1923), i, 80, 380). In England this kind of motto was rare, though there are examples: *Autre que elle* (Lord Scrope), *Plus est en vous* (Louis de Bruges, the Flemish Earl of Winchester), and *Une sanz pluis*, the motto adopted by Henry VI at the time of his marriage (see *Encyclopaedia Britannica*, 'Heraldry'; Evans, i, 102). Lydgate offers further examples of the practice in his *Epithalamion* for the Duke of Gloucester and Jacqueline of Hainault: 'And eeke hir word is in verray sooþe/Ce bien raysoun al þat euer she dooþe' (111f); 'For whom he wryteþe *in goode aventure/Sanz plus vous belle* perpetuelly tendure' (160f). However, the use of mottoes in *AL*, and the context, seem to owe most to the *Temple of Glass*, where we find a beautiful lady kneeling with a petition to Venus, her *word* embroidered on her dress.

Therfore hir woord wiþoute variaunce
Enbrouded was, as men my3t se:
De mieulx en mieulx, with stones and perre.
(308–10)

In MSS Gg. 4.27 and Addit. 16165 the last two lines run: 'Was vp and doun as men myghte se/In frens (Addit. ffresshly) enbroudyt *humblement magre*'. The mottoes in *AL* (viz. 88, 208, 308, 364, 489, 583, 590, 598, 616, 627, 645, 666, 675) were probably made up for the purposes of the poem. Some of them, and others very like them, occur as family mottoes, e.g. *Tant que je puis*, *En dieu est* (*ma fiance*, *foy*, *espoir*), *Sans changer, Sans recuiller jamais* (cf. *AL*, 208, 645, 590, 583); but there is no ascertainable significance in the coincidence.

87. **by and by.** See Glossary and *FL*, 59n; the sense here is ' word for word ', as in *RR*, 4581.

88. *Bien loielment*: ' Very loyally '.

95. *Gen.*, 352: ' Whiche is ontrewe and hath be many a daye ' (also 5685).

102. **ussher.** The Usher of the Chamber looked after the food and service in the lord's room.   Social distinctions were carefully observed in the lord's household, and the carrying of a staff of office (*AL*, 103–5) was a jealously guarded privilege.   The etiquette of courts, and the duties of household officers, were elaborately set forth in the fifteenth-century ' Bokes of Curtasye ' (see *Manners and Meals*, ed. Furnivall, e.g. pp. 309–27).

121. **As many as,** ' however many '.   Parallels for this concessive use of *as* are given in *OED*, s.v. *as*, B. 3b; *MED*, s.v. *as*, 4(b).   Dittography might be suspected in MS A, were it not that the second *as* is an inserted correction in the original hand.

131. **I can no better say.** Cf. *CT*, II, 874, IV, 1874, VIII, 651, X, 54, etc.

134. **governaunce.** See Glossary.   This was a word expressing the highest praise in the description of women (e.g. *BD*, 1008; *CT*, IV, 1603; *TG*, 754).

137. *Gen.*, 4845: ' Of all hir manerys callid trew and playne '.
      terewe. Cf. 14, 476, and see Introduction, p. 12.

138. **busy peyne.** Cf. *CT*, V, 509; *Pity*, 2, 119.   A favourite expression in Lydgate, e.g. *BK*, 241, 338; *RS*, 177, 511, 597, etc.

148. **benedicite.** This common exclamation usually has only three syllables in Chaucer (e.g. *CT*, I, 2115, 4220, III, 1456, 1584); here it has five, as in *CT*, I, 1785.

151. ' (Men have done nothing *wrong*) but I am always ready to believe that there is something (about them that cannot be trusted) '.   The lady's language is very guarded, as if she were anxious not to give offence.

157. A similar *topos* occurs in *GL*, 462f; for the one in the next line cf. *FL*, 172.

161. **fanes.** A typical late-fifteenth-century detail.   Cf. Hawes, *Example of Virtue*, stanza 27: ' with fanis wavering in the wind '; Douglas, *Palice of Honour* (ed. Small, 1874), i, 55: ' goldin fanis waifand in the wind ' (Hammond, p. 491).

163. **bay wyndowes.** *Bay*, not a familiar word, could easily have been omitted by the scribe of MS A, though it might be a later interpolation. Bay windows, projecting windows differing from oriels in that the projecting wall below is carried to the ground, are named in building contracts and other official documents from the fourteenth century onwards (see L. F. Salzman, *Building in England* (Oxford, 1952), pp. 94, 417, 434, etc.), but the reference in *AL* appears to be the earliest literary use of the word; the next is *CL*, 1058.   Bay windows, although they are in the palace of Plesaunce at Greenwich before 1447 (Seaton, *Sir Richard Roos*, p. 297), did not become popular or widely known until the late fifteenth and sixteenth centuries, when they assume a new

importance and splendour in the design of the great Tudor houses. See J. H. Parker, *Domestic Architecture, Richard II to Henry VIII* (1859), p. 54; N. Lloyd, *History of the English House* (1931), pp. 55, 333–5; J. Lees-Milne, *Tudor Renaissance* (1951), pp. 133f.

165. **galaries.** Sheltered walks along the side of a house, like a cloister, ' partly open at the side, or having the roof supported by pillars ' (*OED*). Another feature of early Tudor domestic architecture, very popular with Wolsey (Cavendish, *Metrical Visions*, 113).

168. Cf. *Eye and Heart*, 37f: ' And eke so swete was thair mery report/ That it me thought a verrey paradyse '.

170. **Plesaunt Regard.** Intended, not to describe the palace, but allegorically, as one of the attributes of ideal womanhood (' Pleasant Looks '); line 172 may be taken as a play on the allegorical and literal meanings. *Doux Regard* is one of the followers of Love in *RR* (Chaucer, ' Swete-Lokyng ', 920), but the name here is from Charles d'Orléans, *Rondeaux*, No. 231 (ed. Champion, ii, 422): ' Par l'aumosnier Plaisant Regart/Donnez l'aumosne de Doulceur '; cf. No. 323 (ii, 476): ' plaisant Actrayant Regart '. Allegorical names were often given to the symbolic places of Love (cf. *Joyeux Gard* in Malory), though usually gloomy ones, like ' la forêt de Longue Atente ' (*Rondeaux*, ed. Raynaud, pp. 30, 32–4, etc.) and ' la fortresse de Desespoir en la montaigne de Tristesse ' (pp. 73, 78). Miss Seaton (*op. cit.*, pp. 297–8) recognises the architectural model for Plesaunt Regard in Duke Humphrey's palace at Plesaunce; but the impartial observer will find the comparison more interesting than convincing.

178. **erly or late.** Cf. *RR*, 5859; *Pearl*, 392. A very common tag also in Lydgate's *Pilgrimage* (360, 469, 488, 2785, 4393, 6429, 6507, etc.).

192. **verray.** The only clearly adverbial use in *AL* (cf. 479). See *FL* 10n; the usage in *AL* is more conservative.

202. **Looke what,** ' Whatever service . . .'. Cf. *CT*, III, 517 (' Wayte what '), V, 771 (' Looke who that '), and see *MLR* 3 (1907), 72. The idiom is common in OE and in Shakespeare, but not in ME: see *MLN* 31 (1916), 442.

211f. ' It would be a very good thing in my opinion if we now set off within a little while.' For this sense of *toke*, ' went, made a start, set off,' see *OED*, s.v. *take*, 63.

217. **for nothyng,** ' not for anything '; cf. *BD*, 691; *CT*, III, 1121; *LGW*, 1853.

219. **a soft and esy pase.** As in *Beryn*, 1471; *Gen.*, 4953; *CL*, 567f.

220f. *Gen.*, 632–4:

> To that contre they toke the wey full right,
> And on hir wey so ferre fourth were thei goon,
> That of the Citee sone they hadde a sight.

Cf. 5705.

224. **seynt Julyan.** St Julian the Hospitaller, patron saint of hospitality. After accidentally killing his parents, Julian set up a hospital to harbour poor people, and bore travellers across a nearby river as a penance. See Caxton's *Golden Legend* (ed. F. S. Ellis), i, 377; also *CT*, I, 340; *HF*, 1022; Skeat, *Chaucer*, iii, 265. The medieval belief in St Julian's power is illustrated in a passage from the *Decameron* quoted by Manly in his note to *CT*, I, 340: ' And pray, sir, what sort of prayers do you

use when you are upon a journey? . . . On a journey I have always
been accustomed to say in the morning a Pater Noster and an Ave
Maria for the souls of the father and mother of St Julian; after which
I prayed God and him to give me good lodging for the coming night.
And many a time have I been in great danger, but have always escaped,
and when night came on, I always had a good lodging, which favour I
firmly believe St Julian obtained of God for me, nor do I think I should
ever travel serenely or have good lodging at night were I to forget this
prayer.'

225. **I gre me wele**: ' I willingly agree '. *gre* is taken direct from OFr
gréer, ' agree ', and the reflexive use here, which is very rare, suggests a
knowledge of the English poems of Charles of Orleans, where it is used
reflexively in 6076, and elsewhere in other ways. Cf. *Gen.*, 1141: ' Quod
he, madame, I gre me wele ' (also 5294).

231. **hospital**. In the Middle Ages the monastic and military-religious
orders set up ' hospitals ' all over the country for the accommodation
of poor travellers and pilgrims, for the sick, aged, and insane, and for
lepers.   There were as many as six hundred hospitals of various kinds in
the fourteenth century, though the number of foundations dwindled sub-
sequently.   The comparison expressed in *AL*, perhaps partly suggested
by the mention, a stanza earlier, of St Julian (the Hospitaller), refers to
the continuous high walls surrounding leper hospitals, which can be
seen in contemporary illustrations, e.g. Plates 12, 21, 22, Figs. 21, 22,
in R. M. Clay, *The Medieval Hospitals of England* (1909); see also D.
Knowles, *Medieval Religious Houses* (1953), pp. 45–8, 250–324.

241. **myne array.** The blue clothes she was told to wear by Perseverance in 116.

243. Cf. Orleans, 5176: ' Madame alle this it nedith not no no ' (also
of a superfluous request).

244. **com of.** This expression was originally used for calling dogs off
game, and acquired the sense ' have done ' (*PF*, 494; *CT*, I, 3728); this
shades off to ' come on, come along ' (*CT*, III, 1602; *TC*, ii, 1738, 1742,
1750), with the sense ' hurry up ', as here (cf. *TC*, ii, 310; *TG*, 1272n;
Skeat, *Chaucer*, v, 110).

256. **dare**, ' need '. The loss of *f* or *v* from the stem of OE *þearf* (pres.
3 sg.), ' needs, it is needful ' (and from other parts of the same verb),
giving ME *þar*, led to confusion between *þar* and *dar* in ME, so that
dar(e) is often used with the sense ' need ' (cf. *RR*, 1089, 1324, and see
OED, s.v. *dare*, *tharf*).

259. **broke.** Literally ' make use of, profit by ': ' You profit well by
your new clothes ', i.e. they suit you well. Cf. *Thebes*, 96: ' Wel broke
ye youre name ' (as in *Beryn*, 66). MnE *brook* retains only the sense
' tolerate ', in negative constructions.

265. **this office of purchase,** ' this job of procuring (supplies   and
provisions) '.

287. **To,** ' till ' (*conj.*). See *OED*, s.v. *to*, C. 1.

289. **without wordes mo.** Cf. *CT*, I, 3408, 3650, 3819, etc.

294. **I can nomore.** Cf. *TC*, iii, 390, 1193, 1273, etc.; *Gen.*, 1015: ' I
canne noo more but Ihesu be your spede ' (also 4270).

300. **ever among,** ' continually ': a common phrase in Lydgate's

octosyllabic verse, e.g. *RS*, 615, 1172, 2241; *Pilg.*, 2485, 11046, 18269, 21499.

305. gray. Commonly used as a noun to mean ' gray fur '—usually understood to be of badger skin.

308. *A moy que je voy*, ' What I see is mine ', makes a kind of sense as a motto for Countenance the Porter.

309. ferforth as. By itself *ferforth* means ' far, far on, to a great degree or extent ', but the usual construction in ME is with clauses of comparison or degree, *as ferforth as, so ferforth (that)*, etc. Here it means ' to the very degree that, or exactly as (she came straight to me) ', i.e. ' in the very action of coming towards me '. The sense is strained, but the reading of A seems authentic and meaningful; the version of T is a typical scribal alteration of an unfamiliar or difficult word.

311. Forsoth. MS *Forferth* conforms to no known ME usage, and is easily explicable by reference to the *ferforth* of 309, an unfamiliar usage which stayed in the copyist's mind.
  know and se. Cf. *Fall*, iii, 2893; *Beryn*, 3666; *Gen.*, 3190: ' Here afterward ye shall wele know and see ' (also 5263). MS *she* is possible neither as a word nor as a spelling, though it reappears in 345; *sh* for *s* is an occasional Northern spelling (see *AL*, 332n), but only before *u*, *ew*, etc.

322. Bealchiere. Cf. *CT*, VII, 409; Lydgate, *Horse, Goose and Sheep*, 120f: ' In Wyntir seson for to make *bele cheer,*/Than is neede wode and stuff to carie '.
  marchal. In the later Middle Ages the *marchal of the halle* was one of the chief functionaries of a royal or noble household, being charged with the arrangement of ceremonies, and especially with the ordering and serving of guests at banquets. See 102n; *CT*, I, 752, IV, 1930.

325. bille is the usual word in fifteenth-century literature for a written petition or statement of complaint, especially one concerning faithless or unrequited love, but there is much in *AL*, in the administrative arrangements for the presentation of the bills (337–45, 540–81) and in the bills themselves (582–707), to suggest that the poet is aware too of the stricter legal sense of the word (for derivation of which from Lat. *libellus* rather than Lat. *bulla*, as in the *OED*, see *Select Bills in Eyre*, ed. W. C. Bolland (Selden Society, 30, 1914), pp. xi–xv), and that he is making some attempt to imitate current legal procedure. In law, we are told, ' A Bill of complaint is a declaration in writing, shewing the plaintifes griefe, and the wrong which he supposeth to be done unto him by the defendaunt, and what damages he susteineth by occasion thereof, praying processe against him for redresse of the same ' (W. West, *Symbolaeography* (London, 1594), part 2: A Treatise of Equitie, section 71). As such, the bill, consisting essentially of a statement of complaint and a prayer for redress (as in *AL*), was the initiatory action and the distinguishing feature of all procedure in equity; it is only semi-legal in form, ' always retaining a greater lack of formality than was permitted to other legal documents ' (*Select Cases before the King's Council 1243–1482*, ed. I. S. Leadam and J. F. Baldwin (Selden Society, 35, 1918), p. xxxv); it is written in French or English as well as Latin; it tends to be vague in point of fact but vehement in presenting the enormity of the offence (as in *AL*). In style as well as content the bills of *AL* recall those of fifteenth-century law, especially those presented before the King's Council: there is the same semi-legal parlance, with its profusion of loosely related participles (e.g. *AL* 584, 588, 608, 622–3, etc.), the same choked and circuitous movement and convoluted syntax. The characteristic opening of the bill, ' In full humble wyse complenyng shewith unto your good and gracious lordship your pour Oratour and bedman ', etc. (*Select Cases in the Council of Henry VII*, ed. C. G. Bayne and W. H. Dunham (Selden Society, 75, 1958), p. 61), is more than reminiscent of the phrasing of *AL*. It is worth remembering, too, in this context that the King's Council, like the court of Lady Loyalty, was conceived of in rather vague and general terms, and was approached by suitors as ' the supreme authority in the state, superior to the ordinary law and able to right wrongs of every kind ' (*ibid*., p. lxxxi).

332. **shewe,** ' sue '; cf. *sewe, sue,* 117, etc. This spelling, which is of N or EM origin, has many parallels (see Dobson, *op. cit.*, pp. 706, 947), including one in the preceding note.

334. **me must knowe.** See 22n.

336. **Without feyneng.** Cf. 340; *FL*, 549n; *Gen.*, 1214, 1290, 1347, etc.

337. ' The name of secretary ', says Sir Robert Wingfield in a letter to Henry VIII, 26 June 1516, ' hath the foundation upon the knowledge of such thinggis as ought to be kept secret ' (J. Otway-Ruthven, *The King's Secretary and the Signet office in the XV century* (Cambridge, 1939), p. 63). But although this *secretarye* may have some of the traits of the confidante and the influential personal adviser (see 338), and in this sense be linked with the king's secretary and the great Tudor secretaries, her most important tasks in *AL* are administrative and clerical, to collect and read out the bills (553, 564), and here the closest parallel is again a legal one (see 325n), with the work of the clerk of the King's Council. Litigation in the King's Council began, as we have seen, with the presentation of a petition or bill, and the most normal method of presentation was for the bill to be handed to the clerk of the Council, who would read it out, whether or not the plaintiff were present. From the early fifteenth century ' the office of clerk of the Council was a conspicuous post of trust and honour. . . . His duties consisted especially in conveying confidential messages, not merely delivering the letters but " demonstrating and declaring " them ' (J. F. Baldwin, *The King's Council in England during the Middle Ages* (Oxford 1913), p. 367). Several of these clerks were men of distinction and rose to higher positions in the government.

346. **goode.** Cf. 689; this use as a vocative is found also in, e.g., *TC*, i, 1017, iv, 1660; Orleans, 372.

360. **God yield it yow.** Cf. *CT*, III, 1772, 2177; *TC*, i, 1055.

364. *Plus ne purroy*: ' I could (do) no more '.

377f. ' She will tell you everything about the rules and formalities you have to observe now that you have arrived.'

388. ' Do not grow impatient with your wait '. The sense of *think long*, ' to grow weary with waiting, to be impatient ', still current in some dialects, arises from a perversion of an earlier impersonal construction, e.g. *me þenkiþ long*, ' it seems a long time to me ', by substitution of the nominative for the dative (see *OED*, s.v. *think, v*[1], B. 3, *v*[2], B. 10. c; *long, a*[1]. 9. b).

394f. Cf. *Gen.*, 2669f: ' They sawe comyng along in a valay/A grete peopill, wele dressed in ther geere ' (cf. 4973).

406. Cf. *Gen.*, 287: ' Whiche shall it kepe right wele o warantyce '; also 5938, 6470, 6803.

419f. A medieval audience would need little reminding of the notorious dilatoriness of the law, whether in civil or criminal actions. Opportunities for delay occurred at every stage of a trial and cases dragged on from year to year without coming to a conclusion. Sir John Fortescue, in his *De Laudibus Legum Anglie* (1471), quotes examples of actions in the French high court which lasted thirty years (ed. S. B. Chrimes (Cambridge, 1942), pp. 131–5). The Pastons knew well, and to their cost, of the law's delay, for after the death of Sir John Fastolf in 1459 John Paston spent the remaining seven years of his life in a turmoil of litigation trying to obtain recognition for his inalienable right to the Fastolf estate. His efforts, which made deep inroads into the family fortunes, were not crowned with success, and it was not until 1476 that Caister Castle, the prize of the inheritance, was finally secured by his son (see H. S. Bennett, *The Pastons and their England* (Cambridge, 1932), pp. 10–26). Actual legal expenses, though heavy, were perhaps more readily borne by the litigant than the continual favours and bribes that were expected from him. A typical ' bill of costs ' of the time of Henry VI includes not only legal and secretarial expenses but also other, more expressive details, such as, ' Item in wyne gyeve to squyers and others, xij*d.*, Item for fysh to my lord chaunceler at Hoke, iijs.iiijd' (J. F. Baldwin, *The King's Council*, pp. 533f).

419. Proverbial: ' Long tarrying takes all the thanks away '. See M. P. Tilley, *Proverbs in England in the sixteenth and seventeenth centuries* (Ann Arbor, 1950), p. 652.

425–7. They hope that allowances will be made for their lack of eloquence, and that their complaints will not be ignored or rejected merely because they are crudely expressed.

443. Cf. *Gen.*, 6567f: ' Full umbely besechyng your goodnes,/ That of all this I may haue forgevenes '.
hir goodenesse. For this use of the abstract as a form of title see also *BDM*, 576, and cf. *TG*, 977 (' ʒoure heigh nobles ') and MnE ' Your Highness ', ' Your Excellency '.

455. **berel and cristal.** This detail is from Lydgate; see *Troy*, ii, 970, where windows are so described; *BK*, 37 (water); *Churl and Bird*, 93 (pinnacles); *Pilg.*, 18117 (decoration of ' relics '). **Cristal** was regarded by the Middle Ages as a kind of ice, petrified by some long-continued natural process (Bartholomew, *De Prop. Rerum*, xvi, 31); it was used for vases, caskets, and other ornaments, and for glazing windows (e.g. *Past. Pleas.*, 1416, 1524, 2558). **Berel**, which does not refer to our precious stone but to a form of crystal, was similarly used. Leland describes the windows of Sudeley Castle (near Winchcomb in Gloucestershire) as being ' glazed with berall ' (*Itinerary*, ed. Toulmin-Smith, ii, 56; see also Wm. Harrison, *Description of England*, ed. Furnivall, New Shakespeare Society, 1877, p. 237). The idea of walls of beryl and crystal in *AL* is a fantasy, reminiscent of Chaucer's *House of Fame* (*HF*, 1184, 1288–91) and Lydgate's *Temple of Glass*, which in their turn form part of a descriptive tradition considerably influenced by Revelation 21 (for further references see Sypherd, *House of Fame*, p. 86; he points out, p. 133, that beryl was closely associated with Love: ' Per sua vertute fa crescer l'amore '). Precious metals and stones are lavished ' with the cheap magnificence of fiction ' on the palaces and

temples of medieval romance and allegory, especially in the fifteenth century (see Hammond, p. 490).

456. Mural decoration in domestic interiors, as distinct from churches, was not nearly as common as hanging with tapestries and painted cloths (see Joan Evans, *English Art 1307–1461* (1949), p. 137), but in literature wall-paintings were frequently described, sometimes merely as a means of extending the scope of a poem, but usually in order to enrich or expand its fundamental theme, as here (e.g. *CT*, I, 1918–46, 1994–2038, 2056–74; *BD*, 321–34; *RR*, 135–474; *Assembly of Gods*, 1510ff; see Sypherd, pp. 82–6; Elizabeth L. Harris, *The Mural as a Decorative Device in Medieval Literature*, Nashville, Tennessee, 1935). Often, in love visions, the paintings represent famous lovers of the past (e.g. *PF*, 284–94; *TG*, 42–142; *CL*, 229–38), usually the faithful and unfortunate, as in the crystal engravings (another touch of fantasy; cf. the walls ' enamelled ' with the story of Troy in *Past. Pleas.*, 5234) of *AL*. This whole technique for introducing illustrative material is a patent device, but it is worth remembering that in the Middle Ages pictures were far more frequently used for communication than words (see Triggs, *Assembly of Gods*, p. lviii). The **storyes**, as befits the allegory, are of love's martyrs, true and faithful women unfortunate or wronged in love. Chaucer often finds occasion for introducing such lists of unfortunate women (e.g. *BD*, 726–39; *HF*, 388–426; *PF*, 284–94; *CT*, II, 60–76, V, 1367–456; *LGW*, 249–69), while *LGW* is a systematic martyrology, based on the elaborate compilations of Ovid (*Heroides*) and Boccaccio (*De Claris Mulieribus*). Phyllis, Thisbe, and Cleopatra usually figure in Chaucer's lists, and their stories are told in *LGW*: the list of names was largely stereotyped, partly through being used as a *topos* of eulogy (cf. Nine Worthies, *FL*, 504n)—a woman would be said to possess the outstanding qualities of each in turn (see e.g. Lydgate, *Epithalamion for Gloucester*, 71–84, and Hammond's note; *Ballade of her that hath all the Virtues*, 8–28, in *Minor Poems*, ii, 379). Melusene, however, is a new addition to the martyrology (she is included also in *CL*, 233–5), while *Anelada* is from Chaucer's *Anelida and Arcite*, much of which is devoted to her *Compleynt* (cf. *AL*, 466).

457. **of wommanly pite.** The idea is, probably, that Phyllis's misfortunes were all due to her first taking pity on Demophon when he was shipwrecked on the shores of her kingdom (*LGW*, 2404–53).

460. **under a tre.** The mention of the mulberry tree is interesting, since, although it figures prominently in Ovid's story of Pyramus and Thisbe, it receives no more than a casual mention in Gower and Chaucer (*Conf. Am.*, iii, 1381; *LGW*, 785).

463. **Melusene.** MS *Enclusene* is a scribal error. The legend of Melusine appears in ME in two fifteenth-century translations from the French, one in prose (*Melusine*, ed. A. K. Donald, EETS (E.S.) 68, 1895), and one in verse (*Romans of Partenay*, ed. Skeat, EETS (O.S.) 22, 1866). The story ran that Melusine, owing to a spell cast upon her by her mother, used to turn into a serpent from the waist down every Saturday, and, when she eventually marries Count Raymond, makes him vow not to ask where she goes on Saturdays. She proves a loyal and faithful wife, and bears him ten children; but finally Raymond's curiosity gets the better of him. He follows her one Saturday, hacks a hole with his sword in the door of the room in which she locks herself, and sees her in the bath, with her serpent's tail, ' gret and orrible ' (*Part.*, 2808; cf. *Melusine*, p. 297). His later betrayal of the secret brings about her perpetual damnation.

howenclusene was probably the reading in the exemplar copied by the later scribes, and the best they could do with it was *Hawes the shene*: *Hawes*, or *Hawyse*, was indeed a character in the romance of *Fouke FitzWarin* (ed. A. C. Wood, 1911; French version, ed. L. Brandin, CFMA, 1930), but she was never ' deceived in her bath ', so far as we know. The misreading was materially influenced by Chaucer's frequent use of *the shene* as a rhyming tag attached to the names of women: *CT*, I, 1068, V, 1045; *TC*, ii, 824, etc.

466. **complayne.** As in 584, 590, 599, etc., the reference is to the formal, literary statement of complaint (*Anel.*, 211–350) popular in medieval courtly love poetry: see *FL*, 320n.

471. **umple:** OFr *omple*, ' a fine kind of linen stuff ' (*OED*), fine gauze or lawn. The word is also used in *London Lickpenny*, 76 (in Hammond).

477. Mandeville describes an elaborate throne set on seven ' degrees ' or steps in Prester John's palace (*Travels*, i, 183), very similar to the throne of Darius in the Alexander legend, where each of the seven steps has a different symbolic significance (*Wars of Alexander*, ed. EETS (E.S.) 47, 3336ff).

478. Cf. *Gen.*, 72: ' Of sylk and gold full curyously wrought '.

cassidony: OFr *cassidoine*, a semi-popular form of *calcidoine*, from Lat. *c(h)alcedonius*, the Latinised form of the Greek name given in Revelation 21:19 to the precious stone forming the third foundation of the new Jerusalem. From the thirteenth century (see *Pearl*, ed. Gordon, 1003n) the name was applied to a semi-transparent white quartz, tinted yellow or blue: ' a ston of white pale coler, as it wer a trobel whitnes ' (*English Medieval Lapidaries*, ed. EETS (O.S.) 190, p. 75). A main virtue attributed to the stone in the lapidaries was its power to give ' maystre in causes ' (p. 75; cf. p. 30), a symbolism peculiarly appropriate to its use here as the foundation of the seat of authority.

480. **saphirs.** Though the title was disputed (as by Lydgate in favour of the ruby, *TG*, 259; *RS*, 6603; *Fall*, iii, 3412), the sapphire was regarded by the encyclopaedias (*De Prop. Rerum*, xvi, 87) and lapidaries as *gemma gemmarum*, the most precious of all jewels. It was a token of truth and constancy, e.g. Lydgate, *Gloriosa Dicta*, 161–8 (*Minor Poems*, i, 321); Orleans, 2310.

482. **Ynde.** For the medieval imagination India was the extreme limit of remoteness, the end of the world (as in *Aeneid*, vi, 794): e.g. *RR*, 624 (' Although he sought oon in-tyl Ynde '); *RS*, 2362 (' Thogh men soughten into ynde '); *CT*, III, 824, VI, 722; *BD*, 889; *TC*, v, 971. The name was also, of course, the symbol of fabulous splendour; see Caxton's *Mirror of the World* (ed. Prior, EETS (E.S.) 110, 1913), pp. 70–90; *FL*, 202n.

486. **cloth of state.** The name given to a rich canopy of great splendour over a throne; cf. *GL*, 484; Cavendish, *Met. Visions*, 123.

489. *A Endurer:* ' (Ever) to endure '.

496. **bi goodely warnyng.** This describes what she had to say, not how she said it: the reading of *with* for *bi* in T makes the sense clearer.

507. **chaunceler.** Lat. *cancellarius*, the usher in law courts whose station was *ad cancellos*, the bars or grating separating the public from the judges; in medieval households, an important official who supervised the running of the household and the estate.

509. **us must.** See 22n.

510. Cf. *Gen.*, 5119: ' Moche pepyll slayn And Alway moo And moo '.

511. Cf. *Gen.*, 4971: ' And so furth on to telle yow ferthermore '; also 4852, 5302; and cf. 5110, 5775, 5855, 6027.

515f. Cf. Orleans, 5051f: ' So inly fayre so fulle of goodlynes/ So wel enswerid bothe of port and chere '. **Inly fayre** was a very common phrase, e.g. *TC*, iii, 1606; *RS*, 265, 951, 1796, 1978, etc.

519–32. The scribe of A evidently missed these two stanzas in turning the leaf.

523. **In taberd wyse.** The *tabard* was a short sleeveless coat (originally simply two panels of cloth joined over the shoulders), emblazoned with armorial bearings and worn by heralds. The word was used also of a ploughman's loose smock (e.g. *CT*, I, 541), and, in the later Middle Ages, of a more elaborate short blazoned surcoat worn by knights over their armour, with open wing sleeves hanging loosely down below the elbow (see Fairholt, *Costume*, i, 209; Houston, *Medieval Costume*, p. 213; *P.Pl.*, C, vii, 203). The **slevys hangyng don** are probably of this type, though *in taberd wyse* may indicate simply that the gown was open below the arms, with front and back joining at the waist, as in the late-fifteenth-century surcoat (*FL*, 141n), in which case the sleeves referred to might hang to the ground, a fashion at once very popular and bitterly criticised in the fifteenth century (e.g. Hoccleve, *Reg. of Princes*, 533–9; Barclay, *Ship of Fools*, 515, and the note in Hammond).

526–30. The sense is, that the borders of her gown, which would normally have been trimmed with ermine, were decorated with rows of pearls according to a certain pattern, with diamonds set between them; see C. Köhler, *History of Costume* (1928), p. 206; *FL*, 145n. This passage echoes Charles of Orleans's description of Fortune (4988–94).

> And as the surcot forgoth in substaunce
> Of ermyn and is powdrid round abowt
> So was it wrought with fyn pynche and plesaunce
> And in the stede of powdryng alle without
> As y biheld right wel persayue y mought
> How it was sett ful thikke with laughyng eyene
> But many moo that wepte y myght aspien.

vent. The opening at the neck of the gown, the V-neck which became popular at the end of the fifteenth century (Fairholt, *Costume*, i, 188f, ii, 405).

528f. Cf. *CT*, I, 2161: ' Couched with perles whyte and rounde and grete '; cf. *FL*, 145n, 148n.

530. **pouderyng.** Originally a heraldic term; a common variant of charges and fields was sowing or ' powdering ' them with a small charge repeated many times, e.g. ' gold powdered with fleurs-de-lys sable ' (Mortimer of Norfolk). The term came to be closely associated with the ermine tails (also a heraldic device) which flecked with black the white ermine borders, e.g. *Assembly of Gods*, 266: ' purfylyd with poudryd hermyne '; *Past. Pleas.*, 2041: ' With armynes powdred bordred at the vent '. The sense was also generalised to describe the ' sprinkling ' of a garment with precious stones or ornaments (e.g. *Fall*, iv, 541). In *AL*, just as rows of pearls took the place of the usual ermine border, so diamonds take the place of ermine tails.

531. **of assyse.** Cf. *in assise*, ' in (due) order ', *RR*, 900, 1237, 1392. Here the reference is to manner rather than position, ' in the same

fashion ' (i.e. the sleeves and hems were ornamented in the same way as ' the coler and the vent ').

533. serpe. Some kind of collar or neck-ring is here described, probably a circlet of precious metal, chased out or engraved, and set at intervals with white enamel flowers, each with a ruby in the centre. *Serpe*, a word taken from French, is often used in wills and inventories of the fifteenth century to denote a (serpentine) collar; cf. Orleans, 5021–4:

> Abowt hir nek also she ware
> A serpe the fasson to declare
> Hit wrought was fulle of broken balis/Of dise. . . .

Shaw (*Dresses and Decorations*, 2 vols., 1843, vol. ii, Fig. 40) reproduces a painting by Lucas van der Leyden of St Agnes, wearing a serpentine collar, with white flowers at intervals, set with jewels. For similar jewelled collars see *KQ*, 330–3; *CL*, 813f; Friedländer, *Van Eyck to Bruegel*, Figs. 91, 103, 105; and cf. *LGW*, 534; *Pilg.*, 690. Charles of Orleans himself had a collar set with fourteen rubies and sixty-two large pearls, ' environné de fleurs de geneste esmaillées de blanc et de noir ' (Evans, *Pattern*, i, 96).

536. balays of entaile. The strict sense of *entaile* is intaglio or incised work, as opposed to cameo or relief carving; however, *of entaile* here may mean simply ' carved, cut '. Cf. *RR*, 162, 1081; *TG*, 37n; *Churl and Bird*, 235 (' garnetes of entaile '); and see *MED*. The balas is ' a delicate rose-red variety of the spinel ruby ' (*OED*), highly valued in the Middle Ages as the stone of peace, security, and chastity (*Lapidaries*, pp. 29, 48, 73), and frequently mentioned in literature, e.g. *Rom.*, 19925; *KQ*, 319; *Eye and Heart*, 410; Orleans, 4982; *GL*, 1144; *CL*, 80. A long description of a *cercle*, with a large jewel set in the front, is given in *RR*, 1107–28.

538. yong and old. For this intensive formula see *CT*, II, 417, 820, V, 88, VII, 2161, etc. Cf. *Gen.*, 2831 (' Of yong and old and euery maner of age '), 6937 (' Bothe yong and old and euery maner of age ').

539. This expression seems to have been modelled on earlier formulas using *hevene* and *paradise*, e.g. *TC*, ii, 637 (' It was an heven upon hym for to see '); *Troy*, i, 1590 (' paradise '). Cf. *Gen.*, 2205: ' It was a world to here the sperys breke '.

540. This: ' thus '—a common spelling (it is habitual in Charles of Orleans). It may be from OE *þys, þis,* inst. of the demonstrative pronoun *þes;* or merely an alteration of *thus* (*OED*, s.v. *this, adv.*).

549. a-pace. Chaucer's phrase ' goon a pas ' means ' to walk at a foot-pace ', which may be the sense here, ' with measured step', as would be appropriate in the ceremonial of the court. However, the modern sense, ' quickly ', developed during the fifteenth century, and would fit well.

550. at al. This phrase began to assume its modern usage, with negatives (as here) and interrogatives only, after *c.* 1450: Chaucer uses the phrase as an intensive, but in a rather different way (e.g. *CT*, IV, 1222, VII, 170).

576–8. Perhaps an allusion to the proverb ' First come, first served ' (Tilley, *op. cit.*, p. 111).

582–707. The lines that follow mark a low ebb in fifteenth-century verse. The complaints are repetitive, imperfectly distinguished, monotonous, and imprecise, and the poet's attempt to impart a legal flavour to the style of the bills (see 325n) is ill-considered. Beyond this, it was an error of judgment for the poet to suppose that he could excite interest in nine separate and similar petitions of complaint summarily presented, especially when the complaints themselves have no more than general and typical significance in the scheme of the poem. The language, indeed, is so colourless that it would be charitable to assume that perhaps the complaints had once a topical and personal significance, which is now lost (see Stevens, *op. cit.*, pp. 212, 215).

583. *Sanz que jamais*: ' Without ever (giving occasion) '; see 587.

590. *Une sans chaungier*: ' One without changing '.

592. A difficult line. The versions of Tr and L are meaningless, and Thynne showed his usual skill in making some sense of an inferior copy text by emending *playn* to *payne*; Skeat paraphrases: ' Yet nothing like she (i.e. herself) deserved, since she took all the trouble '. However, A does not need emendation: *takith* means ' considers ' (as frequently), and *pleyne* ' fully ' (an unusual sense, but one for which there is evidence in *OED*, s.v. *plain*, adv. sign. 6; *plain*, a2. 1). Hence: ' She still considered that the reward she had had for her devotion was inadequate '.

593. Cf. Suffolk, B, XVI, 3f: ' And in no wyse I can not me restrayn/ But alle way styll to be faythfull and trewe '.

598. *Oncques puis lever*: ' I can (not) ever rise ' (i.e. succeed).

607. **ill.** See *FL*, 395n.

nov, ' now '; not an uncommon spelling (see *OED*).

608. **humble,** ' humbly ': trisyllabic. For the spelling see *OED*.

611–16. However angry or displeased she showed herself, she could not see the person she loved when she wanted to, and consequently she was reluctant to admit that her motto was ' Entirely yours '.

615. **and forsoth.** The reading of T makes good sense with a full stop after *ernest*.

627. *C'est sanz dire*: ' It goes without saying ' (i.e. my case speaks for itself).

633–7. She was by now impervious to misfortune, and neither joy nor grief affected her. Her devotion had gone unrewarded for so long that she had given up hope of any consolation, and was past caring.

634. **joy or smert.** Cf. *RR*, 2860, 3414; *Troy*, ii, 4057; *Fall*, i, 3450; Orleans, 2713.

639. **se.** An early use of the idiom (*OED*, s.v. 8b) where *see* means ' to ensure that something is done '; see Glossary. Lydgate uses the word in this sense, but always with *to* or an infinitive (e.g. *Troy*, i, 946, 2632, iii, 4833, 5056).

640. **she.** For this impersonal use (' one ') of the personal pronoun, compare *CT*, I, 964, II, 1090, V, 1053, 1088, etc.

645. *En dieu est*: ' In God is (my trust) '; see 655.

649–51. The main inspiration for this melancholy reflection is Charles of Orleans.

> As for my service spent Ʒus alle in vayne
> Rebuke and skorne is payment of my fee
> But pite is allas trouth may not rayne.
> (6052–4)

See also Suffolk, B, XVIII, 12–14. The idea, however, is not un-common; cf. Chaucer's *Lak of Stedfastnesse*, 15; Hoccleve, *Male Regle*, 281f.

For trowth somtyme was wont to take availe. Speght's revised edition of 1602 announces on its title page several new and attractive features, including ' Sentences and Prouerbes noted '; so, through the volume, we find in the margin little hands pointing magisterially to some particularly pithy saying (e.g. *CT*, I, 443). This line in *AL* is the only one, in either *FL* or *AL*, dignified in this manner. Urry in 1721 prints *AL* 665 in italics as another gnomic saying.

655f. This explicit recognition in the complaint of the significance of the motto is not usual (cf. 138, 208).

663. **it sat hir passyng neere**: ' it affected her very deeply, it grieved her sorely '. For this impersonal use of *sat* cf. Chaucer, ' sat him sore ', *TC*, iii, 240, iv, 231; *BD*, 1220.

665. This proverbial saying is quoted in John Ray's *English Proverbs* (1678), and also used in *Every Man in his Humour*, II, ii, 53. It is a variant, of which *AL* provides the first recorded instance, of the common proverb ' Need knows no law ' (e.g. *P.Pl.*, B, xx, 10; Skelton, *Colin Clout*, 864; cf. *CT*, I, 4026, ' nede has na peer '). See *Oxford Dictionary of English Proverbs* (1948), p. 446; Tilley, *op. cit.*, pp. 491, 493. The particular form adopted in *AL* is popular in *sententiae* of other kinds: ' But Fortune wil haue hir cours alwey ' (*Troy*, ii, 3307); ' Kynde woll have his cours ' (*Beryn*, 86); ' For loue will haue his course for eny thing ' (*Gen.*, 896).

666. **Sejour ensure**: ' Rest assured '. All other MSS and editions read *Soyes*, ' be ', but *sejour* is a possible corrupt form from OFr *sejourner*, ' rest, stay '.

668. Cf. Suffolk, B, XVI, 19f: ' " I trow," quod he, " thy labour ys in vayn ";/ And I answerd that I non othir knewe ' (cf. also *AL*, 67).

670. **humble**. See 608n.

674. Cf. *Gen.*, 431–4:

> A very goodly man, I you ensure,
> With good vesage, full metely of stature,
> His porte, his chere, and all his behavinge
> Full like a Ientilman in euery thyng.

Cf. also *AL*, 79, 192.

havyng suggests N influence, since, although Chaucer uses a verb *have* meaning ' behave ', the noun *havyng*, ' behaviour, demeanour ', was chiefly confined to Scotland, and even there examples in the singular are rare (*OED*).

675. **Bien monest**, ' Well-advised ': the more usual meaning of OFr *monester*, ' warn, admonish ' (Godefroy), fits less well.
   as ferre as I cowth feele. *Gen.*, 5431: ' as ferre as I canne fele '.

679. Cf. *CT*, V, 680: ' And in vertu sende thee continuaunce '.

680. Lady Loyalty speaks, turning to the fifth lady, the authoress, who has not yet presented her complaint. She is reluctant to do so and replies rather rudely (682, 690), but is eventually prevailed upon.

689. **hate**. A Northern form (of *hoten*, ' bid, order '), though Skeat suggests that it is due to confusion with the preterite *hatte*.

M

seynt Jame. St James (the Greater), the brother of St John the Evangelist. A legend arose in the seventh century that he had made an evangelising visit to Spain, and that after his death his body had been transferred there. His remains were supposed to lie at Compostella, in Galicia, where during the Middle Ages the relics of Santiago became one of the greatest of all Christian shrines and places of pilgrimage (see *CT*, I, 466). For the use of his name in oaths cf. *CT*, I, 4264, III, 312, 1443, VII, 355, etc.

691f. The sense of these lines would be improved if *ye* (691) were emended to *me* (cf. 22, 749), and the two lines given to Lady Loyalty.
  bi reason and bi skil. Cf. *CT*, IV, 1678, VII, 1809, 1869.

693. it sayde. The reading of A is quite clear: the authoress steps back from participant to narrator, and introduces her own bill which, like the others, was read by the secretary. The other MSS confuse the situation.

696. as seme ye. An example of the personal use of an impersonal verb, which arose from the substitution of the nom. for the dative. Skeat noted that *seem* was still used in Devon to mean ' think, suppose '.

697f. ' If you knew fully all the circumstances, I know that you would think so ' (i.e. that I could desire no more).

699f. Cf. *CT*, II, 229–31:

> Saveth my lyf, and beth noght recchelees
> To geten hire that hath my life in cure;
> For in this wo I may nat longe endure.

See also *TG*, 819.

707. desert deservith. These and other cognate forms were one of the favourite sources of *annominatio* or *paronomasia* in French verse.

713. both oon and al. Cf. *Troy*, iii, 951, iv, 6379; *Fall*, ix, 279.

714. in general, ' collectively '. They had been having audience one by one.

718. pitous for to here. A phrase common in Chaucer (*CT*, I, 2345; *HF*, 180, 189, etc.). Cf. 660; *FL*, 37n.

720–8. The postponed judgment is a frequent convention in poems involving an assembly or debate: it avoided commitment, preserved the poet's freedom, and prevented too great an irruption into reality. *PF* and *The Owl and the Nightingale* are well-known examples; see also *CN*, 272; *Eye and Heart*; *Parlement*, Suffolk, B, XX (a close parallel); Pisan, *Livre des Trois Jugements, Dit de Poissy*.
  parlement. The usual sense in ME, even as late as Lydgate, is simply ' talking, conversation ' (e.g. *Pilg.*, 3977, 9124, 10250), but it is evidently to be understood here in its more formal sense, a judicial assembly, to follow the preliminary hearing of complaints which has just been held. The same distinction, between *assembly* and *parliament*, seems to be made in *Isle of Ladies*, 1967–72.

735. furth withal. Taken here as limiting **toke:** ' And straightway each took the other by the sleeve, as if to leave '. Alternatively, a verb of motion could be understood in 735 (as often in ME, e.g. *CT*, V, 604; cf. 742, 755, *infra*); or a dash after **leve,** as if to symbolise in the narrative the interruption of the dream (unlikely).

736. water. Skeat suggests that the water was thrown in her face by her companions to wake her up; this seems rather drastic. Perhaps the spray from the fountain caught her face as her head nodded in sleep. The waking of the dreamer was often carefully worked into the narrative in medieval dream allegories. One of the neatest, and simplest, examples is *PF*, 693f, where it is the noise of the birds flying away that awakens the dreamer; elsewhere it is the sound of a bell (*BD*), the blast of a bugle (*Parl. of Thre Ages*), the noise of guns (Dunbar's *Golden Targe*), or, as in *AL*, the shock of water (Douglas's *Palice of Honour*, Skelton's *Bowge of Court*).

740. **this booke.** She seems to have forgotten that she is supposed to be telling her story orally (see 22–8).

743. The lady's story, which has occupied the greater part of the poem (29–742), and included the dream (78–735), ends here, and the knight or squire who originally accosted her (15) speaks. With the effusive self-congratulation of this conclusion should be contrasted the conventional modesty of the *FL* epilogue.

744. This recalls the pilgrims' comment on the *Knight's Tale*: ' a noble storie,/And worthy for to drawen to memorie ' (*CT*, I, 3111f).

747. **inly grete plesaunce.** The reading of T agrees with a known Lydgate idiom (see *FL*, 113n), besides improving the metre.

749. **me must wite.** See 22n.

752. **La semble.** This is the reading of the MS, and there seems little reason for substituting *L'asemble*, since *semble* is well attested in OFr, as well as *sembly* in ME. The custom of introducing the title of a poem in its concluding lines is common amongst fifteenth-century French poets, and Sir Richard Roos, in his translation of *La Belle Dame sans Merci*, leaves the title in French at the end of the poem (see Seaton, *op. cit.*, p. 96).

756. The transition from interlocutor to reader, if it is a transition (cf. the confusion in 740), is abrupt.

GLOSSARY

The Glossary records words which might in form or meaning present difficulty to the reader, though it does not aim to repeat what is already in the Notes. The cross-references ignore variation of *i/y*, and variants current in MnE. Grammatical variants are not glossed if they bear the same basic meaning as the head-word. † is attached to emended forms; n after a line-reference indicates that the note to that line should be referred to. Where a word occurs more than three times in each text, the first three examples are given (two from FL, one from AL), followed by etc. Where a word occurs more than three times in only one text, the first three examples from that text are followed by etc. AL is prefixed to references to *The Assembly of Ladies*; references without prefix are to *The Flower and the Leaf*.

a, an, *indef. art.* a, an, 6, 16, AL 4, etc.; the same, 59

abasshed, *past part.* afraid, over-awed, AL 120

abidyng, *n.* abode, dwelling, AL 264

accord, *n.* concord, harmony, 132

according, *pres. part.* agreeing, matching, 227; blending (with), 112

acertained, *past part.* made certain, apprised, 568

a(c)queyntaunce, Acqueyntaunce, *n.* acquaintance, AL 179, 233, 376, etc.; (*personified*) Friend-ship, AL 269

aferd, *past part.* afraid, AL 332

affiaunce, *n.* trust, AL 655

affray, *n.* quarrel, tumult, storm, 374

afore, *adv.* before, AL 210, 412, 692; in advance, before (them), AL 252

aforne, *prep.* before, leading up to, AL 697

after, aftir, aftyr, *prep.* after, 24, 194, 219, etc.; according to,

267, 552, AL 9, 11, 33, etc.; in pursuance of, 425; *adv.* AL 459, 545, 643, etc.; *conj.* AL 200

agayne, ageyn(e), *see* **ayen**

Agnus castus, *n.* agnus castus, ' tree of Chastity ', 160n, 173, 475

agone, *past part.* gone, AL 393

aire, *n.* air, scent, 6, 79

aleys, *n. pl.* alleys, paths, AL 10

alway, alwey(s), *adv.* always, ever, 478, 511, AL 364, 419, 510, etc.

amased, *past part.* stunned, bewildered, AL 739

among, *adv.* at times; **ever among,** every now and then, AL 300

amyddis, *adv.* in the middle, AL 35

an, *see* **a**

and, *conj.* if, 528, AL 157, 697

annoy, *n.* trouble, suffering, 389

anon(e), *adv.* at once, forthwith (*often much weakened*), 293, 346, AL 22, etc.; **anon right,** immediately, 397, 402; **right**

anon, AL 37; **anon(e) withal,** straightway, AL 560, 579

apayde, apayed, *past part.* satisfied, pleased, AL 208, 612

appaired, *past part.* impaired, spoilt, withered, 553

apparaile, *n.* ornament, AL 476

appese, *v.* mitigate, AL 671

arbere, *see* **herber**

armes, *n. pl.* arms; coat of arms, 213; **men of armes,** warriors, 196; **kings of armes,** chief heralds, 220

arraied, (a)raied, arrayed, *past part.* arrayed, equipped, decked out, 233, 262, 426, AL 205

array, aray, *n.* array, attire, 26, 139, AL 232, etc.; state, condition, 395

as, *conj., adv., rel. pron.* as, 17, 20, AL 5, etc.; as if, 101, 143, 197, AL 735; like, 65; such as, 148, 337; as far as, AL 615; (*pleonastic*) 241, 355n, AL 286, 359, 619; **as by,** according to, to judge by, 416; **as for,** with regard to, 117, 118, 533; **as in,** judging by, AL 674; **as of,** in respect of, 76; as for, AL 726; **as many as,** however many, AL 121n; **so as,** as far as, 205, AL 485, 525; in the same way as, 330, 528

aspy, *v.* spy, see, 108; **aspied,** *past part.* AL 193

assaile, *v.* assail, 366; provoke, irk, AL 41

assay, *v.* try, 452, AL 433

assent, *n.* assent; **bi on(e) assent,** with one accord, by common consent, AL 30, 730

assyse, *n.* order, position; **of assyse,** in their turn, in the same fashion, AL 531

astate, *n.* state, nobility, AL 97, 516, 540

astonied, *past part.* astonished, 102

Attemperaunce, *n.* (*personified*) Temperance, AL 508

attendaunce, *n.* attendance, wait, AL 388

attones, *adv.* at once, at the same time, AL 546

availe, *n.* avail; **take availe,** prevail, AL 649

avaunce, *v.* (*trans.*) advance, promote, 578; (*refl.*) get on, prosper, AL 180

avauntage, *n.* advantage, AL 44

aventure, *n.* fortune, 460; **at aventure,** by chance, AL 260

avise, advise, *n.* advice, AL 189; sense, consideration, AL 559; **be oon avise,** of one opinion, AL 379; **be myn advise,** in my opinion, take my advice, 331; **take . . . avise . . . of,** take counsel with, consult with, AL 565f

avise, *v.* (*trans.*) consider, look over, 187; (*refl.*) discern, determine, AL 88

avisement, *n.* consideration; **toke goode avisement,** considered carefully, AL 709

Avisenesse, *n.* (*personified*) Prudent Consideration, AL 343

awaiting, awaityng, *pres. part.* waiting, in attendance, 252, 382, 535; watching, taking a look, AL 300

aye, *adv.* ever, 487, 551, 554

ayen, *prep.* against; **ayen the sonne,** to greet the sun, 34

ayen, agayne, ageyn(e), *adv.* again, AL 392, 414, 421, etc.; in reply, 419, 466, 572, AL 16, 19, 94, etc.; yet again, 105n

ayenst, *prep.* against, contrary to, 291, AL 586

bad(de), *see* **bid**

balays, *n.* balas, balas ruby, AL 536n

banere, *n.* banner, 211

bare, *adj.* bare, 338

bare, *see* **bere**

bargaret, *n.* pastoral song, 348n

bayne, *n.* bath, AL 464

be, bien, *v.* to be, 75, 88, AL 80, etc.; **be,** *pres. subj. sg.* 528, AL 101, 252, 294, etc.; *pres. pl.* 10, 465, 468, etc., AL 24; **bien,** *pres. pl.* AL 110, 121, 247, etc.; **ben,** AL 283, **beene,** 535; **be,** *imper.* AL 120; **be,** *past part.* 44, 308, 314, AL 95, **ben,** 197, **bene,** 390, **ybe,** 375, **bien,** AL 591, 640, 701; **beyng,** *pres. part.* AL 556

be, *see* **by**

Bealchiere, *n.* (*personified*) Good Cheer, AL 322

behielde, *pret.* beheld, AL 191

behight, *pret. as pres.* promise, assure, 396

behynd(e), *adv.* behind, AL 36; backward, remiss, AL 326; **forgete behynd,** forgotten, left out, AL 113

belongyng, *pres. part.* befitting, suitable, AL 676

ben(e), *see* **be**

benched, *past part.* provided with benches of turf, 50

benedicite, *interj.* bless ye (the Lord)! AL 148

bere, beare, *v.* bear; *pres.* 479, 512, 517, AL 103, 115, 404; **bereth,** *pres. 3 sg.* 474; **bare, bere,** *pret.* 213†, 223, 254, etc.; **bore,** *past part.* 507; **bearing, beryng,** *pres. part.* 173, AL 493, 582

berel, *n.* beryl, AL 455n

beseene, *past part.* provided, adorned, 169

besprad, *pret.* covered, 266

bete, *past part.* embroidered, 212n

bi, *see* **by**

bid, *v.* to bid, AL 321; **bad(de),** *pret. sg.* bade, 460n, AL 368; commanded, AL 111; **bode,** *past part.* commanded, AL 555

bien, *see* **be**

bigone, *past part.* provided; **wel bigone,** well situated, fortunate, 186n

bil(le), *n.* bill, petition, statement of complaint, AL 325, 345, 583, etc.; **billes, billis,** *pl.* AL 542, 553, 557, etc.

blew(e), bliew, *adj.* blue, AL 83, 116, 206, etc.

bloody, *adj.* warlike, fearsome, 275

bode, *see* **bid**

boistously, *adv.* rudely, roughly; in homely, unpolished fashion, 595

bone, *n.* boon, request, petition, AL 621

Boole, *n.* Bull (the sign Taurus), 3

boose, *n.* boss, round metal stud or knob, 246n

bord, *n.* board, 59

bore, *see* **bere**

bote, *n.* healing, relief, 83

bouȝt, *past part.* bought, 203

brake, *pret.* broke, 284; **brake of,** broke off, ceased, 300; **broken,** *past part.* AL 586

brast, *pret.* burst, broke, 490n

bre(a)de, *n.* breadth, 43, 305

brenning, *pres. part. as adj.* burning, 408

brid, *n.* bird, 94; **birds,** *pl.* 127; **briddes, birds,** *gen. pl.* 37, 119

brode, broad, *adj.* broad, 33, 211, 215

broke, *v.* use, profit by, AL 259n

busily, *adv.* intently, assiduously, eagerly, 41, 106, AL 302

busines, busynesse, *n.* business, occupation, 537; work, tasks, AL 31, 184

busy, *adj.* industrious, AL 138

but, *conj.* but (*often with little meaning*), 18, 70, AL 26, etc.; *prep., adv.* (*after neg.*) otherwise than, any more than, except, 190, 538, 562, AL 84, 114; *adv.* only, AL 40, 144, 150, etc.

by, be, bi, *prep.* by, by means of, according to, 58, 96, AL 10, etc.; near, beside, 105, 110, 431; with, AL 496; **by and by,** in succession, in order, one by one, AL 410, 717; one after another, side by side, 59n, 145; precisely, to the letter, AL 87n; bit by bit, in detail, AL 485; *adv.* by, past, 455, 465, AL 247; near by, 134, 304

cam, *see* **come**

can, *v.* can, 205, 393, AL 122, etc.; can say, AL 152, 294; **coud, cowde, couth(e), cowth,** *pret.* could, 39, 42, AL 70, etc. (*shading off to* knew how *in* 461, 585)

case, cace, *n.* case, affair, matter (*often very loosely*), AL 429, 594, 609, etc.; incident, 451; point, AL 145; suit, AL 359; circumstance, plight, AL 461; **cace,** *pl.* events, AL 75

cassidony, *n.* chalcedony, AL 478n

cedule, *n.* written statement, petition, AL 345

cercle, *n.* circlet, diadem, AL 536

certaine, certayne, certeyne, sertayne, *adj.* certain, particular, 16; *adv.* certainly, indeed, 504, AL 55, 172, 243, etc.; **in, for certayne** etc., for certain, certainly, indeed, AL 102, 135, 298, etc.

certeynte, *n.* truth, AL 751; **in certeynte,** in truth, indeed, AL 17

chaire, *n.* chariot, 1

chap(e)let, *n.* wreath of flowers or leaves for head, garland, 154, 236, 260, etc.; *pl.* 159, 161, 209, etc.

chayer, *n.* throne, AL 476

chere, cheare, chiere, *n.* face, look, mien, AL 662; disposition, demeanour, behaviour, 420, AL 138; **make chere,** give good cheer, comfort, 385

cherisshed, *past part.* loved, held dear, AL 135

child, *n.* young man, 259

cle(a)ne, *adv.* entirely, 292, 372; neatly, AL 49

closed, closid, *pret.* enclosed, AL 52, 230; *past part.* 55

coast, *n.* region, 76

cold, *adj.* cool, 122, 443

coler, *n.* collar, AL 526; **colers,** colors, *pl.* 147, 215

com(e), *v. inf., pres.* come, 207, AL 108, 116, 147, etc.; **com of,** *imp.* come on, be quick, AL 244n; **com(e), cam(e),** *pret.* 136, 183, AL 47, etc.; **com(en),** *past part.* AL 110, 201, 287; **com(m)-ing, comyng,** *pres. part.* 196, 383, AL 73, 297, 347, etc.; to come, AL 636; **of your comyng,** when you come, AL 378; **in your comyng,** to get here, to come, AL 727

combraunce, *n.* burden, bother, AL 430

comfort, *n.* consolation, AL 636, 671; contentment, AL 604; encouragement, AL 187

compas, compace, *n.* circuit; **in, of compas,** all around, 54, 343, AL 53; **in maner of compace,** in circular formation, 163

complayne, compleyne, *v.* complain, make (formal) complaint, AL 466, 590, 652; **compleyn-eng,** *pres. part.* AL 584, 603

compleynt, *n.* formal complaint, AL 599, 628

contenaunce, Co(u)ntenaunce, *n.* face, looks, AL 82; (*personified*) Self-control, Self-possession, AL 177, 277, 295, etc. (*cf. MnE* out of countenance, *etc.*)

contenuaunce, *n.* continuance, AL 679

contraire, *adj.* contrary, disagreeable, 82

contre, *n.* country, AL 482; place, AL 371

convenient, *adj.* suitable (to my mood), congenial, 119

corage, *n.* disposition, impetuosity, AL 41

corsere, *n.* courser, charger, 264

cost, *n.* expense, 215; harm, AL 419

couchyd, *past part.*, set, studded, AL 529

coud, *see* **can**

counsaile, *n.* advice, AL 189; council, AL 109, 566

counseil(e), *v.* advise, AL 250, 372

Countenaunce, *see* **contenaunce**

cours, *n.* course; **have his cours**, take its course, have its way, AL 665

couth(e), cowde, cowth, *see* **can**

craftily, craftely, *adv.* skilfully, 339, AL 49

crosse, *adj.* crossing, intersecting, AL 10

crown(e), *n.* crown, 172, 380; wreath, 508; *pl.* heraldic crowns, 223; garlands, 249

cunningly, *adv.* skilfully, 57

cure, *n.* care, pains, 61; charge, care, AL 699

curiously, *adv.* skilfully, intricately, AL 478

curteys, *adj.* courteous, AL 387; **curteisly**, *adv.* AL 94

dare, *v.* dare, AL 353, 403, 517; need, AL 256n; **darst**, *pres. 2 sg.* 592; **durst**, *pret.* AL 485; **if (that) I durst**, if I might be so bold as to . . . 463, 544

debonaire, *adj.* courteous, 501

de(e)de, *adj.* dead, 11, 481

degre(e), *n.* rank, status, 552, AL 99, 272, 404; *pl.* 267

dele, *n.* part, bit; **every dele**, everything, AL 703; **right through**, AL 227

deme, *v.* deem, suppose, 81; **demed**, *pret.* 124; **demed wel**, judged for certain, concluded, 381

demure, *adj.* serious, sober, composed, 459, AL 82

departed, *pret.* departed, AL 393; *past part.* split, AL 275; rent, 193

desert, *n.* deserving, merit, worth, AL 587, 635, 707

devise, devyse, *v.* devise, plan, contrive, AL 51, 122; describe, relate, 97, AL 525; tell, imagine, AL 70; say, suggest, AL 333; **devised**, *past part.* planned, designed, AL 159

deyd, *pret.* died, AL 458

did(e), *see* **do**

dight, *past part.* arrayed, decorated, 254

dints, *n. pl.* blows, strokes, 290

disceyved, *past part.* deceived, AL 464

discryve, *v.* describe, AL 512

disease, *n.* grief, sorrow, 21; discomfort, distress, 377

disguising, *n.* strange mode of dress, 276n

disloged, *past part.* displaced, excluded, AL 62

displesaunce, *n.* distress, AL 661

disport, *n.* amusement, AL 164

do, doo, *v.* to do, perform, execute, AL 138, 174, 189, etc.; **do ease**, comfort, 392; **have to do**, have dealings, AL 509; **doth**, *pres. 3 sg.* AL 6; **do(e), doo, pres. pl. and subj.** 542, 572, AL 552, 561, 748; *imper.* cause, enable, AL 155; *pres. subj. sg.* give, AL 293; **did(e)**, *pret.* 62, 230, AL 41, etc.; sufficed, looked, 332; **do, don(e)**, *past part.* 61, 448, AL 149, etc.; finished, AL 2, 31, 139, etc.

do(u)ghter, *n.* daughter, 462, 467, 500, etc.

dome, *n.* judgment; **to my dome**, in my opinion, 306

don, *adv.* down, AL 523

don(e), doo, *see* **do**

Douseperis, *n. pl.,* the Twelve Peers, 516n

dou(b)t, *n.* doubt; **out of dout,** without doubt, doubtless, 73, 146

dowte, *v. refl.* fear, AL 246

dread, drede, *n.* fear, 592; doubt, 152

dresse, *v.* to dress (*refl.*), AL 381; *pres.* go, proceed, AL 215; **dressid, drest,** *pret.* (*refl.*) dressed, AL 253; went, advanced, 456; **dressed,** *past part.* arrayed, made, bedecked, 249, AL 206

dropping, *pres. part. as adj.* dripping, soaked, 371

drow, drew, *pret.* drew, 284, 588

durst, *see* **dare**

ech(e), iche, yche, *adj.* each, 400, AL 33, 404, 545, etc.; **eche a,** every, AL 454

ech(e)on(e), *pron.* each one, 142, 184, AL 288, etc.

eet, *pret.* ate, 90

eglentere, eglatere, *n.* eglantine, sweet-briar, 56, 80, 112

eie, *n.* eye, 85, 323

eke, *adv.* also, 37, 123, 162, etc.

ellis, *adv.* else, AL 326

embrouded, enbrowdid, *past part.* embroidered, 330, AL 85

encombraunce, *n.* burden, bother, AL 653, 746

endite, *v.* write, AL 307

enemayle, *n.* enamel, AL 534

ensure, *v.* assure, 60, 287, 457, AL 52, 199, 495, etc.

entaile, *n.* carving; **of entaile,** of engraved design, ornamented with incised or intaglio work, AL 536n

entent(e), intent, *n.* purpose, 118, 425, AL 472, 550, 568, etc.;

plan, AL 33; mind, consideration, AL 711

entuned, *past part.* kept in tune, harmonising, 180

environ, *adv.* round about, AL 53

environing, *pres. part.* surrounding, 321n

ernest, *n.* earnest; **in (verray) ernest,** in truth, truly, AL 537, 614

espide, *past part.* seen, 75

est, *n.* east, AL 39

even, *adv.* right (by), 105, 110, 134, etc.

evenly, *adv.* equally, regularly, 278n

everiche, *pron.* each one, 151, 331, AL 9, 117, 397

everichon(e), everychon(e), *pron.* every one, without exception, 168, 227, AL 73, etc.

exemplaire, *n.* model, pattern, 502

ey, *interj.* oh!, AL 148

fable, *n.* fictitious story; false statement, AL 685

facion, fassion, *n.* fashion, workmanship, AL 305, 522

faine, fayne, *adj.* glad, eager, 378; *adv.* gladly; **wo(u)ld . . . faine,** would be glad to, 464, AL 100, 173, 242, etc.; *superl.* **wold faynest,** AL 613

fair(e), fayre, feyre, *adj.* fair, fine, gracious, 93, 304, AL 48, etc.; *adv.* finely, beautifully, 7, 426

falle, *v.* befall, come, AL 6; **fil,** *pret.* fell, AL 77; came, AL 16

fanes, *n. pl.* vanes, weathercocks, AL 161

fantasye, *n.* fancy, inclination, AL 597; *pl.* AL 11†

fare, *v.* go, 341, 401

fassion, *see* **facion**

fast, *adv.* quickly, 199, 410, 587; right, close, 304; firmly, AL 276

feare, feere, *see* **fe(e)re**

feintise, *n.* deceit, evasion, 549

felawship, felawshyp, *n.* company, band of friends, AL 30, 73, 216, etc.; friendship, AL 136

fe(e)le, *v.* feel, AL 125; perceive, AL 675; **felt,** *pret.* 374, AL 661; smelt, 79; *past part.* 311; smelt, 84

fele, *adj.* many, 5

fer(re), *adv.* far, 191, AL 36, 141, 213, etc.; **ferther,** *comp.* farther, 116

fe(e)re, feare, *n.* company; **in fere,** together (with them), completely, as well, 57, 351, AL 407, etc.

fere, *n.* fear, 487

ferforth, *adv.* far, AL 273; forward, well advanced, AL 37; exactly, just, AL 309n

ferther, *see* **fer(re)**

feyneng, *n.* pretence, evasion; **without(e) feyneng,** without hesitation, frankly, AL 336, 340

feyre, *see* **faire**

figured, *past part. as adj.* formed, fashioned, 166

fil, *see* **falle**

fle, *v.* fly, 444

flit, *v.* shift, waver, vary, 489

fonde, *see* **fynde**

for(e), *conj.* for, because, 19, 21, AL 184, etc.; **for bicause,** because, 473, AL 26; **for to,** (in order) to, 6, 37, AL 27, etc.; *prep.* for, because of, for the sake of, etc., 172, 198, AL 39, etc.; on behalf of, AL 392; **for any thing,** on all accounts, by all means, 417

forgete, *past part.* forgotten, AL 113, 337

forgrowen, *past part.* overgrown, 45n

forshronke, *past part.* shrunk up, shrivelled up, 358

forsoth, *adv.,* verily, indeed, AL 21, 157, 269, etc.

forth, furth, *adv.* forth, away, out, onward, 295, 303, AL 40, etc.; immediately after, then, 585; further, AL 511; **furth, forth withal,** forthwith, straightway, AL 193, 643, 735

forthright, *adv.* straight, directly, 439

for-weryed, *past part.* exhausted, completely worn out, AL 45

fres(s)h, *adj.* fresh, bright, refreshing, 30, 52, 109, etc., AL 2; spirited, 264; new, untarnished, AL 161; *superl.* finest, AL 535

freshly, *adv.* freshly, newly, 51; briskly, vigorously, 274

fret, *n.* jewelled gold hair-net, caul, 152

fro(m), *prep.* from, 90, 195, AL 183, etc.; away from, apart from, 32; *adv.* **to and fro,** 68, AL 43, 58

froward, *adj.* adverse, unpleasant, 82

ful(l), *adv.* very, quite, 17, 41, AL 36, etc.

furred, *past part.* trimmed with fur, 243, AL 305

furth, *see* **forth**

further, *adj.* more forward, nearer, 110n

fynde, *v.* find, AL 160, 177, 327, etc.; **fonde,** *pret.* found, AL 232, 606

gadred, *past part.* gathered, AL 3; **gadering,** *pres. part.* gathering, 411

galaries, *n. pl.* galleries, porticoes, AL 165n

gan, *pret.* began (*shading off to auxiliary usage*), 438, 446, 586, AL 739; did (*auxiliary to form pret.*), 27, 108, 444, AL 501

garnishing, *n.* ornamentation, decoration, 143

gate, ya(a)te, *n.* gate, AL 176, 274, 281, etc.

gate, *pret.* got, AL 44

geare, *n.* gear, equipment, 226; apparel, 26

gentillesse, gentilnesse, *n.* courtesy, AL 186, 342

gent(i)ly, *adv.* courteously, AL 282, 577

gesse, *v.* guess, suppose, AL 212; conceive, 525

glad, *adj.* glad, pleased, 14, 15, 570, AL 127; cheerful, 301, AL 138; gay, 35

goddes(se), *n.* goddess, 472, 534

good(e), gode, *adj.* good, 10, 77, AL 39, etc.; *as n.* (*as a form of address*) good lady, AL 346, 689

good(e)ly, *adj.* comely, pleasant, pretty, fine, 135, 333, AL 163, etc.; polite, AL 367, 496n; *superl.* finest, AL 452; *adv.* rightly, reasonably, decorously, 299; duly, dutifully, AL 549; *superl.* most elegantly, AL 384

governaunce, *n.* control; management, conduct, (of the fight), 286; discreet, well-controlled behaviour, AL 134; arrangement, AL 235

grace, *n.* grace, favour, AL 608, 658; honour, distinction, 557

gramercy, *interj.* many thanks, 462

graven, *past part.* engraved, AL 456, 467

gray, *n.* grey fur, AL 305

gre, *v. refl.* agree, consent, AL 225n

gret(e), great, *adj.* great, 29, 113, AL 26, etc.; many, AL 395; *adv.* greatly, considerably, AL 46

gretely, greatly, *adv.* very much, 22, 44, 441, AL 246

gre(e)vance, *n.* grievance, complaint, AL 659; distress, hardship, 311, 560

greves, *n. pl.* bushes, thickets, 367

grevously, *adv.* grievously; **toke grevously,** took to heart, AL 633

ground(e), *n.* ground, 5, 245, AL 477; place, spot, 126

ground, *past part.* ground, whetted, 258

guiding, *n.* office, duty, 230

guyse, *n.* manner, fashion, AL 9, 381, 603

gwerdoned, *past part.* rewarded, AL 591

han, *pres. pl.* have, 478, AL 688

happe, *v.* (*used both personally and impersonally*) happen, AL 178, 682; **happed,** *pret.* 354, 456, AL 29; *past part.* (*passive construction*) circumstanced, befallen, 16

hardily, *adv.* certainly, assuredly, 234

hardy, *adj.* bold, resolute, 480

hardynesse, *n.* boldness, courage, AL 187

harneis, *n.* gear, accoutrements, trappings, 218, 226, 235, etc.

hate, *v. pres. sg.* bid, order, AL 689; **hight,** *pret.* (*in pres. passive sense*) is called, AL 133, 169, 318, etc.

havyng, *n.* behaviour, demeanour, AL 674n

hauke, *v.* hawk, hunt with hawk, 538

hearb(e), *n.* plant, 477; shoot, 13; *pl.* herbs, 407

heavenly, *adv.* exquisitely, 166

hegge, *n.* hedge, 54, 66, 402; *pl.* 367

hem, *see* they

hensh-men, *n. pl.* squires or pages on horseback, 252n

her, *see* she, they

herauds, *n. pl.* heralds, 232

herbegyer, herbergier, *n.* lodgings-warden, AL 268, 389

herber(e), arbere, *n.* arbour, bower, shady retreat, 49n, 55, 64, etc., AL 48

here, *n.* hair, 332; **haires,** *pl.* 260

hertily, *adv.* heartily, earnestly, AL 285, 292, 316, etc.

hew(e), *n.* hue, colour, 30, 52, 317, AL 65

hie, *v.* to hurry, hasten, 586; *imp.* (*refl.*) AL 244

hie, hye, high, *adj.* high, 1, AL 160, 272; exalted, AL 121; **on hye,** above, on top, 222; *adv.* richly, gaudily, AL 81

hield(e), *see* **hold**

hight, *see* **hate**

hir, *see* **she, they**

hold, *v.* hold; judge, think, AL 287; **hield,** *pret. sg.* held, AL 499; **hielde,** *pret. pl.* considered, AL 733; **holde,** *past part.* held, AL 721

hole, *adj.* whole, AL 340

hond, hand(e), *n.* hand, 174, 303, 326, etc.; AL 499; **in hond,** by the hand, 334; **of ther hond,** in deeds of valour, 482n; **honds,** *pl.* 270

hong, *v.* hang, 245

hors(e), *n.* horse, 218, 226, 237, etc.; **horse,** *gen. sg.* 280; **horse,** *pl.* 201, 274†, 293, etc.

humble, *adv.* humbly, AL 608n, 670

hyt, *pron.* it, AL 521, 525

iche, *see* **ech**

ill, *adj.* ill, wretched, 395; badly off, unhappy, AL 607; *adv.* ill, badly, AL 612

inly, *adv.* inwardly, deeply, 113, AL 686; truly, AL 515, 747

intent, *see* **entent**

iwis, *adv.* certainly, truly, AL 283

jape, *n.* jest, AL 348, 349

Jhesu, *n.* Jesus, AL 294

journay, journey, *n.* journey, AL 214, 220

joyning, *pres. part.* adjoining, 92

just(e)s, *n. pl.* jousts, 282, 288, 403n

justing, *n.* jousting, 292

kene, *adj.* keen, sharp, 258, 556; bold, brave, 271n

knowen, *pres. 2 pl.* know, AL 719

knowlache, knowlachyng, *n.* knowledge; **have knowlache, -yng,** know, get to know, hear, AL 235, 630, 684

konnyng, *n.* knowledge, skill, AL 513

lade, *past part.* laden, covered, 33, 305

laft, *see* **left**

langage, *n.* language, style, 595

large, *adj.* large, wide, 201, 245, 266; open, frank, AL 153; *comp.* larger, AL 552

Largesse, *n.* (*personified*) Liberality, Generosity, AL 318

lasse, *see* **litel**

last, *adj.* last, AL 217; (*as n.*) **at the last,** at last, eventually, presently, 43, 94, 108, etc., AL 220

late, *see* **lete**

laud, *n.* praise, honour, 522

laurer, laurey, *n.* laurel, 109, 158, 249, etc.

left, laft, *pret.* left, AL 441; (*in passive sense*) was left, remained, 364, AL 190; *past part.* left (off), 292

lenger, *comp. adj.* longer, 423; *comp. adv.* longer, 582

lere, *v.* learn, 229n

lesse, *see* **litel**

lesyng, *n.* falsehood; **without lesyng,** truly, AL 263

lete, late, *v.* let, AL 25, 222, 570; **late se,** let me see, AL 23, 681

lete, *v.* refrain, spare, 215

leve, *n.* leave, 586, AL 290

licence, *n.* permission (to go), AL 200

lief, *adj.* dear, desirable, AL 694

lif(e), live, *n.* life, 87, 131, 182, AL 150, 514; **lives,** *pl.* 490n

lightly, *adv.* quickly, deftly, 281

like, lyke, *adj.* like, similar, 53, 133, AL 231, etc.; *adv.* **like as,** in such a way as, (in the same way) as, AL 104, 527, 632, etc.

liked, *pret.* was pleased, satisfied (*pers.*), AL 673; *past part.* pleased (*impers.*), 494

list, lust, *v.* wish, desire (*pers.*), 204, 590, AL 354; **yow list** (*impers.*), it pleases you, AL 291, 424; **list,** *pret.* wished, chose (*pers.*), 67; **him list** (*impers.*), it pleased him, 90

lite(l), lit(t)le, *adj.* little, 43, 190, AL 25, etc.; *adv.* 594, AL 214; **lesse, lasse,** *comp. adj. as n.* AL 214, 439 (*see* more)

lith, *pres. 3 sg.* lies, hangs, AL 21

live, *see* life

live, *v.* live, AL 672; **al hir dayes livyng,** all the days of her life, AL 640

loggyng, *n.* lodging, AL 390

Loiaulte, *n.* (*personified*) Loyalty, Faithfulness, AL 98†

lond, *n.* land, AL 157

long, *v.* to belong, (ap)pertain, 427; **longith,** *pres. 3 sg.* AL 266; **longged,** *pret.* AL 518; **longing,** *pres. part.* 437, 503

loth, *adj.* reluctant, AL 664

lough, *pret.* laughed, AL 279

lust, *see* list

lustily, lustely, *adv.* lustily, joyfully, 136, 176, 430

lusty, *adj.* joyful, 324; vigorous, 553

Male Bouch, *n.* (*personified*) Wicked Tongue, Slander, 580

maner(e), *n.* manner, kind (of), 143, 170, AL 89, etc.; way, fashion, 39, 419, AL 206, etc.; form, 163; bearing, behaviour, AL 137, 270

manerly, *adv.* properly, 230

many, *adj.* many, 6, 145, AL 65, etc.; **many one, oon,** many a one, 225, 336, AL 14, 456

manyfold, manifold, *adj. as n.* manifold; **by manyfold, many fold, manifold,** by far, 96, 120, 169

marchal, *n.* marshal, AL 322n

margarites, *n. pl.* marguerites, daisies, AL 57

margoleyne, *n.* marjoram, AL 56

marshall, *adj.* martial, 523

mase, *n.* maze, AL 17, 32

mased, *past part.* bewildered, perplexed, AL 38

matere, matier(e), *n.* matter, business, affair, 453, AL 28, 588, 650; suit, petition, AL 117, 340, 409, etc.; *pl.* suits, AL 324, 328, 444, etc.

maystresse, *n.* mistress, AL 445

meat, *n.* food, 121

mede, *n.* meadow, 9, 184, 279, etc.; *pl.* 538

mede, *n.* reward, AL 293

medill, medle, *n.* medlar, 86, 442

medle, *v. refl.* meddle, AL 154

merry, *adj.* sweet, pleasant, 99

mervaile, *v.* marvel (at), 22; **marveled,** *pret.* 441

mervaile, *n.* marvel; **I have mervaile,** I marvel, AL 234; **had mervaile,** marvelled, AL 648

mervelously, *adv.* marvellously, 156

mesure, *n.* measure; **by mesure,** according to a set pattern, 58; soberly, AL 81

metely, *adj.* moderate; **metely of stature,** of well-proportioned medium height, AL 79

mid, *n.* middle; **in mid,** in the middle of, 164, 342

middes, myddes, *n.* midst, 184, 279, AL 55

might, *n.* might, power, 138; utmost, 436

mightily, *adv.* strongly, assuredly, 518

mo(o), *adj.* more, (*often as n.*) others, 220, 273, AL 60, 84, 143, etc.

moche, *adj.* (*often as n.*) *and adv.* much, AL 226, 338, 417, etc.

more, *adj.* (*often as n.*) more, 20, 204, AL 118, etc.; **more and lasse,** great and small, one and all, AL 439; *adv.* more, 97, 119, AL 251, etc.; furthermore, AL 111, 461

musike, *n.* music, tuneful harmony, 132

must, *pret. as pres.* must, 583, AL 116, 145, 422; (*impersonal use with dat.*) AL 22n, 74, 334, etc.; *pret. subj.* might, 461n

mys (of), *v.* miss, AL 129; lack, AL 358

nad(e), *pret.* had not, 21, 370

nas, *pret.* was not, 19

nat, *adv.* not, AL 13, 62, 70, etc.

nay, *adv.* no, AL 349; *n.* denial; **it (hyt, this) is (ys) no nay,** there is no denying it, AL 306, 351, 521

ne, *adv.* not, nor, 18, 19, AL 272, etc.

ne m'oublie-mies, *n. pl.* forget-me-nots, AL 61

nede, *adv.* needs, of necessity, AL 74

nedil, *n.* needle, AL 487

nedith, *v. impers.* is necessary, AL 243, 413

neede, *n.* necessity, AL 665

ne(e)re, *adv.* near, AL 204, 484; nearly, deeply, AL 663

new(e), niewe, *adj.* new, fresh, 8, 33, 50, etc., AL 69; (*as n.*) new clothes, AL 259; **of new,** anew, afresh, 319; *adv.* **newe and newe,** ever afresh, continually, AL 68

nie, nigh, nygh, *adv.* nigh, nearly, 360, 588, AL 113

nis, *pres. 3 sg.* is not, 555

nombre, *n.* number, AL 6, 504

nombre, *v.* count, AL 395

nones, *n.* nonce; **for the nones,** for the purpose, occasion, 198n

not, *v.* know not, 354

notable, *adj.* remarkable, renowned, 513

nothing, nothyng, *n.* nothing, 374, 427, AL 550, 694; **for nothyng,** not for anything, on no account, AL 217; *adv.* not at all, in no way, in no degree, 229n, 234, AL 18, 153, 495, etc.

o, *see* one

observaunce, *n.* duty, homage, 576

occupacion, *n.* function, 565

of, *prep.* of, 1, 4, AL 1, etc.; about, concerning, 204, 320, AL 195, etc.; because of, 14, 15; from, 80, 312, 532; as regards, 168; at, 22, 441; by, 126; for, 420, AL 186, 293; out of, for, AL 342, 457, 705; caused by, 408; during, 40, 448, AL 703

of, *adv.* off, 191, 292, 300, AL 244

officer, *n.* court official, AL 261

one, on, oon, o(o), *adj. and pron.* one, 70, 74, AL 15, etc.; a single, 370, AL 162, 507; the same, AL 634; unbroken, a single whole, AL 67; **the on,** the first, 253†; **one and one,** one after another, in rows, 144; **by oon and oon,** one by one, AL 368, 543

ones, *adv.* once, 84

open, *adj.* definite, explicit, AL 723

opyn, *v.* open; broach, make known, AL 409; **opened,** *pret.* opened, AL 281, 491

or, *conj.* ere, before, 28, 125, AL 110

ordynaunce, *n.* arrangement; organisation, AL 267; orderly

patterns, AL 57; regulation, decree, AL 575; order, array, AL 500

orient, oryent, *adj.* precious, of supreme excellence, lustrous, 148n, AL 528

other, *adj.* other, 121, 226, AL 31, etc.; the other, AL 596; a different, AL 33; *pron.* the other, AL 734; others, AL 38, 143; else, AL 67

ought, *n.* anything, 571

out(e), *adv.* out, 34, 195, AL 34, 493; **out of,** 12, 134, 206, etc., AL 742; without, 73, 146; deprived of, lacking, AL 607

overlaid, *past part.* oppressed, 83

oversprad, overspredde, *past part.* covered, 343, AL 471

pace, pase, *n.* pace, movement, 165; **a great pace,** at a great pace, 449; **a soft and esy pase,** at a gentle, easy pace, AL 219

pained, *pret.* exerted, 447

paitrell, *n.* poitril, breast-piece of horse's harness, 246

paleys, *n.* palace, AL 721

palfray, *n.* palfrey (a saddle-horse for ordinary riding, especially for ladies), 425

parde, *interj.* (by God), indeed (a petty oath, suitable for women or in their company), 47, AL 684, 753

parfit, *adj.* perfect, 524

party, *n.* part, portion, 203; part, side, AL 587

pase, *see* **pace**

passage, *n.* alley, AL 47

passing, passyng, *adv.* surpassingly, very, 96, 111, 434, AL 344, 663, 743

passingly, *adv.* exceedingly, very, 352

Pater Noster, *n.* (Our Father), the Lord's Prayer, AL 224

pay, *n.* pleasure, satisfaction, AL 255

peine, peyne, payne, *n.* labour, trouble, utmost exertions, 62, AL 138, 240, 359, etc.; pain, suffering, AL 695

penses, *n. pl.* pansies, AL 62

peraventure, *adv.* perhaps, AL 682

Perseveraunce, *n.* (*personified*) Constancy, AL 91, 236, 375, etc.

Phebus, *n.* Phoebus, the Sun, 1, 310

pitous, *adj.* piteous, pitiful, AL 461, 584, 660, etc.

pitously, *adv.* piteously, pitifully, AL 458, 631

plain, playne, *adj.* plain; clear, AL 103; open, frank, AL 137; flat, smooth, 59; *n.* plain truth, AL 28

plaining, pleyneng, *pres. part.* complaining; making a formal 'complaint', 320; (*as adj.*) sorrowful, AL 611

playne, pleyne, *adv.* plainly, openly, AL 170, 328, 425, etc.; fully, AL 592n

pleasa(u)ntly, *adv.* pleasantly, 352, 432; contentedly, happily, 158, 446, 454

ple(a)sa(u)nce, *n.* pleasure, delight, 287, 487, AL 59, etc.; will, AL 373; ease, 309

pley, *v.* play, disport themselves, 538

pleyne, *see* **playne**

pleyneng, *see* **plaining**

pomels, *n. pl.* pommels, rounded knobs, AL 479

port(e), *n.* bearing, demeanour, AL 137, 674

pouderyng, *n.* sprinkling with bright ornaments, spangling, AL 530n

poynt, *n.* jot, whit, AL 606

prees, prease, *n.* throng, 592n, AL 429, 551

presence, *n.* presence, AL 121, 181, 201, etc.; (*as form of address*) majesty, AL 594

present, *adj.* present, in presence, AL 108, 556, 683; *adv.* here, in this very place, AL 721

present, *past part.* presented, AL 570

pretile, *adv.* daintily, 89

prety, *adj.* dainty, elegant, 65, 356

preved, *past part.* proved, tested, AL 701

prien, *v. inf.* pry, peer, 68

prise, *n.* prize, 290

proces(s)e, *n.* course of events, story, AL 27, 602

promesse, *n.* promise, AL 585

proporcioun, *n.* proportion; **a bettir by proporcioun,** one better proportioned, AL 51

purfil, purfyll, *n.* embroidered or furred hem of a garment, AL 87, 524; **purfiles, purfyllys,** *pl.* 146, AL 531

purfiled, *past part.* ornamented (*probably at the hems*), 328n; **purfelyng,** *pres. part.,* hemming; **made in purfelyng,** used in trimming borders, AL 527

purvey, *v.* provide, 429, AL 390

purviour, *n.* purveyor, steward, AL 266

quantity, *n.* abundance, 76

raied, *see* **arraied**

rather, *adv.* sooner, AL 418; rather, 546

raunsoun, *n.* ransom, 255

reason, reson, *n.* reason, cause, AL 600; **by no way of reason,** in no reasonable way, 564; **as reason wold,** as was only reasonable, AL 595; **as reson wold it soo,** as good sense bade, AL 442; **reason it wold,** it were reasonable, AL 578; **bi reason and bi skil,** in all reason, AL 691

record, *n.* testimony, 532

rede, *v.* read, 509, 590, AL 564, etc.; advise, AL 182, 215, 339;

red, *pret.* read, AL 581; **redde, past part.** AL 473, 576, 643, etc.

Regard, *n.* (*personified*) Aspect, Looks, AL 170n

rehearse, reherce, *v.* recount, tell (of), repeat, 205, AL 468, 644, 725; **rehersed,** *past part.* AL 680; **rehersyng,** *pres. part.* AL 622, 659, 741

rejoice, *v.* make joyful, delight, 313; **rejoised,** *past part.* 38

remembraunce, *n.* remembrance, memory, 579, AL 742, 744; (*personified*) AL 336; memorial, record, AL 656; knowledge, AL 90

renueth, *pres. 3 sg.* renews, 11

reson, *see* **reason**

rest, *n.* rest for couching spear, 282n

rich(e), ryche, *adj.* rich, splendid, precious, 145, 152, 153, etc., AL 476, 486, 521; rich, luxuriant, 75; rich (enough), 172

right, *n.* truth, AL 750

right, ryght, *adv.* truthfully, correctly, AL 132; truly, 36; properly, 262; very, 49, 135, AL 46, etc.; right, just, 110, AL 616; **now right,** just now, 298

rome, roome, *n.* room, space, AL 497, 552

roming, *pres. part.* wandering, strolling, 325

rong, *pret.* rang, echoed, 100

rought, *pret.* cared; **nothyng rought,** had no cares, AL 18

roundell, *n.* rondeau, dance-song with refrain, 176n

rout, *n.* host, crowd, 196, 265, 450

routh, *n.* ruth, pity, 376

rude, *adj.* rough, crude, 595

rule, *n.* rule, custom, AL 104; discipline, 286

sad, *adj.* sober, serious, AL 82

sadly, *adv.* soberly, gravely, 159

salades, *n. pl.* salad herbs, 412

saluted, salwed, *pret.* saluted, greeted, 460, AL 442

sat, *see* **sit**

sautry, *n.* psaltery, 337n

save, sauf, *prep.* save, except, 240, 365, AL 284, 507

savour, *n.* smell, odour, 84, 313; *pl.* 123

say, sey, *v.* say, tell, 563, AL 36, 66, 93, etc.; **say we,** let us say, AL 223; **said (e), sayde, seyde,** *pret.* 298, 350, AL 16, etc.; **said, seyd,** *past part.* 570, AL 622; **saying,** *pres. part.* 421

scochones, *n. pl.* escutcheons, heraldic shields, 216, 223, 237

se(e), *v. inf. and pres.* see, 46, 69, AL 23, etc.; see out, ensure provision of, AL 639n; **sene,** *inf.* 157n; **see, sie,** *pret.* 60, 78, 87, etc.; **saw(e),** AL 191, 229, 258, etc.; **sen,** *past part.* AL 717, **sene,** 250, 399, 451, AL 515, **seen,** 125, 307, 589, **seyne,** 63

seeme, seme, *v.* seem, appear, 216; *(personal use)* think, suppose, AL 696; **semed,** *pret.* seemed, AL 67, 80; **seeming, semyng,** *pres. part.* seeming, AL 231; by appearance, AL 261; **by seeming,** as it appeared, 229; **to my seeming,** as it appears to me, 415

seemely, semely, *adj.* comely, handsome, 240, AL 492

se(e)ke, *v.* seek, 74, 234n, 549; **sought,** *pret. and past part.* sought, AL 19; searched, scoured, AL 157; *(refl.)* looked for an advantage for themselves, AL 43 (cf. *MnE* self-seeking); **yif it were thurgh sought,** if one searched thoroughly, AL 481

semblance, *n.* appearance, looks, 301, 459

seme(d), semyng, semely, *see* **seeme, seemely**

semes, *n. pl.* seams, 142

sen(e), *see* **se(e)**

serpe, *n.* collar, neck-ring, AL 533†

sertayne, *see* **certaine**

service, servise *n.* service, AL 104, 202, 731; allegiance, devotion, 566, 573, AL 591; religious service, 437

set, *v.* set, put, 235; **set,** *pret.* *(refl.)* sat, settled, 440, 445, AL 77; **set(te),** *past part.* set, placed, AL 477, 535; adorned, AL 476; studded, 144, 153, 214, etc., AL 480; settled, AL 547; planted, 56; fixed, stuck, 146; **he was sette,** his heart was set, engaged, AL 669

sete, *see* **sit**

sewe, *see* **sue**

sey, seyd(e), *see* **say**

seyne, *see* **se(e)**

shape(n), *past part.* shaped, formed, 64, 167

sharpe, *adv.* sharply, 258

she, *pron.* she, 105, 109, AL 80, etc., **shee,** 547; **her,** *acc., dat.* 107, 351, 382, etc., AL 677, **hir,** AL 89, 93, 98, etc.; **her,** *gen.* 42, 151, 155, etc., AL 603, 608; **hir,** 445, 458, AL 82, 83, 84, etc., **hyr,** AL 519, 520

shene, *adj.* fair, beautiful, 270n; bright, 34

shent, *past part.* destroyed; exhausted, 360

shewe, *v.* show, AL 58, 328, 658; offer, AL 609; show up, stand out, AL 490

shewe, *see* **sue**

sie, *see* **se(e)**

sight, *n.* sight, spectacle, 36, 78, 157, etc.; vision, eyes, AL 472; **to sight,** to the sight, to see, 135; **(as) to my sight,** as far as I could see, apparently, 174, 241

sikerly, *adv.* for certain, AL 504

sikernesse, *n.* certainty, security, AL 607

simple, symple, *adj.* simple, artless, AL 197; weak, feeble, 559, AL 513; *superl.* AL 7

sit, *v.* sit, 540; **sat,** *pret.* 109, 118, 127; (*impersonal use*) affected, AL 663; **sete,** *past part.* sat, 436; **sitting,** *pres. part.* 185, 431; fitting, suitable, 141, 380

sith, *prep.* since, 124; *conj.* since, 494, 501, 594, AL 240, 692

skil(le), *n.* reason, AL 586, 691

slouth, *n.* sloth, 549

slowe, *pret.* slew, AL 460; **slayne,** *past part.* slain, AL 462

small, *adj.* small, 8; short, 52; fine, high (*of the voice*), 180n

smert, *n.* pain, AL 634

sodainly, *adv.* suddenly, 79, 101, 128, etc., AL 736

soft, *adj.* gentle, leisurely, AL 219; *adv.* gently, 4†

somtyme, *adv.* once, at one time, AL 649; in the past, AL 635

so(o)ne, *adv.* soon, 83, 299, AL 126, etc.; **sonner,** *comp.* sooner, AL 418; **sonnest,** *superl.* AL 578

song, *pret.* sang, 105, 162, 298, etc.

sonne, *n.* sun, 28, 34, 355, etc.

sonner, sonnest, *see* sone

soole, *adj.* sole, alone, 165

soot(e), *see* sote

soothly, *see* sothly

sore, *adj.* severe, hard, 290; *adv.* sorely, bitterly, AL 466, 584; hard, strenuously, 447

sorow, *n.* sorrow, AL 671; **sorwes,** *pl.* AL 695

sort, *n.* kind, species; **of oo sort,** of a piece, of the same (high) standard, AL 162; **aftyr a sort,** according to the same pattern, AL 526

sote, *n.* sot, fool, 101

sote, soot(e), *adj.* sweet, 84, 117, 317

soth, *n.* sooth, truth, AL 36, 66, 184, etc.

sothfastnesse, *n.* truth, certainty, AL 446

so(o)thly, *adv.* truly, indeed, 182, 547, 570, AL 508

sought, *see* seke

soupe, *v.* sup, dine, 417

sovenez, *n. pl.* remember-mes, speedwells, AL 61n, 86

sownes, *n. pl.* sounds, 275

space, *n.* space of time, while, 558, AL 74, 144, 211, etc.

spede, *n.* help, AL 294

spede, *v.* prosper, fare, AL 226; **sped(d)e,** *past part.* dealt with, AL 418, 578

spent, *past part.* made use of, AL 732

spe(a)re, spheare, *n.* spear, 258, 281, 284

springen, *v.* to spring, 9; **springeth,** *pres. 3 sg.* 13; **sprang,** *pret. sg.* AL 736; **sprongen,** *pret. pl.* 34; **sprong,** *past part.* 31, 210; **springing, spryngyng,** *pres. part.* AL 69; beginning, dawn, 25, AL 218

square, *v.* make square; cut to size, 404n

squyers, *n. pl.,* squires, AL 14

stabilnesse, *n.* stability, security, AL 606

stages, *n. pl.* steps, tiers, AL 477

stately, *adj.* imposing, splendid, 153, 405

stering, *pres. part.* steering, driving, 199; stirring, urging on, 274

sterry, *adj.* starry, 2

steyres, *n. pl.* stairs, AL 54

straungely, *adv.* unusually, AL 487

streames, *n. pl.* springs, fountains, AL 68n

streyte, *adj.* narrow, AL 47

sturdily, *adv.* strongly, 362

substaunce, *n.* substance; the essentials, AL 741; **in substaunce,** in short, AL 335, 678

succoured, *past part.* protected, 365

sue, s(h)ewe, *v.* sue, make petition, AL 332, 420, 506, etc.; present, AL 117

suerte, *n.* surety, certainty, AL 605

suffred, *past part.* suffered, AL 703; permitted, AL 651

surcotes, *n. pl.* over-garments, 141n, 327, 330

sustene, *v.* sustain, endure, 291

suster, *n.* sister, 388, AL 259, 278, 363, etc.; **sustres,** *pl.* AL 370

sute, *n.* suit, kind; **in a sute,** in accord, of the same kind, 227, 340; **in sute of,** in accord with, matching, 238, 335

swelt, *pret.* sweltered, fainted with the heat, 360

taberd, *n.* tabard, herald's coat, AL 523n

take, *v.* take, 438, 532, AL 286, 303, 372, etc.; **takith,** *pres. 3 sg.* considers, AL 592n; **toke, took(e),** *pret.* took, 61, 279, AL 33, etc.; treated, regarded, AL 633; set off, AL 211n; **take,** *past part.* taken, AL 240; accepted, AL 647

tale, *n.* tale, story, AL 21, 756; **talis,** *pl.* discourse, AL 274

tappet, *n.* tapestry, piece of figured cloth used as a hanging over a door, AL 499, 501; carpet, AL 579

tartarium, *n.* cloth of Tartary, a rich kind of silk, 212n

tene, *n.* trouble, distress, 389

terewe, *see* trewe

than, then, *conj.* than, 21, 97, AL 154, etc.

than, *see* then

thank, *n.* acknowledgment, requital, AL 635, 706

that, *pron. rel.* that, which, 11, 34, AL 18, etc.; what, 11, AL 622; *auxiliary relative (with* **who, whom, what),** 496, AL 175, 238;

who that, whoever, if any one, 67, AL 67; *dem. adj. and pron.* 117, 198, AL 56, etc.; *emphatic,* 345, AL 22, 159, 248, etc.; **tho,** *pl.* 63, 71, 161, etc., **those,** 504

that, *conj.* that, 13, 23, AL 29, etc. *Often used with preps. and advs. to form conjs., e.g.* **when that,** 1, 191; **why that,** 18, 498; **how that,** 510; **sith that,** 494, 594; **where that** (wherever), 410; *and also with* **if, thogh, till, for bicause, now, while**

then, than, *adv.* then, 125, 179, AL 89, etc.

then, *see* than

ther(e), *see* they

ther(e), *adv.* there, 9, 71, AL 62, etc.; *(impersonal use)* 19, 69, AL 5, etc., **theyr,** AL 14, 84; because of that, 490; **where,** AL 668; **there as,** where, AL 108, 438, 611

therate, *adv.* upon it, AL 276

ther(e)to, *adv.* to it, AL 359; in addition, moreover, 122

therwithal, *adv.* with that, at that, AL 279, 737

they, *pron. 3 pl.* they, 142, 163, AL 34, etc.; **them,** *acc., dat.* 219, 371, 376, etc., **hem,** 168, 187, AL 9, etc., **theym,** AL 41, 357, 367; **their,** *gen.* 131, 138, 139, etc., AL 626, **theyr,** AL 9, 11, 38, etc., **ther,** 482, 484, AL 5, 359, **there,** 230, **her,** 275, 357, 371, etc., AL 397, 410, **hir,** 483

theyr, *see* they, ther(e)

thider, *adv.* thither, AL 166, 229

thing, thyng, *n.* thing, 121, 429, AL 25, etc.; anything, 60; **in every (all) maner thing,** in everything, in every way, 170, 550; **thing, thyng,** *pl.* things, 77, 189, AL 677, 699

tho, *see* that

thorow, thurgh, *prep.* through, AL 473; *adv.* through, AL 436; throughout, thoroughly, 103, AL 481

thought, *see* **thynk**

thred, thridde, *adj.* third, 257, AL 659

throughly, *adv.* thoroughly, fully, 568

throw, *n.* short space of time, while, 190, 318, 361

thurgh, *see* **thorow**

thynk, *v.* think, AL 118, 168, 687, etc.; think of, regard, AL 388; believe, AL 354; (*impersonal with dat.*) it seems, AL 374; **thought, thou3t,** *pret.* thought, 47, 79, AL 648, etc.; intended, AL 303; (*impers.*) it seemed, 36, 105, AL 50, etc.; it struck (me), AL 194; **thought,** *past part.* imagined, AL 163, 480

til(l), *conj.* until, 48, 103, 490, AL 220; *prep.* to (*before vowels and h*), AL 155, 289, 332, etc.

to, *adv.* too, AL 469, 513, 653, etc.

to, *conj.* until, AL 287

tobrent, *past part.* burnt, scorched, 358

togider, togyder, to-gydre, *adv.* together, 295, AL 2, 350, 365

toke, *see* **take**

to-tere, *v.* tear to pieces, 488

tother, *pron.* other, 394n

toures, *n. pl.* towers, AL 160

trapped, *past part.* furnished with trappings, 262

trappours, *n. pl.* trappings, 244

travel, *n.* labour, exertions, AL 732

trewe, triew(e), terewe, *adj.* true, AL 210, 312; loyal, AL 641; real, AL 427; honest, AL 137; *adv.* truly, AL 330

trompes, *see* **trumpe**

tronchoun, *n.* headless shaft of spear, 253

trouth, trowth, *n.* truth, 453, 495, AL 13, etc.; fidelity, AL 647, 701; **of verray trouth,** indeed? AL 171

trow(e), *v.* believe, 62, 130, 201, etc., AL 150

trumpe, *n.* trumpet, 211; **trumps, trompes,** *pl.* 192, 275

trumpet, *n.* trumpeter, 213; *pl.* 210, 228

tuft, *n.* hummock, mound, 342n

twain, tweyne, *adj. as n.* two, AL 4, 596; **twain and twain, tweyne and tweyne,** two by two, in pairs, 295, AL 350

umple, *n.* a fine kind of linen or lawn, AL 471n

unconning, *adj.* ignorant, 591

uncouth, *adj.* strange, unfamiliar, 276

understond, undrestond, undrestande, *v.* understand, know; **I woll ye understond,** I wish you to know, realise, 514, AL 502; **do me til undrestond,** let me know, AL 155

unfold, *past part.* unfolded, expressed, set forth, 595

unkindly, *adj.* unnatural, 413

unmete, *adj.* unsuited, remote, 17n

unneth, *adv.* hardly, with difficulty, 203; **well unneth,** hardly at all, 46

unpurvayde, *past part.* unprovided for, AL 382

until, *prep.* unto, AL 594, 619

untrew, untrue, *adj.* unfaithful, 486; (*as n.*) unfaithfulness, 320

untriewly, *adv.* treacherously, AL 464

veluet, welwet, *n.* velvet, 53†, 141, 233, etc.

vent, *n.* slit or opening at neck of gown, AL 526n

vertuous, *adj.* full of virtue, healing power, 315

very, verray, *adj.* genuine, absolute, true, very, 502, 563, AL 42, 168, 171, etc.; *adv.* really, very, 10, 315, 409, AL 192;

ladylike manner, 302, 347, AL 196

wonder, *n.* wonder, cause for wonder, 593, AL 663; *adj.* wondrous, wonderful, 434, 451, AL 429

wone, *n.* wont, custom, AL 5

wones, *n. pl.* dwellings, 201n

wonne, *see* **wan**

woodbind, *n.* woodbine, wild honeysuckle, 159, 272, 485

worchyng, *n.* design, style of workmanship, AL 529

word(e), *n.* word, 486; motto, AL 87, 207, 306, etc.; **wordes, wordis,** *pl.* words, mottoes, AL 119, 182, 282, etc.

world, *n.* world, 74, 125; multitude, 137; thing worth the world, supreme delight, AL 539

worship, *n.* worthiness, dignity, AL 80

worthy, *adj.* worthy, deserving, 575, AL 744; mighty, 482; excellent, splendid, 296†; **the Nine Worthy,** the Nine Worthies 504

wost, wot(e), *see* **wit(e)**

wrath, *n.* anger, impatience, AL 42

wrethen, *past part.* twisted, intertwined, 57

wringing, *pres. part. as adv.* so wet as to need wringing, soaking, 406

wroth, *adj.* angry, AL 612; grieved, AL 614

wrought, ywrought, *past part.* made, fashioned, 49, 156, AL 165, 478; worked, embroidered, AL 487

y, *pers. pron.* I, 62

ya(a)te, *see* **gate**

yaf, yave, *see* **yeve**

ybe, *see* **be**

yche, *see* **ech**

ye(e), *adv.* yea, yes, AL 326, 331, 660

yede, *pret. sg. and pl.* went, 54, 163, 164, etc.; **yeden,** *pl.* 71

yef, yif, *conj.* if, AL 166, 416, 417, etc.

ye(e)re, *n.* year, 40, 574

yet, yit, *adv.* yet, 39, 87, AL 13, 145, 514, etc.; further, 491, AL 337, 461

yeve, *v.* to give, AL 123, 142, 182, etc.; **yaf, yave,** *pret. sg.* AL 196; **yaf in comaundement,** commanded, AL 712; **yeve,** *past part.* given, AL 187

yield, *v.* repay, requite, AL 360

yif, *see* **yef**

yis, *adv.* yes, 471†, AL 236

yit, *see* **yet**

yong, *adj.* young, AL 261, 275; (*as n.*) AL 538

ysent, *past part.* sent, 424

ywrought, *see* **wrought**

Printed in Great Britain by
Thomas Nelson and Sons Ltd, Edinburgh